LIVES AND WORK AT SEA

LIVES AND WORK AT SEA

Herbert Holdsworth, Colin Hannah, and the Ship *Ladakh*

William L.H. Scarratt

Regatta Press Limited
Ithaca, New York

Regatta Press Limited
Phone: +1–607–277–2211
Fax: +1–607–277–6292
Website: *http://www.regattapress.com*

Library of Congress Cataloging-in-Publication Data

Scarratt, William L. H., 1937–
  Lives and work at sea : Herbert Holdsworth, Colin Hannah, and the ship Ladakh / by
William L.H. Scarratt.
      p. cm.
Includes bibliographical references and index.
  ISBN 0-9674826-8-2 (alk. paper)
  1. Merchant marine—Great Britain—History—19th century. 2. Tramp shipping—Great
Britain—History—19th century. 3. Seafaring life—Great Britain—History—19th century.
4. Merchant mariners—Great Britain—Biography. 5. Holdsworth, Herbert, 1880–1935.
6. Hannah, Colin, 1866–1948. 7. Ladakh (Ship) I. Title.
  HE823.S29 2003
  387.5'092'241—dc22   2003020152

Printed in the United States of America

The paper in this publication meets the minimum requirements of
American National Standard for Information Sciences
Permanence of Paper for Printed Library Materials,
ANSI Z 39.48-1984.

In Memoriam

Jane Holland Wood Holdsworth
1917–98
Mary Holdsworth
1919–80

———————

For

Joanna and Victoria,
Great Granddaughters
and
Miranda and Eleanor,
Great-Great Granddaughters
Of
Herbert and Jane Holdsworth

Contents

Preface ix

Acknowledgements xi

Chapter 1. The Strands Coalesce, 1897–98 1
The Ship *Ladakh* 1
Ladakh as Tramp Ship 9
The Men Who Crewed *Ladakh* 11
Voyage to Calcutta 21
Voyage to New York 22

Chapter 2. Herbert Holdsworth, 1880–1935 28
Background and Career after *Ladakh* 28
Cargo Liners 29
S.S. *Bernard Hall*, 1898 30
Voyages, 1898–1906 33
Marriage, 1910 37
Alfred Holt 39
S.S. *Perseus*, 1931 41
Summary of Voyages, 1910–1932 45
Analysis of Voyages with the Blue Funnel Line 50
Summary of Ships in which Herbert Holdsworth Served 51
Herbert Holdsworth's Retirement and Death 60

Chapter 3. Colin Hannah, 1866–1948 66
Family Background 66
Colin Hannah's First Ship: The *Penthesilea* 67
The *Caroline Morris* 75
The *Sierra Parima* 78
Colin Hannah's First Command: *Cabul* 84
Colin Hannah's Career after *Ladakh* 88
S.S. *Imaum* 88
In Command Once More: S.S. *Sierra Morena* 91
Disaster Off the Rebecca Light 101

S.S. *Graciana*   109
S.S. *Ascania*   116
Summary of Voyages   122
Colin Hannah's Retirement and Death   134

Chapter 4. The Voyages of *Ladakh*   142
Ladakh Before Colin Hannah   142
Colin Hannah Joins Ladakh   166
Subsequent Fate of *Ladakh*   173
Summary of Crew Agreements   173
Summary of Voyages   177
Summary for the Period in Edward Bates & Sons' Ownership   181

Bibliography   183

Index   185

About the Author   188

Preface

Sometime in the late 1940s, I went with my mother to Beatie's department store in Wolverhampton to have two photographs copied that had belonged to my late Grandfather Herbert Holdsworth. One photograph was of the ship *Ladakh* (see plate 1, p. 2) and the other was of her Crew. Although they were an ever-present feature of my childhood, they remained enigmatic. A few clues are present. The photographer is William Gray of Brooklyn, New York. William Gray has annotated the pictures, "Ship *Ladakh*, Colin Hannah, Master." My mother could identify her father but knew nothing else about the photographs, and as with any artifact without a provenance, they were largely meaningless.

Over the years, I made desultory attempts to find out more, but it has been only recently that I have had the time to mount a sustained effort. It had long been apparent that the Agreement and Account of Crew, a legal requirement for every voyage in a British merchant ship, would provide a significant amount of the information I was looking for. I became aware of the existence of these documents as long ago as October 1972 when I met, by chance, Dr. Keith Matthews in the National Maritime Museum, London. I learned that he had been instrumental in saving from destruction 70 percent of the British merchant Navy's Agreements and Accounts of Crew and had used them as the basis of a maritime history archive at the Memorial University of Newfoundland. The agreements are, in effect, contracts of employment and as such provide a wealth of information, which I have used extensively in this book. While the majority of the documents are at Newfoundland, others are held at the Public Record Office and the National Maritime Museum in London.

Herbert Holdsworth's career has been examined largely with the aid of his Continuous Certificates of Discharge, which were given to me by my aunt, Mary Roberts (née Holdsworth) shortly before she died. This information, together with other sources, in particular *Lloyd's List,* have I hope helped to remove some of the anonymity that shrouded Herbert Holdsworth, Colin Hannah, and the *Ladakh*.

This story is inevitably disparate. Colin Hannah's life (1866–1948) spans all of it, but within this time scale the three strands only converge for a short time, from 17 August 1897 to 23 June 1898. It seemed sensible, therefore, to begin the story here even though, chronologically, it is almost the middle. The book then continues with Herbert Holdsworth's career until his death in 1935. The third chapter recounts Colin Hannah's life before and after his captaincy of *Ladakh*. The final chapter deals with the voyages of the *Ladakh* while she was owned by Edward Bates & Sons between 1883 and 1902.

Acknowledgements

The majority of the Agreements and Accounts of Crew were obtained from the Memorial University of Newfoundland, and I am grateful to Stephanie Harlick, Archival Assistant, for all her help.

The following agreements were obtained from the Public Record Office:

Tyndareus and *Ascania*	BT99/3162
Sierra Morena	BT99/2415, 2146, 2806
Ladakh	BT99/1628
Imaum	BT99/2325

The remainder were obtained from the National Maritime Museum, London. Also obtained from the Public Record Office were the Closed Registry papers for:

Tyndareus and *Ascania*	BT99/3162
Ladakh	BT110/160
Sierra Morena and *Graciana*	BT110/526
Log book, *Sierra Morena*	BT165/460
and *Imaum*	BT165/153
Colin Hannah's certificates	
of competency	BT122/88

The extracts from *Lloyd's List* and *Lloyd's Captains Register* were provided by the Memorial University of Newfoundland and are reproduced with permission of the publisher, Lloyd's List, London.

Colin Hannah's will is reproduced with permission of the National Archives of Scotland, SC15/47/23, pages 61–63. Also, Catherine Hannah's will, SC15/41/88, pages 415, 417, and 418.

Roy Paton welcomed my wife and I to Summerhill and provided the photograph of the Elders of Urr Kirk and the verse by Colin Hannah.

The letters of Dr. K. Wright to R. Crawford Clarke, Coroner for the Mid and North Division, County of Salop, are reproduced with permission of R.D. Crawford Clarke, the present coroner.

The extract from *The Last of the Windjammers,* by Basil Lubbock, Glasgow, 1927, with permission of the publishers, Brown, Son & Ferguson.

The extracts from *Blue Funnels in the Mersey,* by C.H. Milsom, Isle of Man, 1988, with permission of the publisher, Sea Breezes Magazine.

The photographs of *Sierra Parima* (negative number P5999) and the *Ascania* (negative number P15930) with permission of the National Maritime Museum, London.

Sharon Maxwell, Library Assistant, University of Liverpool Library, provided me with information on the Bates family history.

Fiona Flett, Archival Assistant, Shell Services International, provided information about the oil trade in the late nineteenth century.

Malcolm Darch introduced me to the history of the Salcombe fruit clippers.

Information regarding the ultimate fate of *Ladakh* was obtained from *http://www.uboat.net*

Chapter 1

The Strands Coalesce, 1897–98

Here on this bank and shoal of time
Macbeth, 1. vii. 1

The name *Ladakh* reflects the interests, both general and mercantile, of her owners, Edward Bates & Sons. They, together with other Liverpool ship owners, were still able, at the end of the nineteenth century, to earn a profit with the sailing tramp ship. The relationship of the ship owners, and the men they employed, was strictly regulated by various Merchant Shipping Acts, which laid down in great detail what was expected of both owner and crew. The Agreement and Account of Crew that Colin Hannah and Herbert Holdsworth signed on 17 August 1897 for voyages to Calcutta and New York thus provides a considerable amount of information on the photographs that William Gray took in Brooklyn in June 1898 (plate 1).

The Ship *Ladakh*

When William Gray described *Ladakh* as a ship, he was using a technical term that means a sailing vessel square rigged on all three masts: fore, main, and mizzen. Contrast this, for example, with a barque, which is square rigged on fore and main masts, but fore and aft rigged on the mizzen. There are many different sail combinations and each has its particular name and optimum working conditions. Square sails are at their best when the vessel is sailing down wind and on a broad reach. With fore and aft sails a vessel is much more weatherly, that is, she will approach more closely to the direction of the wind. Consequently, the rig will be chosen that best suits the trade in which the vessel is engaged. For example, the Salcombe fruit clippers, which carried pineapples and other fruit from the Azores to London, had to be fast and perform well on all points of sailing. They were, therefore, rigged as a barquentine, the square sails on the fore mast were ideal for running before the wind, while the fore and aft sails on the main and mizzen masts enabled the vessel to work her way to windward. *Ladakh* was at the opposite end of this scale.

1

The business philosophy of *Ladakh*'s owners, Edward Bates & Sons of Liverpool, is best summed up by Basil Lubbock in his book *The Last of the Windjammers*. On page 346, Lubbock refers to:

> The big Southampton-built full riggers [and goes on to say] Throughout the 80's there were still a number of firms in Liverpool and elsewhere who believed in the big full rigger when the Clyde ship owners were declaring she was uneconomical besides being very un-handy with her huge yards and great height of mast. The chief supporters of the full rigger were R.W. Leyland and Co. for whom Oswald, Mordaunt and Co. built the following huge carriers [nine ships are listed] . . . *These big ships were, of course, carriers with no pretensions to speed.* . . . . Most of them had tremendous royals and single top-gallant sails. . . . Besides the Leyland ships Oswald Mordaunt and Co. built a number of other 2,000 ton three masters for E. Bates and Sons, for example *Kistna,* 2,149 tons, *Ladakh,* 1,942 tons and *Maydown,* 2,381 tons.

Edward Bates & Sons owned a total of 11 ships, and these will be described below.

Ladakh was thus designed to run before the trade winds, which blow steadily in one direction for long periods. They are caused by hot air at the equator rising and being replaced by cooler air. This movement is then distorted by the rotation of the earth, with the result that the prevailing winds blow clockwise in the northern hemisphere and anti-clockwise in the southern. The effect of the trade winds is augmented by the ocean currents they produce.

These movements of wind and water were studied by the American hydrographer Matthew Maury (1806–73). In 1842, he was posted to the Navy Depot of Charts and Instruments where, at the end of a voyage, the captains deposited their logbooks and chronometers, the latter to be checked and serviced. Maury realized that the information contained in the logbooks could be analyzed to provide an overall and coherent picture of the conditions that might be expected in the oceans at different times of year. Thus in 1847, he was able to publish his *Wind and Current Charts of the North Atlantic.* At an international conference on oceanography in Brussels in 1853, his uniform system of recording oceanographic data was adopted for all naval and merchant vessels, and eventually, charts were produced covering the world. This information was of inestimable value to the mariner. The master of a sailing ship planning a voyage could study the winds and currents he was likely to encounter and shape his course accordingly.

Ladakh's *Builders*

Ladakh was built of iron by Oswald Mordaunt & Co. Woolston, Southampton. There were many advantages of building a ship of iron, not least because of its availability, but also, over a certain size, the comparative thinness of the plating results in an iron ship being 75 percent the weight of a wooden ship of equal strength and equal outward dimensions. In addition, the frames, being smaller, take up less hull capacity.

Plate 1. The ship *Ladakh*.

Ladakh was launched in February 1883 and then fitted out. Her Certificate of Registry is dated 12 April 1883, which is when she passed into the ownership of Edward Bates & Sons of Liverpool.

Certificate of Registry

After 1786 all owners of British ships above a certain size were required to register them with the Customs of their home port. Each ship was given a unique Official Number, which in the case of a wooden ship, had to be chiseled into the main beam. *Ladakh's* number was 87,815, and she was the fifty-third ship to be registered in Liverpool in 1883.

Ladakh's *Tonnage*

One of the principle reasons for registration was to determine how much cargo a ship could carry in order that duty, where payable, could be assessed by Customs. This carrying capacity is expressed as *tonnage*. It has nothing to do with the weight of a vessel but is a measure of volume, expressed in tons of one hundred cubic feet, the word originating from a tax levied on wine imported in *tuns* or casks. The volume of the ship below the upper deck is measured in cubic feet and divided by one hundred, and this gives the ship's gross registered tonnage (G.R.T.). The figure for *Ladakh* was 1,998.3. A second calculation is then performed to take into account those areas of the ship that cannot be used for carrying cargo, and this is subtracted from the gross tonnage to give the net registered tonnage (N.R.T.). It is on the latter that duty is assessed and such charges as port and harbor dues, light dues, towage charges and salvage assessments are made.

The "Deductions Allowed" to arrive at the N.R.T. is divided into two on the certificate:

(1) "On account of space required for propelling power." [Not applicable to *Ladakh*.]
(2) "On account of spaces occupied by Seamen or Apprentices, and appropriated to their use, and kept free from Goods or Stores of every kind, not being the personal property of the crew. Officers' cabins in poop, and seamen in deck house."

This volume in *Ladakh* was 55.9 tons giving a N.R.T. of 1,942.4.

The certificate was modified in 1889 when the following spaces were added to the "Deductions Allowed":

Boatswain's store	18.10 tons
Sail room	8.69 tons
Master's cabin	7.29 tons

This reduced the N.R.T. to 1,908.32.

The registered tonnage is also expressed in cubic meters, presumably for the convenience of continental European ports. The figures for *Ladakh* were:

> Gross registered tonnage   5,655.11 cubic meters;
> Net registered tonnage   5,400.55 cubic meters.

Two other meanings of *tonnage* as applied to shipping are:

(1) Dead Weight Tonnage: the number of tons of twenty hundredweight that a ship will carry when laden to her load line (Plimsoll line).
(2) Displacement Tonnage: the number of tons of water displaced by a ship when thus loaded.

These figures are not known for *Ladakh*.

Ladakh's overall dimensions as recorded on the certificate are as follows:

> Length from fore part of stem under the bowsprit
>   to the aft side of the Head of the Sternpost: 269.0 ft.
> Main breadth to outside of plank: 39.5 ft.
> Depth in hold from tonnage deck to ceiling amidships: 24.2.ft.

Ladakh's *Owners*

In 1825, a further Act of Parliament added the requirement for the ownership of a vessel to be divided into 64 shares, which, in the case of Ladakh, were owned by four members of the Bates family. They were described under the heading "Name, Residence and Occupation of Owner" as follows:

> Edward Percy Bates of Liverpool in the County of Lancaster, Ship owner, twenty Shares
> Gilbert Thompson Bates of Liverpool aforesaid, Ship owner, eighteen Shares
> Sidney Eggers Bates of 27 Clements Lane in the City of London, Ship owner, fourteen Shares
> Wilfred Imrie Bates of Liverpool aforesaid, Ship owner, twelve Shares

Ladakh's *Speed Made Good*

It is not possible to know what would have been *Ladakh's* maximum speed. The speed of a displacement hull is directly proportional to the square root of the water line length and this parameter is not known for *Ladakh*. The National Maritime Museum holds the plans of many hundreds of ships, but unfortunately, *Ladakh* is not among them.

An attempt has been made to determine the speed made good for many of the voyages examined. This has been done by taking the (nautical) mileage between ports, usually from *Reed's Marine Distance Tables* and dividing the figure by the number of days taken on the voyage to give a daily mileage. This figure is then divided by 24 to convert to knots. (1 knot = 1 nautical mile per hour, 1 nautical mile = 1 minute of latitude.) This tells us that *Ladakh* criss-crossed the world at an average speed equivalent to a fast walking pace. It is important to realize that the distance covered by a sailing ship to complete a voyage will almost certainly be much greater than the figure suggested by the tables due to the necessity to tack when the wind is ahead, and if extensive calms are encountered, the average speed will be further eroded.

The Appearance of Ladakh

We can only assume that William Gray's photograph is a true likeness of *Ladakh* although it has been extensively retouched: the sail plan and probably the rigging have been inscribed on the negative and the sea made to look rough. Nevertheless, a ship contemporaneous with and possibly similar to *Ladakh* still survives. This is the *Wavertree,* which is presently being restored at the South Street Seaport Museum in New York. The two ships had a great deal in common: they were built at much the same time, by the same builder, of the same material and their owners pursued the same business philosophy. In the case of *Wavertree* the owners were R.W. Leyland who, like Edward Bates & Sons, operated out of Liverpool. When fully restored, she may provide a good idea of what *Ladakh* really looked like.

The Name Ladakh

Ladakh is named for an area of India in the states of Jammu and Kashmir, a land of deep valleys between the Himalayas and the Karakoram (see map 1). Despite its modern political affiliations, it has more in common with Tibet, and its people are Buddhist. The capital is Leh, which used to be an entrepôt for Central Asian commerce at 11,500 feet above sea level. The reason for this choice of name is perhaps due to the interests of the owners of the *Ladakh.*

Edward Bates & Sons

The Bates family dynasty was founded by Joseph Bates of Skircoat, Halifax in Yorkshire (1796–1846). In 1804, he was described as a "cloth-dresser," buying woolen cloth from weavers, probably in Leeds market, and then carrying out finishing processes, such as bleaching and dying. His second son, Joseph Bates Jr. (born 1809) had gone out to Calcutta, where he started business as a free merchant under the East India Company. By 1830 Joseph Bates Senior was being described

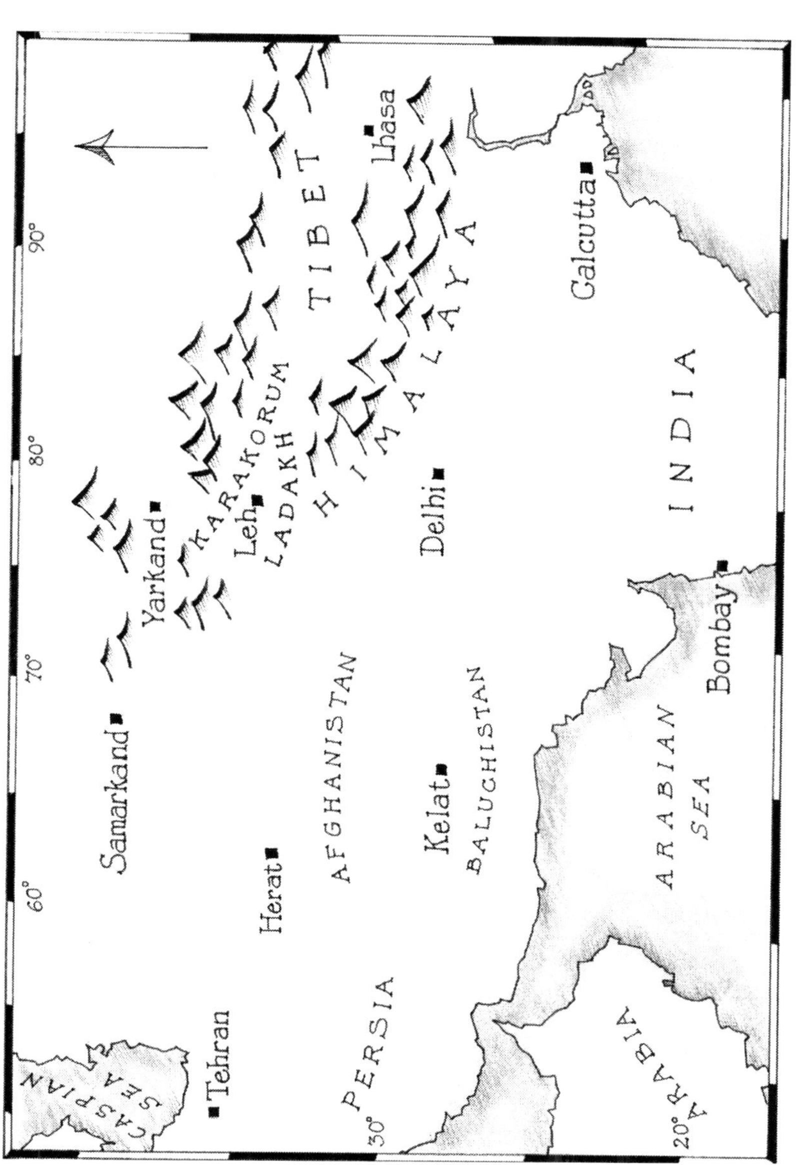

Map 1. Northern India and the area of Ladakh.

as a "woolen and stuff merchant." Together with his sons William and Benjamin, he was exporting the woolen cloth through Liverpool, and Joseph Jr. was selling it in Calcutta.

In 1832/3, Joseph's third son, Edward Bates (1816–96) went out to join his brother in India. The business expanded, and the exports diversified: table covers, hardware, brass and iron wire, axles, pins, shackles, walking sticks, and a variety of colored cloth. Bills could be settled by the remittance of other goods in return such as castor oil, silk, skins, and indigo.

In 1836, Joseph Bates Jr. returned to England to set up as a merchant in Liverpool. Edward Bates remained in India and moved his business to Bombay. In 1848, he also returned to England, and settled in Liverpool as an importer of Indian produce, the Bombay office being left in the care of an agent. Edward also started a packet (courier) service to Bombay with the barque *Simoon.* He built up his fleet of sailing ships and the service was extended to include Calcutta, the Far East, and when the Australian gold rush began, ships sailed direct to Australia and returned via India or South America.

In 1870, the firm was renamed Edward Bates & Sons, and Edward retired to Hampshire. He became a Member of Parliament and, in 1886, received a Baronetcy. The eldest of his four sons, Edward Percy Bates (1845–99) took over the management of the Liverpool office.

In earlier years, Edward Bates had purchased steamers and converted them into sailing vessels, but from 1870, the partners began adding steamers to their fleet. Their main interest, however, remained in sail, so that, by 1897, only four of their eleven ships were steamers, although one of them was a steel screw steamer built to their own design. All the ships were used for general tramping.

The sailing ships, excluding *Ladakh, were:*

- *Cabul*   1,397 G.R.T.   Colin Hannah was master of this ship from 13 February 1896 until he joined the *Ladakh* in August 1897.
- *Herat*   1,400 G.R.T.   Both ships are named after cities in Afghanistan.
- *Kelat*   1,822 G.R.T.   A city in the Baluchistan province of Pakistan.
- *Kistna*   2,149 G.R.T.   Otherwise known as Krishna, a river in India.
- *Manydown*   2,381 G.R.T.   Named after the Bates' family seat.
- *Yarkand*   1,311 G.R.T.   Now called Shache, a city in the north east of China.

The 4 Steam ships were:

- *Idar*   2,595 G.R.T.   A city in the state of Gujarat, India.
- *Imaum*   2,706 G.R.T.   The title of a Mohammedan prince. Colin Hannah served in her from 2 December 1902– 21 April 1903 following the sale of *Ladakh.*

- *Iran*   4,066 G.R.T.
- *Istrar*   2,979 G.R.T.   Provenance unknown.

As can be seen, the names of the ships are a reflection of the Bates family's links with the Far East and central Asia. They would have known about Ladakh as a country, not only because of their trading interests in India, but also because of the strategic role played by the whole region as a buffer zone between Russia and Britain's Indian Empire.

When Edward Percy Bates died in 1899, His eldest son, Edward Bertram Bates (1877–1903), succeeded to the title and management of the family business. He in turn was succeeded by his brother Percy Elly Bates (1879–1946), who, in 1910, joined the board of the Cunard Steamship Company. Percy's shipping interests were widened when he purchased the shares of Sir Alfred Jones (d. 1909), who had been chairman of the Elder Dempster Shipping Company.

In 1911, all three Bates brothers—Percy, Dennis, and Frederick—joined the board of Thomas and John Brocklebank and exchanged their largest vessel for half of the Brocklebank family shares. During World War I, Percy was in charge of the Commercial Services branch of the Ministry of Shipping, and of his two brothers, one was in the Army and the other, the Royal Air Force. With no one to run the business, the ships were sold to Brocklebanks,' and this was the end of their ship-owning activities. The partnership of Edward Bates & Sons continued in business, however, as merchants and private bankers.

After the war, the brothers resumed their interest in shipping but not as owners. Percy Elly Bates became successively Deputy Chairman and, in 1930, Chairman of the Cunard Line. He was, therefore, instrumental in the development of two of Cunard's most prestigious vessels: the *Queen Mary* and *Queen Elizabeth*. When Percy died in 1946, his two brothers Frederick, (1884–1957) and Dennis (1886–1959) succeeded him, the latter in 1953.

Ladakh As Tramp Ship

The *Oxford Dictionary* defines a *tramp ship* as "a cargo vessel, especially (but not necessarily) a steam ship, which takes cargoes wherever obtainable and for any port." The word entered the language in 1880. *Ladakh* sailed 446,311 nautical miles (513,258 statute miles) and visited twenty-eight different ports between 1893 and 1902 while engaged in "general tramping."

The increasing efficiency of the steam engine together with the worldwide installation of the submarine telegraph enabled the concept of the tramp ship to develop. It could wander the world carrying bulk cargoes and always be in touch with its owners, who would organize those cargoes through the Baltic Exchange in London, where ship owners and merchants (or their brokers) met, an uncomplicated and cheap method of doing business.

Ladakh was able to operate as a tramp ship, and compete with steam, by keeping her cost base low. It is possible to glean some idea of the cargoes that *Ladakh* carried by studying *Lloyd's List.* Tramp ships would sometimes load a cargo for which there was not as yet a customer. It would be traded on the Futures Market as speculators gambled on fluctuating commodity prices during a voyage, which, in a sailing ship, could last three or four months. In order to learn the final destination of the cargo, the ship would call at a port "For Orders." The two most popular places in (what was then) the United Kingdom were Falmouth and Cork (Queenstown). These ports owed their popularity to the fact that they have large, safe, easily accessible bays in which a ship could anchor and not have to pay harbor dues, and the assistance of tugs was not required on arrival or departure.

Lloyd's List posted which ships were calling for orders and where, and, crucially, what cargo was being carried. Crucial, because this is one of the few surviving sources of this information. The following references in *Lloyd's List* are to *Ladakh* calling "For Orders":

- On 3 February 1897 *Ladakh* (John Johnson, Master) left Iloilo in the Philippines and 125 days later put into Queenstown (Cork) for orders carrying sugar, which she delivered to Liverpool two days later.
- On 16 March 1899 *Ladakh* (Colin Hannah, Master) sailed from Rangoon; 87 days later on 11 July she put into Falmouth for orders carrying rice. This cargo was delivered to Bremerhaven six days later.
- On 26 September 1900 she was again in Falmouth having left Bassein in Burma on 22 May (127 days out) and she was again carrying rice. She sailed for Rotterdam on 29 September arriving on 1 October 1900.
- Just over one year later, on 5 October 1901 she was back in Falmouth, 114 days out from San Francisco but this time carrying wheat. She was directed to Dublin on 14 October and arrived, towed by the tug *Stormcock,* two days later.
- On 26 October 1902 she was in Queenstown for orders having left Tacoma on 10 June loaded with wheat. (Tacoma is at the head of Puget Sound close to Seattle in the state of Washington on the western seaboard of America.) She left Queenstown on 3 November, again under tow, and was taken to London arriving in Victoria dock on 7 November 1902. This was her last voyage in Edward Bates & Sons' ownership.
- On two occasions *Ladakh* sailed from South Wales ports, and although there is no evidence in *Lloyd's List* or anywhere else, it is likely she was carrying coal.
- *Lloyd's List* also reported disasters, and, again, the cargo may be mentioned, for example, on 26 December 1894 it was noted that *Ladakh* had broken her mooring lines in the Erie basin in New York while loading petroleum at the Anglo-American stores. Her anchors held her until a tug arrived and towed her back to the quay. When *Ladakh* eventually sailed on 5 February 1895, she was caught in a severe storm and had to jettison 600 cases of petroleum.

Some factors common to the cargoes listed above are that they do not demand swift transit, they stow cheaply and easily, bagged or loose, and a full cargo could be obtained at a single loading port and carried direct to a single port of discharge. Furthermore, the loading port may well be in an out-of-the-way place and the cargo will have to be stowed by hand, a process which could take weeks and would be prohibitively expensive for a steamship with its high overheads in terms of coal and engine maintenance. Almost one-third of the twenty years that *Ladakh* was owned by Edward Bates & Sons was spent in harbor. The fact that the return voyage could last for three months or more is not necessarily a disadvantage, as this could obviate costly warehousing. When trading with the East, avoiding the Suez Canal would save thousands of pounds, and the crew's wages were much less than could be had on shore.

Thus it was that sail managed to compete with steam, and did so until the advent of World War II. The last sailing ship owner to survive in business up until this time was Captain Gustaf Erikson who was based at Mariehamn in Finland. An astute businessman with an obsessive ability to keep down costs, he was highly successful in the Australian grain trade, but it is questionable how long even he could have survived after the loss of the *Herzogin Cecilie* when she inexplicably struck the Ham Stone off Soar Mill Cove near Salcombe on 25 April 1936.

The Men Who Crewed *Ladakh*

A detailed record of the men who crewed *Ladakh* may be found in documents entitled "Agreements and Accounts of Crew of the Registrar General of Shipping and Seamen of Great Britain," which are, in effect, contracts of employment between the owners of a merchant ship and her crew (plate 2). Seventy percent of the documents that survive are held at the Memorial University of Newfoundland while the remainder are at the National Maritime Museum or the Public Record Office in London. Because they are legal documents, all crew agreements have the same format and wording. The contract that Herbert Holdsworth signed on 17 August 1897 in Liverpool (when he was 17 years old) will be used to illustrate the general arrangement.

At the top of the first page it is stated that "Any Erasure, Interlineation or Alteration in this Agreement will be void unless attested by some Superintendent of a Mercantile Marine Office, Officer of Customs, Consul, or Vice-Consul, to be made with the consent of the persons interested." The document is headed "Agreement and Account of Crew, Foreign Going Ship," followed by "The term-Foreign-going ship means every ship employed in trading or going between some place or places situate beyond the Coasts of the United Kingdom, the Islands of Guernsey, Jersey, Sark, Alderney, and Man and the Continent of Europe between the River Elbe and Brest inclusive."

Plate 2. Agreement and Account of Crew.

AGREEMENT AND ACCOUNT OF CREW.

FOREIGN-GOING SHIP.

Name of Ship	Official No.	Port of Registry.	Port No. and Date of Register.	Registered Tonnage. Gross. Net.	Nominal Horse Power of Engines (if any).
Ladakh	87816	Liverpool	53 1583 1045 1908		

REGISTERED MANAGING OWNER.

Name.	Address. (State No. of House, Street, and Town.)	No. of Seamen for whom accommodation is certified	FOR PARTICULARS AS TO LOAD LINE, SEE PAGE 2.
E. Bates & Sons	3 Row Quay Liverpool	40	

The Several Persons whose names are hereto subscribed, and whose descriptions are contained on page 4 hereof, and of whom ___ are engaged as Sailors, hereby agree to serve on board the said Ship in the several capacities expressed against their respective Names, on a Voyage from¹

Liverpool to Calcutta

if required to any port or ports within the limits of 72 degrees North and 65 degrees South latitude, trading to and from as may be required until the ship returns to a final port of discharge in the United Kingdom for any period not exceeding thirty one months

Continent of Europe between the Rivers Elbe & Brest inclusive.
Calling for orders if required.

And the Crew agree to conduct themselves in an orderly, faithful, honest, and sober manner, and to be at all times diligent in their respective Duties, and to be obedient to the lawful commands of the said Master, or of any Person who shall lawfully succeed him, and of their Superior Officers, in everything relating to the said Ship and the Stores and Cargo thereof, whether on board, in boats, or on shore; in consideration of which Services to be duly performed, the said Master hereby agrees to pay to the said Crew as Wages the Sums against their Names respectively expressed, and to supply them with provisions according to the Scale on the other side hereof.

And it is hereby agreed that any Embezzlement or wilful or negligent Destruction of any part of the Ship's Cargo or Stores shall be made good to the Owner out of the Wages of the Person guilty of the same.

And if any Person enters himself as qualified for a duty which he proves incompetent to perform, his Wages shall be reduced in proportion to his incompetency: And it is also agreed, That the Regulations authorized by the Board of Trade, which are printed herein and numbered²

1 2 3 4

are adopted by the parties hereto, and shall be considered as embodied in this Agreement: And it is also agreed, That if any Member of the Crew considers himself to be aggrieved by any breach of the Agreement or otherwise, he shall represent the same to the Master or Officer in charge of the Ship in a quiet and orderly manner, who shall thereupon take such steps as the case may require: and it is also stipulated that the Seaman shall receive the advances of wages entered herein against their names.

*The authority of the Owner or Agent for the allotments mentioned within is in my possession.

___ Superintendent, Officer of Customs, or Consular Officer.

*This is to be signed if such an authority has been produced, and to be scored across in ink if it has not.

And it is also agreed, that³

The said Master shall be entitled to deduct from the wages of the said Crew respectively the following amounts, viz.: for not joining at the time specified in Column 10, two days pay; or any expenses which have been incurred in hiring a substitute; and for absence from the Ship at any time without leave a sum not exceeding two weeks pay: and it is further mutually agreed that any dispute arising on the subject of these deductions shall be settled by the Superintendent of a Mercantile Marine Office, Consular Officer, or Shipping Master abroad and that his decision shall be final.

The Crew shall consist of ___ hands all told. The Crew mutually agree to assist each other in the general duties of the Ship.

No Cash shall be advanced abroad or liberty granted other than at the pleasure of the Master.

Should any of the Crew fail to join at the time specified, the Master may ship substitutes at once.

In Witness whereof the said Parties have subscribed their Names at page 4 hereof on the days mentioned against their respective Signatures.

Signed by ___ Master,

on the 12th day of Augst 1897

Date of Commencement of Voyage.	Port at which Voyage commenced.	Date of Termination of Voyage.	Port at which Voyage terminated.	Date of Delivery of Lists to Superintendent.	I hereby declare to the truth of the Entries in this Agreement and Account of Crew, &c.
17/8/97	Pool	18/7 1899	Bremerhaven	18/7 99	___ Master.

¹ Here the Voyage is to be described, and the places named at which the Ship is to touch, or, if that cannot be done, the general nature and probable length of the Voyage is to be given; and if the Agreement is to be used as a Running Agreement under sec. 115, Merchant Shipping Act, 1894, the fact should be stated.
² Here are to be inserted the Numbers of any of the Regulations for preserving discipline issued by the Board of Trade, and printed on the third page hereof, which the parties agree to adopt.
³ Here any other stipulations may be inserted to which the parties agree, and which are not contrary to law.

N.B.—This Form must not be unstitched. No leaves may be taken out of it, and none may be added or substituted. Care should be taken at the time of Engagement that a sufficiently large Form is used. If more men are engaged during the voyage than the number for whom signatures are provided in this Form an additional Form Eng. 1 should be obtained and used.

The name of the ship follows with its official number, port of registry, registered tonnage, registered managing owner, and the number of seamen for whom accommodation is certified. On the *Ladakh* this number was 40 although the total complement of crew, including Colin Hannah, was only 29.

"The several persons whose names are hereto subscribed, and whose descriptions are contained on page 4 hereof, and of whom ＿＿＿＿＿＿＿ are engaged as Sailors, [no number was entered here] hereby agree to serve on board the said Ship in the several capacities expressed against their respective Names, on a voyage from LIVERPOOL to CALCUTTA. and/or if required to any port or ports within the limits of 72 degrees North and 65 degrees South Latitude, trading to and from as may be required until the ship returns to a final port of discharge in the United Kingdom or Continent of Europe, between the River Elbe and Brest inclusive. Calling for orders if required. For any period not exceeding 36 months."

Although the agreement lasted for 36 months, a crewmember could leave the ship with the master's permission. The changes were overseen by the British consul and could be numerous. Despite this legitimate means of ending the contract, presumably because the master would not agree or the men simply did not bother to apply, more than 20 percent of those who signed agreements deserted, the problem being particularly acute in North American ports. This voyage was unusual in that only two men deserted. A total of 69 men signed the agreement, 29 of them at the start of the voyage in Liverpool. When the agreement terminated three years later in Bremerhaven only eight remained of the original 29, and this number included the master, both mates, and the sailmaker.

The agreement continues:

> And the Crew agree to conduct themselves in an orderly, faithful, honest and sober manner, and to be obedient to the lawful commands of the said master, or of any Person who shall lawfully succeed him, and of their Superior Officers, in everything relating to the said Ship and the stores and the Cargo thereof, whether on board, in boats, or on Shore, in consideration of which Services to be duly performed, the said master hereby agrees to pay to the said Crew as Wages the Sums against their Names respectively expressed, and to supply them with provisions according to the Scale on the other side hereof.
>
> And it is hereby agreed that any Embezzlement or willful or negligent Destruction of any part of the Ship's cargo or Stores shall be made good to the Owner out of the Wages of the Person guilty of the same.
>
> And if any Person enters himself as qualified for a duty which he proves incompetent to perform, his Wages shall be reduced in proportion to his incompetency. And it is also agreed, That the Regulations authorized by the Board of Trade, which are printed herein and numbered 1 2 3 and 4 (see page 3) are adopted by the parties hereto, and shall be considered as embodied in this Agreement. And it is also agreed, That if any Member of the Crew considers himself to be aggrieved by any breach of the Agreement or otherwise,

he shall represent the same to the master or Officer in charge of the Ship in a quiet and orderly manner, who shall thereupon take such steps as the case may require. And it is also stipulated that the Seaman shall receive the advance of wages entered here in against their names. And it is also agreed that the said master shall be entitled to deduct from the wages of the said Crew respectively the following amounts

viz: for not joining at the times specified: two days' pay, or any expenses which have been properly incurred in hiring a substitute; and for absence from the ship at any time without leave: a sum not exceeding two weeks' pay; and it is hereby mutually agreed that any dispute arising on the subject of these deductions shall be settled by the Superintendent of a Mercantile Marine Office, Consular Officer, or Shipping master abroad, and that his decision shall be final. And it is also agreed that no cash shall be advanced abroad or leave granted except at the master's pleasure.

At the bottom of this, the first page of the agreement is entered: "The date of commencement of the voyage: 17 August 1897, the port at which the voyage commenced: Liverpool, [and] The date of termination of the agreement: 18 July 1899, [at] Bremerhaven."

On page 2 a table of the "Scale Of Provisions to be allowed and served out to the Crew during the Voyage, in addition to the daily issue of Lime and Lemon Juice and Sugar, or other Anti-Scorbutics, in any case required by the Act":

- 3 Quarts of water and one pound of bread daily
- 1½ pounds of beef on Sunday, Tuesday, Thursday and Saturday
- 1¼ pounds of pork on Monday, Wednesday and Friday
- ½ pound of flour on Sunday, Tuesday and Thursday
- One-third of a pint of Peas on Monday, Wednesday and Friday
- ½ pound of rice on Saturday
- Daily: one eighth of an ounce of tea, half an ounce of Coffee and 2 ounces of sugar

Substitutes and equivalents permitted at the master's option. No spirits allowed." There was also a "Bill Of Fare." However, "the act does not require these particulars to be given, but the Table may be filled up if desired." Nothing was entered here.

On page 3 of the agreement there are details of the "Load line and Draught of Water." A requirement of the 1876 Merchant Shipping Act, this is the disc and lines painted on the sides of British merchant ships that indicate the draught levels to which the ship may be loaded with cargo for varying conditions of season and location. The popular name for the load line, the "Plimsoll mark" commemorates Samuel Plimsoll (1824–98) who was responsible for the passage of the 1876 Act (against the bitter opposition of some ship owners), which made the use of the load line mandatory. Plimsoll's reasons for introducing his Act were the so-called "coffin ships," vessels that were unseaworthy, overloaded, and heavily insured against loss. In later years Plimsoll became president of the Sailors' and Firemen's (that is, Stokers) Union, and also campaigned about conditions in the cattle ships.

The agreement states that the center of the disc on *Ladakh* is to be placed "At 5 feet 10 inches below the upper deck line and that the maximum load line in freshwater should be 5 inches above the centre of the disc whereas the maximum load line in winter in the North Atlantic should be 7 inches below the center of the disc."

The summer months are defined as April to September inclusive. The winter months, October to March inclusive.

The Agreement goes on to state "The additional freeboard specified for the North Atlantic trades is to apply to vessels sailing to, or from, the Mediterranean or any British or European Port, and which may sail to, or from, or call at, Ports in British North America, or Eastern Ports in the United States, the entrance to which from the sea, or the entrance from the sea to the estuary or river on which such Port may be situated, is north of 37°30' North latitude from October to March inclusive. The reduced freeboard allowed for voyages in the Fine Season in the Indian sea only applies to vessels trading between the limits of Suez and Singapore."

There then follows: "Regulations For Maintaining Discipline."

Sanctioned by the Board of Trade in pursuance of § 114 (2) of the Merchant Shipping Act, 1894.

These Regulations are distinct from, and in addition to, those contained in the Act, and are sanctioned but not universally required by Law. All or any of them may be adopted by agreement between a master and his Crew, and thereupon the offences specified in such of them as are adopted will be legally punishable by the appropriate Fines or Punishments. These Regulations, however, are not to apply to Certified Officers.

These Regulations are all numbered, and the numbers of such a them as are adopted must be inserted in the space left for that purpose in the Agreement, page 1, and the following copy of these Regulations must be made to correspond with the Agreement by erasing such of the Regulations as are not adopted. If the Agreement is made before the Superintendent of a Mercantile Marine Office, his signature or initials must be placed opposite such of the Regulations as are adopted. For the purposes of legally enforcing any of the following penalties, the same steps must be adopted as in the case of other Offences punishable under the act; that is to say, a statement of the Offence must, immediately after its commission, be entered in the Official Log Book by the direction of the master, and must at the same time be attested to be true by the signatures of the master and the Mate, or one of the Crew; and a copy of such entry must be furnished, or the same must be read over to the Offender before the ship reaches any port or departs from the Port at which she is; and an entry that the same has been so furnished or read over, and of the reply, if any, of the Offender, must be made and signed in the same manner as the entry of the Offence. These entries must, upon discharge of the Offender, be shown to the Superintendent of a Mercantile Marine Office before whom the Offender is discharged; and if he is satisfied that the Offence is proved, and that the entries have been properly made, the Fine must be deducted from the Offender's wages and paid over to the Superintendent.

If, in consequence of subsequent Good Conduct, the master thinks fit to remit or reduce any Fine upon any Member of his Crew which has been entered in the Official Log, and signifies the same to the Superintendent, the Fine shall be remitted or reduced accordingly. If wages are contracted for by the Voyage or by Share, the amount of the Fines is to be ascertained in the manner in which the Amount of Forfeiture is ascertained in similar cases under Sect. 234."

The offences and their fines are then enumerated:

No. 1. Striking or assaulting any person on Board or belonging to the Ship (if not otherwise prosecuted): Five Shillings.

No. 2. Bringing or having on Board spiritous liquors: Five Shillings.

No. 3. Drunkenness. First Offence: Five shillings. Second Offence: Ten Shillings.

No. 4. Taking on Board and keeping possession of any fire-arms, knuckle-duster, loaded cane, slung-shot, sword-stick, bowie knife, dagger, or any other offensive weapon or offensive instrument, without the concurrence of the master, for every day during which a seaman retains such weapon or instrument: Five Shillings."

To put these fines in perspective, an able seaman earned £2:15s per month. Thus a fine of 5 shillings was 9 percent and one of 10 shillings, 18 percent of his monthly earnings.

Finally on page 3 of the agreement there was "Account Of Apprentices On Board (If Any)." There was one apprentice in *Ladakh* at the commencement of the voyage, Alfred Edmund Bridger. He was born in 1877 in Birkenhead and commenced his indentures on 25 January 1894 in Liverpool and completed them on 21 January 1898 in Calcutta, where he was promoted to able seaman.

The following six pages of the agreement are probably the most interesting (plate 3). They contain 80 numbered rows. Each row contains:

- The signature or mark of the crewmember, his age, nationality, port of engagement address, and home address
- The ship in which he last served and the year of discharge therefrom
- The date and place of signing this agreement
- The capacity in which he is engaged
- Date and hour at which he is to be on board
- Amount of wages per calendar month
- Advances made in the United Kingdom of not more than one month's wages, conditional on going to sea

- Other advances not being conditional on the seaman's going to sea from the United Kingdom
- Amount of weekly or monthly allotment [*usually to family at home*]
- Signature or initials of Official before whom the Seaman is engaged
- Date, Place and Cause of leaving this ship or of death
- Balance of wages paid on discharge
- In a column headed "Release" the crew member signs his name again to indicate, "We the undersigned Members of the Crew of this Ship, do hereby release this Ship and the master and Owner or Owners thereof, from all claims for Wages or otherwise in respect of this voyage and I, the master do hereby release the said undersigned members of the crew from all claims in respect of the said voyage"
- The final column contains the signature or initials of the official before whom the balance of wages was paid and release authorized, and the date

During the three years that the agreement lasted 69 men signed it.

At the beginning of agreements analyzed in this account there is an "Equivalent Value of the Pound." This is calculated by the Bank of England (BOE) and is derived from the retail price index (RPI) based at January 1987=100. The RPI is based on the combined cost of a number of specific goods and does not take into account other factors relevant to a comparison of values: for example, the cost of property or the level of wages. The BOE knows of no figures incorporating all possible factors. (Wages in the agreement are per month.) The United Kingdom converted its' currency to the decimal system in 1972. Prior to this, pounds, shillings, and pence were used. In this system there were 12 pence in one shilling, and 20 shillings in one pound. Pence are rarely mentioned in the agreements and will therefore be largely ignored.

Herbert Holdsworth's service in the *Ladakh* commenced on 14 August 1897, which was the day those joining the ship at Liverpool signed the agreement. At number 28, he was the last to sign, and this was the total number of the crew (plus the apprentice.) All agreed to be on board at 6:00 A.M. on 17 August, which was the day *Ladakh* sailed for Calcutta. Three men (including the carpenter) failed, however, to join and these were replaced by one man on 16 August and two the following day. These latter were engaged by Colin Hannah, presumably on board and at the last moment. All the other members of the crew were engaged by H. Brown, who was an official in the Mercantile Marine Office.

Herbert Holdsworth was 17 years old. He gave as his nationality "Egremont"—in Birkenhead, opposite Liverpool, on the River Mersey. (All the English and Irishmen gave their nationality as their hometown or city.) Herbert Holdsworth's address was 22 Rice Hey Road, Egremont. This was his first voyage, and he was the only man in the ship who had not been to sea before. His rank was ordinary seaman, although his discharge certificate issued just under one year later in New York gave

Plate 3. Crew information.

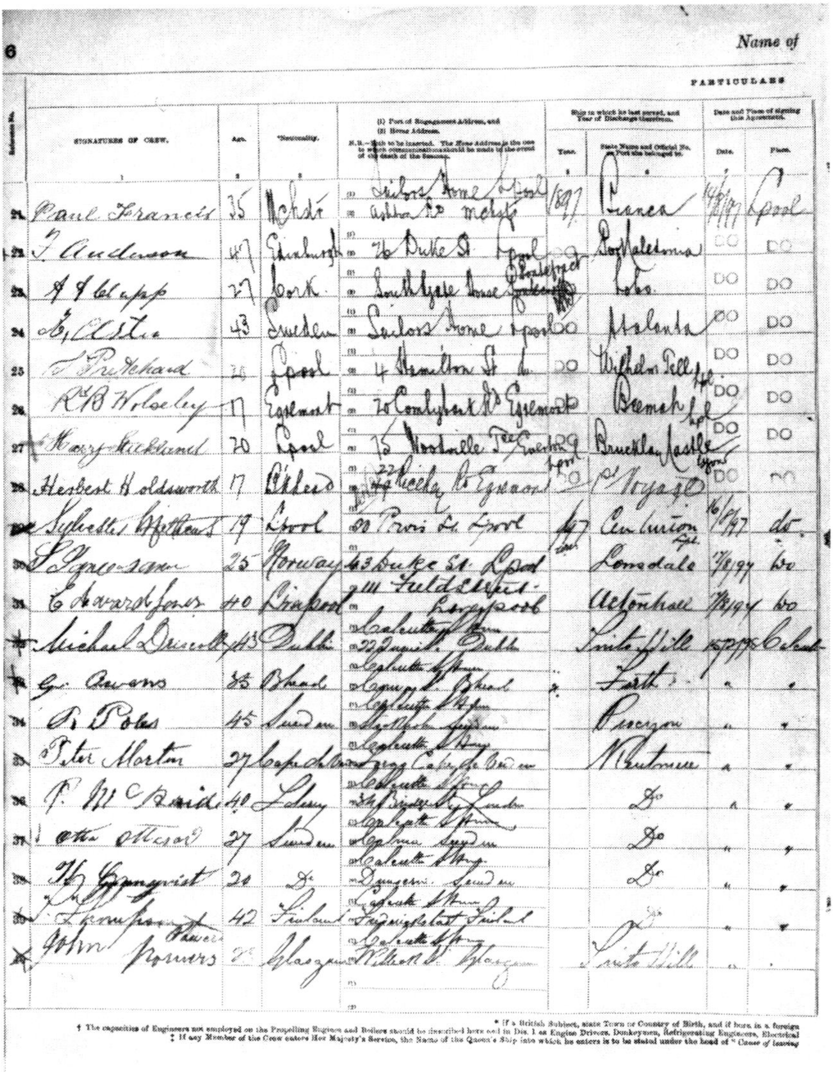

his rank as "Boy," but this had been struck out and replaced by "O.S." (ordinary seaman). His wages were £1:00s per month, and he was advanced the same amount conditional on his going to sea. (£1 in 1897=£54.70 as at March 1999, so that in today's terms he was earning £656.40 a year.

Colin Hannah, as master, signed the agreement first. *Lloyd's Captains Register* records that he was born at *Fort* William but this is erroneous. In the agreements, he gives his place of birth as *Port* William, a small village on the coast of Dumfries and Galloway in the southwest of Scotland. His date of birth was 4 March 1866, so that, at the time of signing the agreement, he was 31 years old. His parents were Thomas Hannah, a tailor and Mary McCourtney. They had married in March 1856 at Glasserton, which is just south of Port William and had six children. Colin was the third boy to be born and, had he remained in Scotland, would probably have spent his life as an agricultural laborer. Catherine, Colin Hannah's wife, is not mentioned in the agreement but is present in plate 4 (see p. 23). She was born on 31 October 1867, the oldest of eight children, of whom five were girls and three were boys. Catherine's father was Thomas McDowall a police sergeant. Her mother Alice's maiden name was McCourtenay. When she registered Catherine's birth, she had to put her mark on the certificate, as she was illiterate. Both parents had been born in Scotland in 1846 and had migrated to Liverpool.

Captain and Mrs. Hannah's address was 8 Northumberland Terrace, Liverpool, which was the family home of the McDowalls. Colin Hannah achieved his master's ticket (number 020322) at Liverpool on 14 December 1891. On 6 February 1892, just before his 26th birthday, he signed the agreement as first mate in the *Sierra Parima* (O.N. 86,212) bound for Mauritius. It was not until four years later in February 1896, that he achieved his first command in the Edward Bates & Sons' ship *Cabul. Ladakh* was thus the third ship he had served in since obtaining his master's ticket and he joined her on 14 August 1897. (Colin Hannah's career both before and after his service in *Ladakh* will be discussed in Chapter 3.)

No details are given in crew agreements of the master's remuneration. It is possible to obtain some idea of the amount involved in steam ships by looking at what the first engineer earned, as he was virtually equal in rank with the master.

The first mate was Robert Pierce, who was 40 years old and had been born on the Isle of Anglesey, North Wales. His address was 12 High Street, Pwhelli, Wales. His wages were £7:10s per month.

The second mate was Thomas Dobson. He was 23 years old and had been born in Liverpool. His address was 41 Winslow Street, Liverpool, and he was paid £6:00s per month. He had been an apprentice in *Ladakh*. His indentures were registered on 24 January 1890 in Swansea and were completed on the 26 November 1895 at sea, shortly after leaving Manila for New York, when he was serving in *Ladakh* under Captain Johnson. He was promoted to third mate with wages of £2:15s, the same as an able seaman. In New York, on 15 May 1896, he was appointed second mate when his wages were raised to £5:00s per month. With his continued service in *Ladakh,* his wages were further increased to £6:00s on the inception of the new agreement of 14 August 1897. He remained in *Ladakh* for the duration of this agreement until it terminated in Bremerhaven on 18 July 1899. With the commencement of another on 1 September 1899 (for a voyage to New York returning to Rotterdam via Bassein in Burma) he was appointed first mate at the age of 25, his wages then being £7:10s. He left *Ladakh* on 2 October 1900 having served in her since 7 November 1894, almost six years.

As described above, Edward Jones, the carpenter, was a last-minute addition to the crew, as the man who had signed the agreement initially had failed to join. Jones was 40 years old and was paid £5:10s, he was thus the most highly paid man after the deck officers.

The sailmaker was Alexander Smith, aged 30. He was the only member of the crew who had been with Colin Hannah in the *Cabul* prior to their both joining *Ladakh*. He was paid £5:00s per month.

The steward was Henry Calway, 43. He was paid £4:15s per month.

The cook was James Anderson, 46; his wages were £4:00s per month.

The bosun had also failed to join. On 1 September, Fred Smith, a Dane (at 50, the oldest man in the ship) was appointed to the post. The original bosun would have been paid £4:00s per month, but Smith's wages remained the same as those he received as an able seaman, £2:15s per month. Including Fred Smith, there were 16 able seamen, each receiving £2:15s per month. The average age of the able seamen was 37 years. To become an able seaman a man must have served for three years before the mast and achieved the following skills:

Understand the compass and be able to steer.
Be competent at whipping, seizing, and splicing ropes and conversant with
    the common knots and bends.
Cast a lead, rig a derrick, launch a lifeboat, and batten down a hatch.

There were five ordinary seamen, and their wages were finely graded. As has been mentioned above, Herbert Holdsworth was paid £1:00s; of the others, one was paid £2:00s, two £1:15s, and one £1:10s. This latter was R.B. Wolseley. He was the same age as Herbert Holdsworth and lived at 20 Comlybank Road, Egremont, which adjoins Rice Hey Road. *Ladakh* was not his first ship, but unfortunately, the name of the previous vessel he served in is illegible. Although several of the Crew have addresses in Liverpool only Herbert Holdsworth and R.B. Wolseley lived in Birkenhead. Surely they must have known each other.

The apprentice, Alfred Edmund Bridger, was, of course, unpaid.

These crew numbers meant that there were probably ten men in each watch, not many to cope with the heavy gear in a ship as large as *Ladakh.*

Thus Edward Bates & Sons' wage bill for this voyage was £83:15s per month (excluding Colin Hannah's emoluments.) The average age of everyone in the crew was 37 years: 19 (68 percent) were older than Colin Hannah; 22 (79 percent) were older than Thomas Dobson the second mate. The Nationalities of the Crew were as follows:

English	14
Welsh	2
Scottish	2
Northern Irish	2
Southern Irish	3
German	2
Finnish	1
Danish	1
Swedish	1
Norwegian	1

Voyage to Calcutta

Ladakh left Liverpool on 17 August 1897. Information about any voyage is minimal. Until 1874 official logbooks were often deposited with the crew agreements, but thereafter, they were mostly destroyed. Positions during the voyage occasionally appear in *Lloyd's List* in a section headed "Ships Spoken." Thus on 13 September (27 days out) *Ladakh* is reported as being in 10°N, 26°W, steering south-southeast. This position is west of Freetown, Sierra Leone.

Ladakh arrived in Calcutta on 15 December, 120 days out, 11,655 miles, 97 miles per day, at an average speed of 4 knots. During the voyage a man had been lost overboard. H. Lindquist, the shipping master, noted in the agreement: "Certified that the death of P. Collins caused by drowning has been duly reported to me by the master and that I have inquired into the death and find no grounds of suspicion. No wages due to him and his effects have been deposited in this Office."

This was not noted in the agreement until 15 February so presumably some legal process, perhaps an inquest, had to be concluded. Patrick Collins was 22 and had been born in Cork. He had been an able seaman and had lost his life on 16 November 1897 (29 days from Calcutta.) Unfortunately, there is no mention of the circumstances of his demise.

Ladakh spent 70 days in Calcutta. On 31 December, nine men were discharged. The British Consul noted: "I certify that the undermentioned seamen have been discharged and left behind at this port on the grounds of mutual consent and I have accordingly granted my sanction to their being so left and their balance of wages have been paid and their effects have been delivered to them." The fee charged by "Consuls or by Officers in British possessions Abroad" for every seaman discharged or left behind was two shillings.

On 21 January 1898 the apprentice, Alfred Edmund Bridger, now aged 21 was promoted to able seaman. He was, therefore, just four days short of serving four years as an apprentice.

On 9 February 1898 H. Lindquist noted: "Certified that A.A. Clapp has been left behind at this port on the ground of his inability from illness to proceed to sea in the vessel, his balance of wages Rs. [Rupees] 105–8-1 paid to him of which sum Rs. 100 deposited in this office and his effects delivered to him." (The rate of exchange was 1 shilling = 1 7/8 Rupees (Rs.).)

On 18 February the 11 men who had left the crew for the reasons mentioned above were replaced by 10 able seamen and a bosun, the latter was Michael Driscoll, 43, from Dublin. Fred Smith, the acting bosun, was, therefore, not promoted. The consul's fee for this transaction was again 2s per crewmember.

All the able seamens' wages were increased to £3:10s but A.E. Bridger was paid at the old rate of £2:15s. For the able seamen this represented an increase of 27 percent and was probably an indication of the difficulty in obtaining crew.

Voyage to New York

On 23 February 1898 *Ladakh* left Calcutta arriving in New York on 13 June, 111 days out, 12,335 miles, 111 miles per day, averaging 4.6 knots. It was here that the photograph (plate 4) of the crew was taken. It contains 26 people (plus Mrs. Hannah), but as there were 29 in the crew, three are missing. It might have been possible to identify who these were if they had left the ship before any of the others. Six left on 16 June, however, which tells us that the photograph was taken before this date but not who the three missing crewmembers are.

The full crew list is as follows, commencing with the number on the crew agreement followed by age, nationality, and rank. Those who joined at Liverpool:

No. 1: Colin Hannah	31 Port William	Master
No. 2: Robert Pierce	40 Anglesey	First mate
No. 3: Thomas Dobson	23 Liverpool	Second mate
No. 6: Henry Calway	43 Cork	Steward
No. 7: James Anderson	46 Glasgow	Cook
No. 8: Alexander Smith	30 Liverpool	Sailmaker
No. 9: Stephen Elebrant	22 London	Able seaman
No. 12: R. Mathias	40 Aberystwyth	Able seaman
No. 13: A. Barr	24 Southport	Able seaman
No. 19: Fred Smith	50 Denmark	Able seaman
No. 24: Paul Francis	35 Manchester	Able seaman
No. 25: S. Pritchard	20 Liverpool	Ordinary seaman
No. 26: R.B. Wolseley	17 Egremont	Ordinary seaman

Plate 4. *Ladakh* crew photo.

No. 27: Harry Strickland	20 Liverpool	Ordinary seaman
No. 28: Herbert Holdsworth	17 Birkenhead	Ordinary seaman
No. 29: Sylvester Matthews	19 Liverpool	Ordinary seaman
No. 31: Edward Jones	40 Liverpool	Carpenter

Those who joined at Calcutta:

No. 32: Michael Driscoll	43 Dublin	Bosun
No. 33: G. Owens	35 Birkenhead	Able seaman
No. 34: R. Poles	45 Sweden	Able seaman
No. 35: Peter Martin	27 (illegible)	Able seaman
No. 36: P. McBride	40 Londonderry	Able seaman
No. 37: Otto Attason	27 Sweden	Able seaman
No. 38: K. Grangrist	20 Sweden	Able seaman
No. 39: Thomas Thompson	42 Finland	Able seaman
No. 40: John Powers	23 Glasgow	Able seaman
No. 41: William Greig	38 South Shields	Able seaman
No. 42: George Kennedy	21 London	Able seaman
No. 43: A.E. Bridger	21 Birkenhead	Able seaman (formerly the apprentice.)

The crew is abaft the main mast so that the camera is looking towards the bows of the ship. The bowsprit is just visible together with the foremast and its lower yard. The twin forestays of the main mast can be seen just to the right of the chimney on the deck house, which possibly houses the galley or perhaps a stove to warm the crew's quarters. The forestay of the mizzen mast is attached to the foot of the main mast to the right of the crewmember behind Mrs. Hannah. In the bottom left-hand corner of the photograph is a hatch with a sail beside it. The size of the boltrope and the cringles on this sail provide some idea of its size and weight. An armchair has been produced for Captain Hannah to sit on, but it is far too low and fit only for his dog and his foot.

Only two people, apart from Captain Hannah, can be identified with absolute certainty: Mrs. Hannah and Herbert Holdsworth, who stands behind and to her left. Captain and Mrs. Hannah are not looking at the camera, as that would have been considered a breach of etiquette. Two other people who may be identified with a fair degree of certainty are the first mate, Robert Pierce, who stands on Herbert Holdsworth's left, is wearing a white uniform and holds a monkey on his left arm. The other man with a white uniform standing with his foot on a box, on which is sitting a man with another monkey, is possibly the second mate, Thomas Dobson. He also avoids looking directly at the camera. Any further identification is, alas, impossible.

Herbert Holdsworth left the *Ladakh* on 23 June 1898 having traveled 23,990 miles. His discharge papers may be seen in plate 5. He had spent 311 days in total

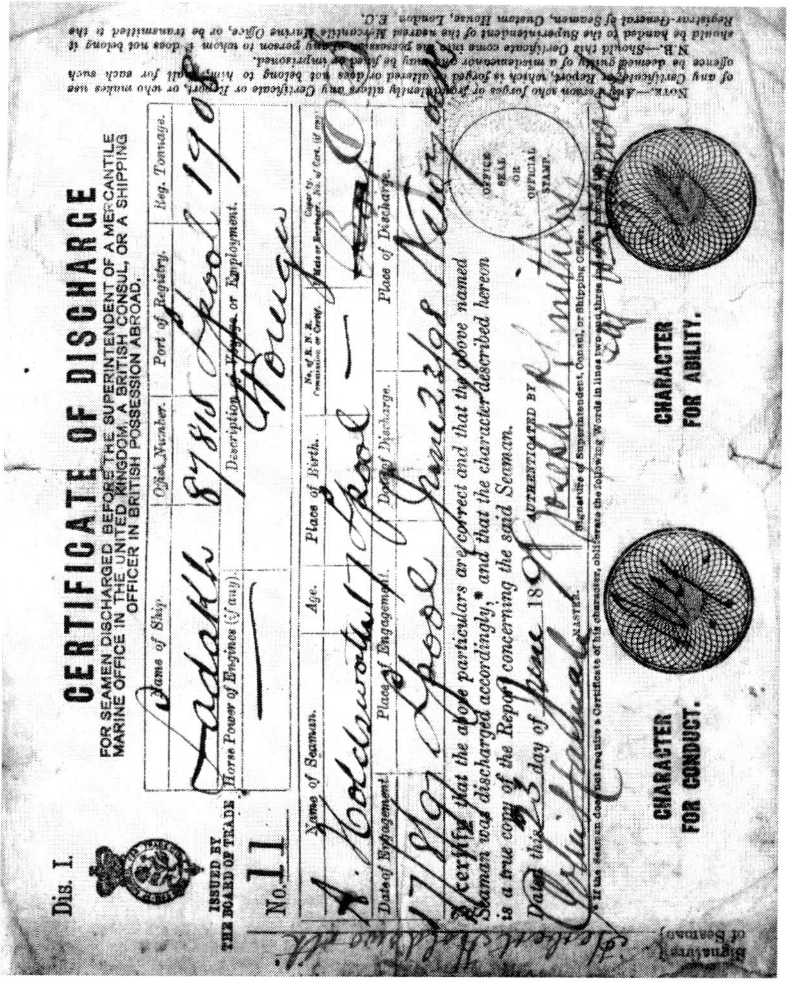

Plate 5. Certificate of Discharge.

as a member of her crew: 231 days were at sea, 70 days in Calcutta, and 10 days in New York. At approximately ten months, his total pay would have been about £10:00s. His balance of wages on discharge was US$28.23. The rate of exchange was approximately $4.86 to the pound so his wages equaled £5:15s. (£1 in 1898 = £54.70 as at March 1999, or in today's terms, £314.50.)

Between 16 and 25 June a total of 21 crewmembers left *Ladakh* in New York by mutual consent. A.E. Bridger was one of them. He appears again in this narrative on 16 March 1915 when he signed the agreement as a refrigerator attendant on the *Ascania,* which suggests his career did not prosper.

The agreement has contradictory entries concerning R.B. Wolseley. Joseph P. Smithers, the British consul-general in New York, states that he was discharged there, but he has signed for his discharge in Bremerhaven, although the British vice-consul there does not record this.

The 21 men who left the ship were replaced by 22, one of whom failed to join. The men signed the agreement on 25 July, and their nationalities were:

German	8
Swedish	3
Norwegian	2
Barbadian	1
Belgian	1
Canadian	1
Finnish	1
French	1
Scottish	1
Illegible	2

On 29 July 1898 *Ladakh* left New York for Bombay arriving on 28 November, 122 days out, 11,430 miles, 94 miles per day, averaging 3.9 knots. She remained here for 33 days. Two men were left behind sick, and two boys—the Barbadian, aged 19, and a German, aged 17—deserted. They were replaced by a 19 year old ordinary seaman from Liverpool.

On 31 December *Ladakh* sailed for Rangoon to load rice. She arrived there on 14 February 1899, 45 days out, 2,117 miles, 47 miles per day, averaging 2 knots.

Three more crew joined the ship: a German, an Irishman from Kinsale, and a Mauritian. *Ladakh* departed Rangoon on 16 March 1899 bound for Falmouth for orders. She was spoken to on 7 May in 35°S, 20°E, which is off Cape Town. On 12 June, she passed Saint Helena and was spoken to again in 8°N, 20°W, south east of Ascension Island. *Ladakh* arrived at Falmouth on 11 July having completed a voyage of 117 days, 11,340 miles, 97 miles per day, averaging 4 knots. She left the following day for Bremerhaven, was off Beachy Head on 14 July, and arrived at her destination on 18 July 1899, 6 days out, 630 miles, 105 miles per day, averaging 4.4 knots. The agreement now terminated and the crew were discharged.

Only six who had signed the agreement at Liverpool in August 1897 were still in the ship:

Colin Hannah	Master
Robert Pierce	First mate
Thomas Dobson	Second mate
James Anderson	Cook, promoted to steward
Alexander Smith	Sailmaker
S. Pritchard	Ordinary seaman
Harry Strickland	Ordinary seaman

Chapter 2

Herbert Holdsworth, 1880–1935

It is impossible to surmise why Herbert chose to become a seafarer. His parents were Matthew Holdsworth (1840–1910) and Jane Pennington (1840–1924). They were married on 25 July 1874 at the Ormskirk Register Office. Matthew lived at 33 Woodville Terrace, Liverpool and gave his "Rank or Profession" as bookkeeper, but he would later describe himself as a corn merchant's cashier. His father, also Matthew, was dead and had been a merchant (whatever that may mean). Jane gave her address as 16 Wellington Terrace, Southport. Her father was still alive and was described as a chronometer maker. The witnesses were Emma Pennington and John A. Clegg. A mere five weeks after the wedding on 31 August 1874, Jane gave birth to their first child, a daughter, Edith. In all they had four children. Emma Jane (1876–1962), Matthew Clement Walker (born 1878), and lastly Herbert Pennington (1880–1935).

Edith married Ernest Micklewright, a designer, on 31 August 1907. Emma Jane was unmarried and worked as a secretary at Liverpool University. Matthew Clement Walker married Annie King, 33, on 15 April 1909. He was working as a bank clerk at the time. Annie gave her father's profession as general contractor.

Thus Herbert Pennington Holdsworth was very much the odd one out. His daughter Jane Holland Wood remembered her uncles and aunts with affection, but there is a definite impression that they disapproved of Herbert and Jane and were constantly helping them with money after Herbert retired.

Background and Career after *Ladakh*

After leaving *Ladakh* Herbert Holdsworth never served in a sailing ship again. For 29 of the 33 years between 1898 and 1932 he was at sea as a purser in steam ships. The possibility of a career as a deck officer may have been considered but there is anecdotal evidence that he was colorblind. The examinations for master and mates consisted of three parts: seamanship, navigation, and the "color test," which was to exclude color blindness. To fail this test was to fail the examination. The other officer group in a steam ship was the engineers, but presumably Herbert Holdsworth lacked the technical bent. It is easy to imagine that his family would have been anxious to persuade him not to continue as a seaman, a group of men with a bad reputation.

Certificates of Discharge

It is from these that an account of Herbert Holdsworth's career at sea can be provided. On leaving a ship each crewmember received a Certificate of Discharge showing the length of the voyage, his rating, and the character given him by the master. A copy was forwarded to the Registrar-General of Shipping and Seamen so that the career of every man was on record. For his own convenience the seaman himself was given a Continuous Discharge Book, in which the particulars of each certificate were entered at the time of discharge, so that he could produce to each employer a running history of the voyages he had made and the character he had borne.

Herbert Holdsworth had 13 individual Certificates of Discharge and two books of the Board of Trade Continuous Certificates of Discharge, the first of these is numbered 102,186 and the second 847,195. Each book records 42 voyages. The first is full, the second contains 39. When these are added to the 13 individual certificates, plus one from an Amsterdam shipping company owned by Alfred Holt and issued in November 1931, the total is 94 voyages, which were completed on 8 May 1932 just after Herbert Holdsworth's 52nd birthday.

Apart from his voyage in the *Ladakh* the whole of Herbert Holdsworth's career was spent in cargo liners for the very good reason that tramp ships do not require the services of a purser.

Cargo Liners

A cargo liner is defined as, "A ship belonging to a shipping company that carries cargo on scheduled routes." The word "liner" originated in 1838 as a steam ship or other vessel, belonging to a "line" of packets. The packet ship was the precursor of the cargo liner. It carried light, high value cargo, in particular mail, and some passengers.

As the technology of ships and shipping progressed and as world trade increased, the packet ship metamorphosed into passenger and cargo liners, and their operation, particularly of the latter, became much more complicated and expensive. The cargo liner must have a constant and permanent berth in those ports where it trades if it is to attract a regular and steady flow of cargo. The loading of this cargo is an immensely complicated business given its disparity and the time available. The ship must enter and leave its berth according to the schedule, or chaos will ensue and business will be lost.

Imagine the problems of having five days to load everything from sewing machines to steel girders, particularly if the girders have to be unloaded before the sewing machines. If you put the girders on top you will dangerously destabilize the ship, and of course, everything that you wish to load first will arrive at the dock last and vice versa. And, the process is then repeated at the several ports to be visited on the voyage.

The first mate is responsible for ensuring that the cargo is loaded safely, but the purser must keep track of it, and all its paperwork. Once the ship is underway again, he will construct, from the notes made while loading and unloading in each port, a stowage plan showing the nature, destination, and stowed position of all the innumerable parcels of cargo in the ship. When the ship arrives in harbor he will have to cope once more with the endless formalities of police, immigration, and customs officials. This then is the job in which Herbert Holdsworth spent his working life.

1898–1906

Until 1906 Herbert Holdsworth sailed mainly with three shipping lines, and all his voyages were in the western hemisphere almost exclusively to the West Indies and North America. Virtually all voyages started and finished in Liverpool or Birkenhead and this includes those undertaken after 1910.

The first two voyages of his new career were to the West Indies in the *Bernard Hall.* The first commenced on 9 November 1898 and was completed on 21 January 1899, and therefore lasted 73 days. After ten days in port the voyage was repeated and again lasted 73 days.

S.S. *Bernard Hall,* 1898

The official number of the *Bernard Hall* was 84,059; port of registry: Liverpool. She was built in 1880 and was therefore three years older than *Ladakh.* Her owner was Samuel Wright of Mersey Chambers, Liverpool. The tonnage figures are significant. Gross tonnage was 2,677 (679 tons more than *Ladakh*) but net tonnage was 1,706 (202 tons less). Only 64 percent of *Bernard Hall's* space could be used to carry cargo compared with 95 percent for *Ladakh.* This is an indication of the amount of space required for engines, boilers, and coal. This figure of 64 percent carrying capacity appears to be the best that can be achieved with a compound steam engine. The ships built for Alfred Holt between 1904 and 1914, all approximated to this figure and the *Perseus,* which was built in 1923 and was the last ship Herbert Holdsworth sailed in, had 62 percent of space usable for cargo. These figures indicate why there were still niche markets in which sail could operate well into the twentieth century. *Bernard Hall's* "Nominal horse power of engines" was 320, 5.3 horsepower per ton.

9 November 1898–21 January 1899, Liverpool–West Indies

The crew agreement for this voyage is broadly similar to those already described, except that it contains the following paragraph:

> The crew shall consist of mate, carpenter, boatswain, 2 stewards, 1 cook, 6 seamen, 2 engineers and 6 firemen and shall appear in the Company's uniform at their own expense. No grog or fat allowed. The Crew also agrees to conform to, and abide by the Rules of the West India and Pacific Steam Ship Company's Mutual Benefit Society. Stewards and cooks liable for lost plate and linen.

> Seamen and Firemen mutually to assist each other and work Coals and Cargo night and day if required. All overtime when engaged in working cargo to be paid at the rate of 6d. [six pence] per hour. If from any cause the said ship cannot sail on the day appointed, or should the vessel put back to port through any accident, the crew shall, if required, be transferred to any other vessel belonging to the same owners or chartered by them, taking the place of the vessel herein named. Also that any member of the crew neglecting to keep a proper look out, shall forfeit to the ship the sum of five shillings for each offence. Any member of the crew using insulting or abusive language to the master or any Officer, shall forfeit to the ship one day's pay for each offence.

Number signing agreement:	47
Failed to join:	5
Number sailing:	42
Deserted:	2
Sick:	1

£1 in 1898 = £54.70 as at March 1999.

J.E. Bartlett	36	Liverpool	Master

He had been master on the previous voyage. His address was 19 Saint Elmo Road, Egremont. Herbert Holdsworth's address at this time was 4 Saint Vincent Road, Egremont. These roads are adjacent and run parallel to one another and at right angles to the promenade.

C.E. Shacklock	29	Birkenhead	First Mate	£11:00s
J. Troughton	29	Liverpool	Second Mate	£8:00s
Arthur Miller	27	Liverpool	Third Mate	£6:00s
Hugh Rennie	24	Barrow	Carpenter	£6:00s
Fred Wilson	28	Sheffield	Bosun	£5:00s
E. Smidt	24	German	Lamp trimmer	£3:15s

Nine able seamen signed the agreement: four were from Liverpool, three were Swedish, and one was German. Their average age was 26. Their wages were £3:10s per month.

The next group to sign the agreement was the engineers and others concerned with the engines:

D. Gordon	30	Liverpool	Chief Engineer	£15:00s
David Gordon	26	Liverpool	Second Engineer	£11:00s
Saul S. Jones	23	Liverpool	Third Engineer	£9:00s
Jacob Birch	23	Liverpool	Fourth Engineer	£7:00s

The wages of the chief engineer are an indication of his status as second only to the master, and his juniors are paid more than the deck officers. The chief engineer also had his own steward, a 15 year old boy who was paid £1:10s per month. This wage differential extended to the five firemen who were paid £4:00s per month and a donkeyman/fireman whose wages were £5:00s. The *Oxford Companion to Ships and the Sea* defines a donkey engine as, "A small auxiliary steam engine with its own small boiler, used for furnishing power for a variety of smaller mechanical duties on board a vessel in harbor for which it would be uneconomic to produce steam from the main boilers."

Finally there were three trimmers who were paid at the same rate as the able seamen. The trimmers had to move coal from the bunkers so that it was readily available for the firemen to shovel into the furnace and also dispose of the ashes overboard, usually at the end of the watch. Six of the ten who stoked the boilers, including the donkeyman were illiterate and their higher wages were almost certainly a reflection of the appalling conditions in which they had to work. Their average age was 26. Seven men and one woman completed the crew, and all were from Liverpool or Birkenhead.

Chief steward	29	£7:00s
Second steward	23	£3:00s
Steward	20	£2:00s
Stewards' boy	20	£1:10s
Chief cook	32	£6:00s
Second cook	26	£3:00s

Finally, we come to the purser, Herbert Holdsworth, now aged 18. His pay was £4:00s per month (£218.80 in today's terms). The stewardess, Elizabeth M. Leather, aged 36, was paid £3:00s. Her presence, together with the other cooks and stewards, suggests that a small number of passengers were carried in the ship. The master and the stewardess were the two oldest in the crew except for a 39 year old able seaman who deserted.

The total wage bill (excluding the captain's remuneration) was £179:15s per month. This is more than double the figure for *Ladakh*.

Bernard Hall left Liverpool on 9 November 1898 and arrived at Barbados on 24 November, where a trimmer was left behind in hospital and another taken on in his place. She remained here for 24 hours before proceeding to La Guaira, which is close to Caracas on the north coast of Venezuela.

One of the trimmers deserted here. This was reported to the British consul in Curaçao on 1 December. On 3 December they were at Puerto Colombia which is just up the coast from Cartagena (both ports are in Colombia), where they arrived on 10 December and reported the desertion of an able seaman.

On 16 December they arrived and departed Cienfuegos, Cuba. Finally the *Bernard Hall* called at Galveston, Texas having done a clockwise circuit of the Caribbean and Gulf of Mexico.

Another trimmer joined the ship in Galveston. Christmas was spent here, and they departed for Liverpool on 31 December arriving on 21 January 1899. Another voyage in the *Bernard Hall* followed but on that occasion their last port of call was New Orleans.

Voyages, 1899–1906

The next four voyages were in the *American* (O.N. 105,345, N.R.T. 5,406) and were unusual in that they commenced in London. All were to New York and lasted on average 34 days. The *American* was owned by F. Leyland & Co. Exchange Buildings, Liverpool, a company that owned 40 ships at this time. Herbert Holdsworth sailed once more from London in the *American*, but this time to New Orleans, leaving on 25 October 1899 and returning to Liverpool on 12 December.

Two voyages to the West Indies followed in the Leyland ship *Nicaraguan* (O.N. 99,347, N.R.T. 2,385) commencing on 4 January 1900. One lasted 70 days, the other 61.

He then joined the *Barbadian* (O.N. 102,072, N.R.T. 2,934), again owned by F. Leyland & Co., for two trips to New Orleans of 46 and 44 days, being back in Liverpool on 26 October 1900. He then left on 1 November for two trips to the West Indies and one, commencing on 13 April 1901, to New Orleans and Cape Town, which was completed on 28 August 1901 after a voyage of 137 days.

There is then a gap of five months before he joined the *Vancouver* (O.N. 87,963, N.R.T. 3,400) on 29 March 1902. This voyage lasted 81 days and was to the Mediterranean and Portland (presumably in Oregon.)

On 10 July 1902 he joined the *Merion* (O.N. 115,257, N.R.T. 7,459) for the first of eight voyages to Boston. The average time for each of these trips was 24 days and only four or five days were spent in Liverpool before they set off again.

The *Merion* was owned by the International Navigation Co. (the American Line) with offices in Liverpool, Southampton, and London. Herbert Holdsworth left the *Merion* on 6 March 1903.

On 9 April 1903 he joined the *Mayflower* (O.N. 15,288, N.R.T. 8,675) for seven voyages to Boston, which were very similar to those in *Merion*. These trips were completed on 18 October 1903. The *Mayflower* was owned by the British and North Atlantic Steamship Company (the Dominion Line) of 24 James Street, Liverpool. She was a virtually new ship having been built in 1902.

On 11 November 1903 he was back in the *Barbadian* for the first of 11 voyages to the West Indies. He also sailed once in the *Colonian* (O.N. 115,222, N.R.T. 4,142), once in the *Louisianian* (O.N. 99,322, N.R.T. 2,385), twice in the *Belgian* (O.N. 113,417, N.R.T. 2,363), five times in the *Jamaican* (O.N. 12,085, N.R.T. 2,947), and once in the *Alexandrian* (O.N. 115,212, N.R.T. 2,898). The longest of these voyages was 90 days and the shortest was 55 days with an average of 67 days. Time spent in port between voyages varied between three days and one month. All the ships were owned by F. Leyland & Co.

Out of a total of 41 voyages: (excluding that in *Ladakh*)

17 (41 percent) were to the West Indies;
15 (37 percent) were to Boston;
4 (10 percent) were to New York;
3 (7 percent) were to New Orleans;
1 was to Cape Town via New Orleans;
and 1 was to the Mediterranean and Portland (Oregon)

An analysis of the days spent on voyages for the years 1897–1905 (including that in *Ladakh*) gives the following results:

1897: 311 days at sea (85 percent of the year)
1898: 227 days at sea (62 percent of the year)
1899: 258 days at sea (71 percent of the year)
1900: 282 days at sea (77 percent of the year)
1901: 209 days at sea (58 percent of the year)
1902: 220 days at sea (60 percent of the year)
1903: 273 days at sea (75 percent of the year)
1904: 313 days at sea (86 percent of the year)
1905: 292 days at sea (80 percent of the year)
1906: 86 days at sea (24 percent of the year)

Herbert Holdsworth was home at Christmas in the years 1898, 1901, 1902, and 1904, although in this latter year he sailed on Boxing Day.

For reasons that are impossible to discover there was a gap in Herbert Holdsworth's sea-going career between 29 March 1906 and 15 April 1910.

Details of Voyages, 1898–1906

Voyages with Individual Certificates of Discharge

Table 1. 9 November 1898–12 December 1899

Name of Ship	From	To	Date of Departure	Date of Return	Days on Voyage	Days at Home
Bernard Hall	Liverpool	West Indies	9.xi.98	21.i.99	73	10
Bernard Hall	Liverpool	West Indies	1.ii.99	13.iv.99	73	22
American	London	New York	5.v.99	7.vi.99	33	7
American	London	New York	14.vi.99	18.vii.99	35	9
American	London	New York	28.vii.99	30.viii.99	33	11
American	London	New York	9.ix.99	14.x.99	35	11
American	London	New Orleans	25.x.99	12.xii.99	49	23

Table 2. 4 January 1900–8 January 1901

Name of Ship	From	To	Date of Departure	Date of Return	Days on Voyage	Days at Home
Nicaraguan	Liverpool	West Indies	4.i.00	14.iii.00	70	8
Nicaraguan	Liverpool	West Indies	22.iii.00	22.v.00	61	57
Barbadian	Liverpool	New Orleans	18.vii.00	2.ix.00	46	10
Barbadian	Liverpool	New Orleans	12.ix.00	26.x.00	44	5
Barbadian	Liverpool	West Indies	1.xi.00	8.i.01	69	6

Voyages recorded in the first Board of Trade Continuous Certificate of Discharge book, number 102,186. The number of the voyage as it appears in the book is given in the first column by the name of the ship.

Table 3. 14 January 1901–28 August 1901

Name of Ship	From	To	Date of Departure	Date of Return	Days on Voyage	Days at Home
Barbadian (1)	Liverpool	West Indies	14.i.01	1.iv.01	72	12
Barbadian (2)	Liverpool	New Orleans Cape Town	13.iv.01	28.viii.01	137	214

Table 4. 29 March 1902–20 December 1902

Name of Ship	From	To	Date of Departure	Date of Return	Days on Voyage	Days at Home
Vancouver (3)	Liverpool	Mediterranean Portland	29.iii.02	17.vi.02	80	23
Merion (4)	Liverpool	Boston	10.vii.02	3.viii.02	24	4
Merion (5)	Liverpool	Boston	7.viii.02	30.viii.02	21	5
Merion (6)	Liverpool	Boston	4.ix.02	27.ix.02	24	5
Merion (7)	Liverpool	Boston	2.x.02	25.x.02	23	5
Merion (8)	Liverpool	Boston	30.x.02	23.xi.02	24	4
Merion (9)	Liverpool	Boston	27.xi.02	20.xii.02	23	11

Table 5. 1 January 1903–18 October 1903

Name of Ship	From	To	Date of Departure	Date of Return	Days on Voyage	Days at Home
Merion (10)	Liverpool	Boston	1.i.03	29.i.03	28	7
Merion (11)	Liverpool	Boston	5.ii.03	6.iii.03	30	34
Mayflower (12)	Liverpool	Boston	9.iv.03	3.v.03	24	4
Mayflower (13)	Liverpool	Boston	7.v.03	31.v.03	24	4
Mayflower (14)	Liverpool	Boston	4.vi.03	27.vi.03	23	5
Mayflower (15)	Liverpool	Boston	2.vii.03	25.vii.03	23	5
Mayflower (16)	Liverpool	Boston	30.vii.03	22.viii.03	23	5
Mayflower (17)	Liverpool	Boston	27.viii.03	19.ix.03	23	4
Mayflower (18)	Liverpool	Boston	23.ix.03	18.ix.03	25	24

Table 6. 11 November 1903–6 December 1904

Name of Ship	From	To	Date of Departure	Date of Return	Days on Voyage	Days at Home
Barbadian (19)	Liverpool	West Indies	11.xi.03	21.i.04	71	7
Colonian (20)	Liverpool	West Indies	28.i.04	23.iii.04	55	8
Louisianian (21)	Liverpool	West Indies	31.iii.04	4.vi.04	65	14
Belgian (22)	Liverpool	West Indies	18.vi.04	16.ix.04	90	7
Belgian (23)	Liverpool	West Indies	22.ix.04	6.xii.04	75	18

Table 7. 24 December 1904–13 November 1905

Name of Ship	From	To	Date of Departure	Date of Return	Days on Voyage	Days at Home
Jamaican (24)	Liverpool	West Indies	24.xii.04	25.ii.05	63	8
Jamaican (25)	Liverpool	West Indies	4.iii.05	29.iv.05	56	28
Jamaican (26)	Liverpool	West Indies	27.v.05	19.viii.05	85	21
Jamaican (27)	Liverpool	West Indies	9.ix.05	13.xi.05	65	17

Table 8. 30 November 1905–29 March 1906

Name of Ship	From	To	Date of Departure	Date of Return	Days on Voyage	Days at Home
Jamaican (28)	Liverpool	West Indies	30.xi.05	24.i.06	55	3
Alexandrian (29)	Liverpool	West Indies	27.i.06	29.iii.06	62	

There now follows a gap of just over four years, between 29 March 1906 and 15 April 1910. What Herbert Holdsworth was doing during this period, it has not been possible to ascertain.

Marriage, 1910

On 8 January 1910, Matthew Holdsworth, Herbert Holdsworth's father, died aged 69. His death certificate gives his occupation as "Corn Broker's Clerk" and the cause of death: "Erysipelas, 3 days, Heart failure, 6 hours." Certified by A.R. Wilson MD.

Erysipelas is an acute, superficial, rapidly spreading (in pre-antibiotic days) infection of the skin caused by the Streptococcus bacterium. The disease was untreatable in 1910 and would have resulted in multi-organ failure with, in the case of Matthew Holdsworth, the heart being the first to fail. The death was registered by Matthew's elder son, Matthew Clement, who gave as his address "In attendance, 10 Ball Avenue, Liscard." Liscard is an area in Birkenhead, which still exists, but Ball Avenue has disappeared. The registration district was Birkenhead, subdistrict of Wallasey in the County of Chester.

Two months later, on 11 March 1910, Herbert Holdsworth and Jane Holland (plate 6) were married in the registry office in Birkenhead. Herbert Holdsworth was 29. He had been living with his parents at 10 Ball Avenue. He gave his rank or profession as purser (despite the fact that he had not been to sea for four years) and his father, Matthew Holdsworth (deceased), corn merchant's cashier.

Plate 6. Herbert Holdsworth and Jane Holland.

Jane Holland was 24 years old, and her address was 53 Rundle Street, Birkenhead. This street still exists and is just south of the docks. Jane Holland's father was William Holland, a master mariner on a coasting steamer.

At the bottom of the certificate it states: "Married in the Register Office by Certificate before me, A.R. Gregory, Registrar." The certificate is also signed by S.R. Carter, Deputy Superintendent Registrar. The section "According to the Rites and Ceremonies of the _____________________ Church" has been struck out. The witnesses of the marriage were Wm. Holland and H.J. Thurlow.

Thirty-five days after the wedding Herbert Holdsworth sailed on the *Cedric* (O.N. 115,354) for New York. He was back in Liverpool on 8 May, but on 14 May he left for Montreal in the *Megantic* (O.N. 127,981, N.R.T. 9,183), returning on 4 June.

Sometime between 4 June and 6 August 1910, Herbert Holdsworth joined the Alfred Holt Ocean Steam Ship Company (the "Blue Funnel Line") and remained with it until he retired 22 years later. It was one of the most prestigious and successful shipping companies in Britain, if not the world. In 1910 it owned 60 ships; in 1932, when Herbert Holdsworth retired, the figure had increased to 80.

Alfred Holt

Alfred Holt (1829–1911) was the third son of George Holt, a successful Liverpool businessman with interests in cotton, banking, and insurance. Alfred did not intend to follow his father into commerce but wished to become a civil engineer and was apprenticed to Edward Woods, an engineer with the Liverpool and Manchester Railway Co. When Alfred completed his apprenticeship in 1851, there was a temporary depression in the railway industry, and he took employment as a shipping clerk. This introduced him to steam ships, and his future career was decided.

In 1852, the sailing ship still reigned supreme on the long distance routes of the world. This was the heroic age of sail when men, such as Donald McKay (1810–80) of Boston, designed and built such magnificent ships as the *Lightning, Sovereign of the Seas,* and *James Baines.*

Two fundamental problems confronted the designers and builders of early steam engines. These were their gross inefficiency and the difficulty in building boilers and cylinders that could safely withstand the high pressures required for efficient working. Thomas Newcomen (1663–1729), who built the world's first practical steam engine in 1712, relied on atmospheric pressure to drive it. Steam was introduced into the cylinder and then condensed with cold water. Steam occupies ten times the volume as the same weight of water so the effect was to produce a vacuum and atmospheric pressure drove the piston down. This engine was 1 percent efficient, that is to say only one ton of coal out of a hundred produced any usable energy. This was plainly not a suitable engine for a ship.

As boiler designed improved, steam could be injected into the cylinder under pressure, and thus move the piston. By 1840, however, the steam engines used in ships were still very inefficient. The *Britannia,* designed for the Atlantic, had to use 640 of her total capacity of 865 tons for coal, leaving only 225 tons for cargo. Furthermore, the engine compartment occupied half the total space in the ship.

Common sense dictated that trade with the Far East must remain the preserve of the sailing ship for the foreseeable future. Alfred Holt's realization that this was not the case enabled him to build one of the great shipping lines. His understanding of the potential of the compound steam engine was the key to his success. Advances in boiler design had resulted in much greater steam pressures, but it was still considered too dangerous to inject steam at very high pressure into a single cylinder. To obviate this problem the steam was first injected into a small (and therefore strong) cylinder and, still retaining much of its potential energy, was immediately evacuated into a larger cylinder. This proved to be a satisfactory solution to the problem since both cylinders could be used to drive the crankshaft. Eventually this compound, or tandem, engine was superseded by the triple expansion engine, which, as its name implies, had three cylinders, the second cylinder exhausting into the third. Now three cylinders were driving the crankshaft all from one initial jet of steam into cylinder number one.

The compound engine was markedly more efficient than its predecessors, so much so, that together with other developments in ship design, it at last became possible for steam ships to trade efficiently with the Far East. Thus on 19 April 1866 the *Agamemnon* of Holt's Ocean Steam Ship Company inaugurated a regular service to China and the Far East. The opening of the Suez Canal in 1869 signaled the final victory of the steam ship, and Alfred Holt was superbly placed to take advantage of it.

Alfred Holt was not only an astute businessman, but his engineering background enabled him to appreciate the vital importance of what we now call research and development. He constantly sought to improve his ships and made a point of overseeing their construction. (He must have been a very difficult client.) Holt also insisted that his ships were built to "Passenger Certificate" standards despite the fact that they were primarily for carrying cargo. This provided him with an unexpected opportunity when the Suez Canal was opened in 1869.

Every (male) Muslim is expected to make a pilgrimage to Mecca at least once in his lifetime. Holt ships carried these pilgrims to and from Jeddah, which is on the Red Sea coast of Saudi Arabia and the nearest port to Mecca. Eventually as many as a thousand would be transported in each ship (on deck) and this trade was still continuing when Herbert Holdsworth was serving with Alfred Holt.

Alfred Holt was an Old Testament figure, and this lent his decisions an apparent ruthlessness. Thus, while he was always kind and considerate to his captains, an error of judgment that hazarded any of his ships would result in dismissal, whatever their length of service. Alfred Holt felt that he must act impartially when assessing his obligations to shareholders and crews, as well as his captains.

His tenure of the chairmanship of the Mersey Docks and Harbor Board, which commenced in 1889, lasted only fifteen months before he resigned, as he considered the Board was failing to match his own strict business ethics. For Alfred Holt, conscience was the final arbiter, and he refused to accept that anyone or anything, particularly the government, had the right to override it. This was the basis for his resistance to the various merchant shipping acts, which he regarded as setting disgracefully *low* standards.

The problem with men like Alfred Holt is their inability to realize that their high principles are likely to be the exception rather than the rule. When Alfred Holt retired in 1904, his son, Richard Durning Holt (1868–1941) became the driving force behind the company and would have been the man whom Herbert Holdsworth would have recognized as the ultimate head of the organization.

S.S. *Perseus*

Crew Agreement, 26 December 1931–9 May 1932

Before going on to record and analyze the voyages that Herbert Holdsworth made in the service of Alfred Holt & Co., the crew agreement of his last voyage (see map 2) will be recorded.

This was made in the steam ship *Perseus,* built in 1923, O.N. 10,286, registered in Liverpool. She was managed by the China Mutual Steam Navigation Company, a subsidiary of Alfred Holt, based at the group's headquarters, India Buildings, Water Street, Liverpool; Gross tonnage 10,286, net tonnage 6,335. Thus 62 percent of the ship's volume was available to carry freight and passengers. The nominal horsepower on the engines was 1200—that is, 5.2 horsepower per ton. These ratios are virtually the same as the *Bernard Hall,* which suggests that the efficiency of the compound steam engine had remained unaltered for fifty years. The voyage commenced on 26 December 1931 at Birkenhead, terminating on 9 May 1932 at Victoria Docks in London.

A total of 48 men signed the agreement in Liverpool, but this was not the total of the crew. On the last page there is a note: "Remainder of crew on Chinese agreement." These must have been the stokers and trimmers.

Thirty-seven crewmembers remained in *Perseus* from her previous voyage, and although some "Names of last ship" are illegible, everyone else in the crew had also been serving in Alfred Holt ships. No one failed to join, and there were no deserters.

Nationalities were as follows:

English	37, 24 of whom were from Liverpool, Birkenhead, or Wallasey.
Scottish	4, including a Shetland Islander.
Isle of Man	2

Welsh	2, including a man from Anglesey.
Southern Ireland	2
American	1

£1 in 1931 = £30.96 as at March 1999.

J. Davies	45	Master	Liverpool	
Ramsey Brown	46	First mate	Forfar	£31:00s
G.T. Morgan	33	Second mate	Birkenhead	£25:00s
J.B. Marshall	31	Third Mate	Paisley	£21:00s
J. Gibson	40	Carpenter	Liverpool	£13:10s
T. Proswell	46	Bosun	Chester	£11:10s
P. Cringle	50	Lamp trimmer and able seaman	Isle of Man	£9:10s

There are then listed ten able seamen, with an average age of 37. Four were paid £9:10s and the remainder £9:00s. Two ordinary seamen, aged 18 and 21, were each paid £5:17s:06d and a deck boy, 19, whose wages were £2:10s.

The agreement then lists the engineers:

C.E. Melville	41	Chief engineer	Birkenhead	£41:00s
J. Blackstock	39	Second engineer	Birkenhead	£30:10s
G. Nisbet	35	Extra second engineer	Birkenhead	£24:10s
G. Barr	34	Third engineer	Bootle	£23:00s
Herbert Shaw	27	Fourth engineer	Sunderland	£19:00s

Four assistant engineers are then listed. Their average age was 23 and their wages were £12:00s per month.

There then follow the stewards:

| Chief steward | 52 | (place of birth illegible) | £21:00s |
| Second steward | 41 | Newport (Monmouthshire) | £10:00s |

Six assistant stewards follow, average age 24, each paid £8:05s. Three junior assistant stewards, average age 22, £5:00s

Chief cook	43	£14:00s
Second cook and baker	24	£10:10s
Assistant cook	24	£9:00s
Scullion	19	£5:00s
First wireless Operator	37	£19:00s

A supernumerary wireless operator aged 27 was paid £11:00s

The American in the crew was Samuel Henry Kalen aged 27. He was the ship's doctor, and *Perseus* was his first ship. His address was the West London Hospital, Hammersmith, and his wages were £10:00s.

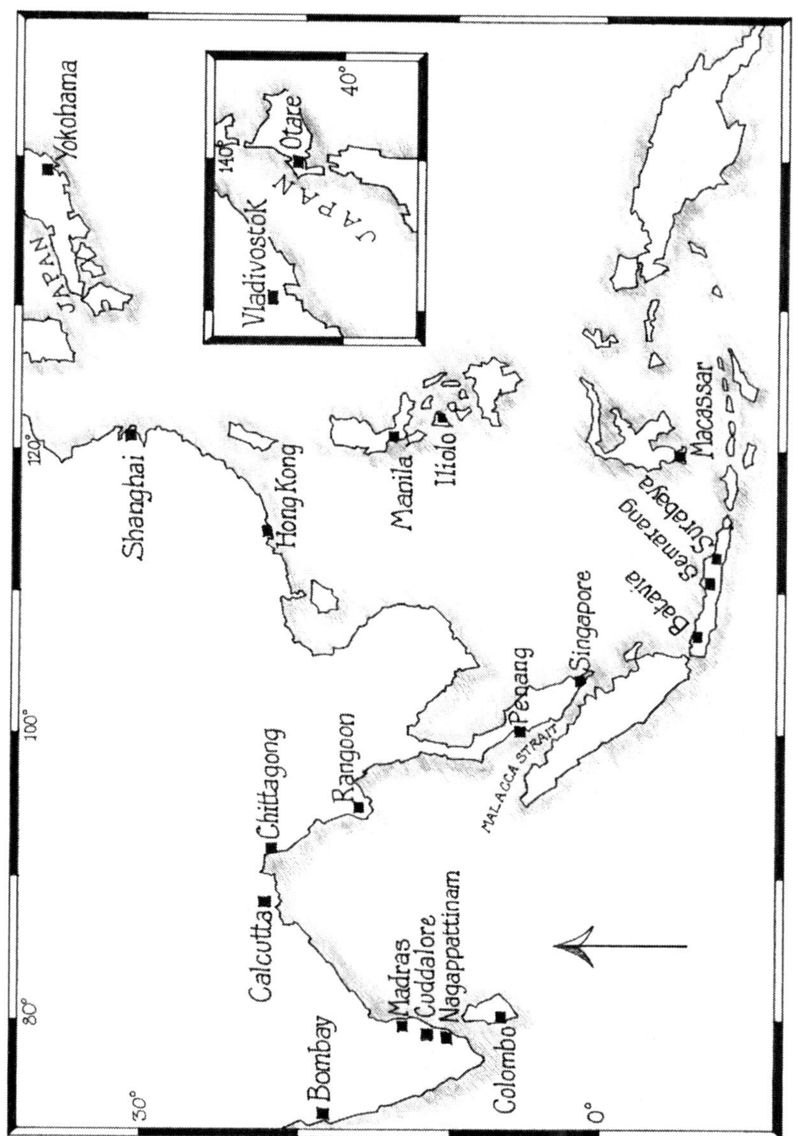

Map 2. Herbert Holdsworth's last voyage.

43

The last person to sign the agreement in Liverpool was Herbert Pennington Holdsworth, as purser, then aged 50. His address was Oak House Lane, Over, Winsford, Cheshire. (Winsford is approximately 32 miles from Birkenhead.) His wages were £21:00s per month (£7,801.92 a year in today's terms). This is the same as the third mate and the chief steward.

Perseus left Birkenhead on Boxing Day 1931.

Arrived	Port Said	6 January 1932
Departed		7 January
Arrived	Penang	25 January
Departed		29 January
Arrived	Hong Kong	3 February
Departed		4 February

The supernumerary radio operator left the ship here.

Arrived	Shanghai	9 February
Departed		13 February
Arrived	Yokohama	23 February
Departed		24 February
Arrived	Vladivostok	28 February
Departed		5 March
Arrived	Otare	8 March
Departed		14 March
Arrived	Shanghai	23 March
Departed		25 March
Arrived	Hong Kong	29 March

A supernumerary third mate (£21:00s per month) and supernumerary wireless operator (£13:10s) were taken on here. Date of departure not recorded.

Arrived	Penang	5 April
Departed		7 April

The British consul recorded "I hereby certify that I have placed on board the within named vessel one distressed British seaman named W. Bibby for conveyance to United Kingdom in accordance with section 48 of the Merchant Shipping Act."

Arrived	London, Victoria Docks,	9 May 1932

The Mercantile Marine Office recorded, "D.B.S. W. Bibby landed at this port today."
Herbert Holdsworth was discharged and never went to sea again.

Summary of Voyages, 1910–1932

Voyages recorded in the first Board of Trade *Continuous Certificate of Discharge* book, number 102,186. The number of the voyage as it appears in the book is given in the first column beneath the name of the ship.

Table 9

Name of Ship	From	To	Date of Departure	Date of Return	Days on Voyage	Days at Home
Cedric (30)	Liverpool	New York	15.iv.10	8.v.10	23	6
Magantic (31)	Liverpool	Montreal	14.v.10	4.vi.10	21	

After 63 days in England, Herbert Holdsworth began his service with Alfred Holt's Ocean Steam Ship Company. Almost all voyages were to the Far East, and consequently, voyage times were much longer.

Table 10

Name of Ship	From	To	Date of Departure	Date of Return	Days on Voyage	Days at Home
Ajax (32)	Glasgow	Australia	6.viii.10	31.xii.10	147	20
Ajax (33)	Birkenhead	Straits of Mallaca China, Japan	21.i.11	24.v.11	124	19
Peleus (34)	Birkenhead	China, Japan	12.vi.11	17.x.11	127	24
Peleus (35)	Birkenhead	China, Japan	10.xii.11	9.iii.12	120	29

Thomas Herbert conceived.

Table 11

Name of Ship	From	To	Date of Departure	Date of Return	Days on Voyage	Days at Home
Peleus (36)	Birkenhead	China, Japan	7.iv.12	7.viii.12	91	32
Peleus (37)	Birkenhead	China, Japan	8.ix.12	30.xii.12	11	33

Thomas Herbert was born on 8 December 1912. He was three weeks old when Herbert Holdsworth first saw him.

Table 12

Name of Ship	From	To	Date of Departure	Date of Return	Days on Voyage	Days at Home
Titan (38)	Birkenhead	Japan, Pacific	2.ii.13	24.viii.13	204	34
Titan (39)	Birkenhead	Japan, Pacific	27.ix.13	5.iii.14	161	29
Agapenor (40)	Birkenhead	China, Japan	3.iv.14	21.vii.14	109	109

Great Britain declared war on Germany on 4 August 1914. Herbert Holdsworth remained ashore for 139 days before his next voyage began, on 6 December 1914.

Table 13

Name of Ship	From	To	Date of Departure	Date of Return	Days on Voyage	Days at Home
Oanfa (41)	Birkenhead	China Puget Sound	6.xii.14	3.vii.15	204	14
Protesilaus (42)	London	China, Japan	17.vii.15	26.xii.15	132	22

This completes the entries in the first Continuous Certificate of Discharge book. A new one, number 847,195, was issued on 16 December 1915.

Table 14

Name of Ship	From	To	Date of Departure	Date of Return	Days on Voyage	Days at Home
Protesilaus (1)	London	Straits China, Japan	18.xii.15	8.v.16	142	23

Herbert Holdsworth spent 23 days at home, and Jane Holland Wood was conceived. She was born on 10 February 1917. He went to sea again on 31 May 1916, and did not return home until 461 days later on 4 September 1917, nearly seven months after Jane's birth (Voyages 2–4).

Number two ended prematurely when *Ping Suey* went aground on Dasseneiland, near Cape Town, on 24 June 1916. The crew were taken off, and Herbert Holdsworth arrived in Cape Town on 6 July. He left the same day.

Table 15

Name of Ship	From	To	Date of Departure	Date of Return	Days on Voyage	Days at Home
Ping Suey (2)	Birkenhead	Cape Town	31.v.16	6.vii.16	33	
Agapenor (3)	Cape Town	Hong Kong	6.vii.16	8.viii.16	33	
Talthybius (4)	Hong Kong	Japan Puget Sound	9.viii.16	4.ix.17	392	57
Talthybius (5)	Birkenhead	China	31.x.17	14.iv.18	167	8
Talthybius (6)	On His Majesty's Service		22.iv.18	12.vi.18	51	6
Talthybius (7)	On His Majesty's Service		18.vi.18	28.vii.18	40	11
Talthybius (8)	On His Majesty's Service		8.viii.18	13.ix.18	36	7

After the war Herbert Holdsworth was awarded the Mercantile Marine War Medal. There were two criteria for this award:

- Making one or more voyages through a danger zone.
- Serving with His Majesty's Commissioned Ships and Auxiliaries under special Naval engagement.

Table 16

Name of Ship	From	To	Date of Departure	Date of Return	Days on Voyage	Days at Home
Talthybius (9)	Birkenhead	New York	20.ix.18	15.xii.18	86	104

During this voyage the war ended on 11 November 1918. Herbert Holdsworth spent 104 days at home, and Mary was conceived. She was born on 4 November 1919.

Table 17

Name of Ship	From	To	Date of Departure	Date of Return	Days on Voyage	Days at Home
Talthybius (10)	Birkenhead	China, Japan	28.iii.19	7.ix.19	163	84

Eighty-four days were spent on leave, so that Herbert Holdsworth would have been at home for Mary's birth on 4 November 1919.

Table 18

Name of Ship	From	To	Date of Departure	Date of Return	Days on Voyage	Days at Home
Belerophon (11)	Birkenhead	China, Japan	28.xi.19	25.iv.20	149	14
Belerophon (12)	Birkenhead	China, Japan	9.v.20	20.x.20	164	19
Belerophon (13)	Birkenhead	Straits, Japan	8.xi.20	15.iii.21	128	25

After 25 days at home, Herbert Holdsworth now embarked on the longest voyage of his career. It lasted 477 days, over fifteen months (Voyages 14–17).

Table 19

Name of Ship	From	To	Date of Departure	Date of Return	Days on Voyage	Days at Home
Belerophon (14)	Birkenhead	Japan	9.iv.21	5.vi.21	57	
Belerophon (15)	Yokohama	Hong Kong	6.vi.21	30.vi.21	24	
Tyndareus (16)	Hong Kong	Transpacific	1.vii.21	26.vi.22	361	

The voyage began, and finished, in Hong Kong, but Herbert Holdsworth joined his next ship in Singapore.

Table 20

Name of Ship	From	To	Date of Departure	Date of Return	Days on Voyage	Days at Home
Atreus (17)	Singapore	Birkenhead	19.vii.22	23.viii.22	35	52

Table 21

Name of Ship	From	To	Date of Departure	Date of Return	Days on Voyage	Days at Home
Meriones (18)	Birkenhead	China	14.x.22	31.i.23	109	52
Meriones (19)	Birkenhead	Straits China, Japan	23.iii.23	8.vii.23	107	27
Meriones (20)	Birkenhead	China, Japan Australia	4.viii.23	16.xii.23	130	34
Meriones (21)	Birkenhead	China, Japan	19.i.24	14.v.24	116	52
Meriones (22)	Birkenhead	Australia	5.vii.24	8.xi.24	126	34

On 19 October 1924, 19 days before Herbert Holdsworth arrived home from voyage number 22 his mother, Jane Pennington, died. Her death certificate recorded that she had been living at 40 Ashdale Road, Wavertree, Liverpool (no longer on the street map). The cause of death was "Decay of nature," and the death had been notified by her elder daughter, Edith.

Table 22

Name of Ship	From	To	Date of Departure	Date of Return	Days on Voyage	Days at Home
Meriones (23)	Birkenhead	Singapore China, Japan	12.xii.24	10.iv.25	120	35
Meriones (24)	Birkenhead	Singapore China, Japan	15.v.25	11.ix.25	119	43
Meriones (25)	Birkenhead	China	24.x.25	? 1.ii.26	≅ 100	35
Meriones (26)	Birkenhead	China	6.iii.26	25.vi.26	111	33
Meriones (27)	Birkenhead	Australia	28.vii.26	5.xii.26	130	41
Meriones (28)	Birkenhead	China, Japan	15.i.27	6.v.27	112	51
Meriones (29)	Birkenhead	Australia	26.vi.27	18.x.27	114	25
Meriones (30)	Birkenhead	Straits, Manila Japan	12.xi.27	11.iii.27	120	26
Meriones (31)	Birkenhead	China, Japan	6.iv.28	27.vii.28	112	32
Meriones (32)	Birkenhead	Singapore China, Japan	28.viii.28	28.xii.28	123	43
Meriones (33)	Birkenhead	China, Japan	9.ii.29	29.v.29	110	159

Following this long period of leave, nearly six months, the pattern of the next six voyages changes, in that the destination is Java, and the port of departure, is often Hamburg.

Table 23

Name of Ship	From	To	Date of Departure	Date of Return	Days on Voyage	Days at Home
Persander (34)	Hamburg	Java	4.xi.29	2.iii.30	119	50
Eurymedon (35)	Hamburg	Java	1.iv.30	21.viii.30	123	14
Eurymedon (36)	Hamburg	Java	4.ix.30	7.i.31	125	38
Eurymedon (37)	Birkenhead	Java	14.ii.31	? 1.vi.31	≅ 107	55
Stentor (38)	Birkenhead	Java	25.vii.31	6.ix.31	43	

This voyage ended in Macassar (Ujung Pandang), which is on Celebes, an island close to Java.

The next Certificate of Discharge is Dutch and is issued by the Nederland-sche Stoomvaat–Maatschappij (NSM) "Oceaan." This was a Dutch subsidiary of Alfred Holt, which had been formed in 1891 to compete with Dutch companies that were infiltrating what was regarded as the Ocean Steam Ship Company's territory, on the east coast of Sumatra. The ship that Herbert Holdsworth now joined on 7 September 1931 was the *Melampus,* which had been built specifically for the NSM "Oceaan" in 1924.

Melampus arrived in Amsterdam on 17 November 1931, a voyage of 71 days. After 39 days in England Herbert Holdsworth's last voyage commenced.

Table 24

Name of Ship	From	To	Date of Departure	Date of Return	Days on Voyage	Days at Home
Perseus (39)	Birkenhead	Straits China, Japan	26.xii.31	8.v.32	134	

Analysis of Voyages with the Blue Funnel Line

1910:	191 days at sea	(52 percent of the year); includes 44 days in the *Megantic* and *Cedric,* which were not owned by Alfred Holt.
1911:	303 days at sea	(83 percent of the year)
1912:	275 days at sea	(75 percent of the year)
1913:	300 days at sea	(82 percent of the year)
1914:	199 days at sea	(54 percent of the year)
1915:	330 days at sea	(90 percent of the year)
1916:	343 days at sea	(94 percent of the year)
1917:	309 days at sea	(85 percent of the year)
1918:	318 days at sea	(87 percent of the year)
1919:	196 days at sea	(54 percent of the year)
1920:	333 days at sea	(91 percent of the year)
1921:	341 days at sea	(93 percent of the year)
1922:	313 days at sea	(86 percent of the year)
1923:	272 days at sea	(75 percent of the year)
1924:	268 days at sea	(73 percent of the year)
1925:	287 days at sea	(79 percent of the year)
1926:	272 days at sea	(75 percent of the year)
1927:	275 days at sea	(75 percent of the year)
1928:	305 days at sea	(84 percent of the year)

    1929:   167 days at sea   (46 percent of the year)
    1930:   323 days at sea   (88 percent of the year)
    1931:   235 days at sea   (64 percent of the year)
    1932:   129 days at sea   (35 percent of the year)

This is an average of 273 days at sea for each of the 23 years he served, which is 75 percent of each year or nine months. To a certain extent this average obscures some very long absences. For example, 31 May 1916–4 September 1917, a period of 461 days, when Herbert Holdsworth was absent for the birth of Jane Holland Wood (plate 7) on 10 February 1917.

He was home for Jane Holland Wood's birthday in 1923, 1926, and 1931, but in 1929 he sailed the day before. He was home also for Mary's birth in 1919 and other birthdays in 1920 and 1927. In 1929, he set off on her birthday.

He was home for Christmas in 1923 and 1926, and in 1931, he sailed on Boxing Day for his last voyage.

His longest absence was that from 9 April 1921 to 23 August 1922—477 days. This voyage is of interest because the only surviving communication between Herbert Holdsworth and Jane was written on 15 July 1921, 97 days out. It is a postcard of Winsford, Cheshire. (Where the family was living at the time.) It is addressed to: "Mr. H.P. Holdsworth, Purser, S.S. *Tyndareus,* Blue Funnel Line, C/O Messrs. Wodwell and Co, Victoria, B.C." This latter has been crossed out and replaced by "Seattle Coast." The card reads:

> My dearest H./
>
> You will wonder at a postcard, but not having received any letters from you and not getting addresses, I am sending postcards to Seattle and Victoria to let you know we are all well, waiting to post long letter to you. I had a postcard from the office saying you transferred to *Tyndareus* 6 June so surely I should get letter from you soon. In the meantime I am risking sending you p.c. so you will not worry,
>
> Hope you are well
> Love and kisses J.

Also surviving from this voyage is a photograph of the officers of the *Tyndareus* taken at Manila at Christmas 1921 (plate 8). Unfortunately the picture is annotated by rank rather than by name, and as the crew agreement cannot be found, the subjects remain anonymous.

Summary of Ships in Which Herbert Holdsworth Served

Together with a brief history of their ultimate fate, this section is excerpted from *Blue Funnels in the Mersey* by C.H. Milsom, 1988.

Plate 7.

MARY   HERBERT   JANE

Plate 8. Officers of the S.S. *Tyndareus.*

Number 1, Meriones

Eight of the 17 ships in which Herbert Holdsworth served were sunk during the course of World War II, including the *Meriones,* the ship in which he spent just over five years, between 1922 and 1928. This represents 30 percent of his time at sea with the Blue Funnel Line.

There are two photographs of the *Meriones.* One (plate 9) is annotated *"s/s Meriones* Bay of Biscay, Outward bound" [undated].

The other (plate 10) is a postcard (undated) produced by a commercial photographer whose address was Mount Studio, Clifton Cottage, 35 Rowson Street, New Brighton.

It reads as follows:

> To the Purser, S.S. Meriones (Holt Line)
>
> Dear Sir, Having taken the accompanying snap of your boat whilst entering dock on Sunday last, I should be pleased to execute any orders you could obtain for me at the following rates
>
> P/cards 4d each
> 8½ x 6½   1/- each [one shilling.]
> larger sizes in proportion
>
> Thanking you in anticipation
> Yours Faithfully
> A.P. Pullan

Meriones was built in 1922 by Palmer and Co., Newcastle. O.N. 145,974, N.R.T. 4,810. On 22 January 1941 she ran aground on the South Haisborough Bank, off Cromer. Attempts to salvage the ship were unsuccessful and on 25 January the crew was taken off by the Cromer lifeboat. The following morning she was bombed, set on fire, and was declared a total loss

Number 2, Talthybius

Herbert Holdsworth spent just over two and a half years (15 percent of his sea time) in this vessel. There is a photograph of her (plate 11). The picture is annotated *"s/s Talthybius* North Pacific," which appears to have been taken in a typhoon.

Talthybius was built in 1912 by Scotts of Greenock. O.N. 131,411, N.R.T. 6,522. On 4 and 5 May 1941, she was bombed in Liverpool but escaped serious damage. On 3 February 1942, she was bombed and severely damaged in Singapore. Despite heroic efforts by the officers to save her, she fell into the hands of the Japanese who were able to repair her, and she was renamed *Taruyasu Maru.* On 30 June 1942 she struck an American mine in Toyama Bay on the northern coast of Honshu (the main island of Japan) and was beached in Maizuru harbor. After the war she was salvaged and renamed *Empire Evenlode* under *(text continues on p. 58)*

Plate 9. S.S. *Meriones* on the Bay of Biscay.

Plate 10. S.S. *Meriones* being docked.

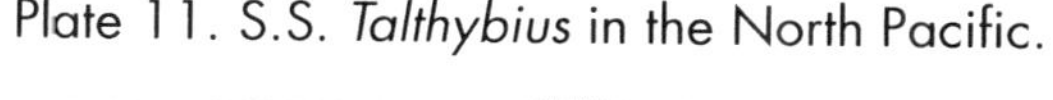

Plate 11. S.S. *Talthybius* in the North Pacific.

the ownership of the Ministry of War Transport. On 1 December 1948, she arrived at Hong Kong and was placed under the management of Alfred Holt & Co. who, after many vicissitudes, got her back to England, but she had to be scrapped.

Number 3, Belerophon 498 days (8.1 percent of sea time)

Built in 1906 by Workman, Clark & Co., Belfast. O.N. 120,915, N.R.T. 5,743. Sold for scrap in 1948 and broken up at Barrow in Furness.

Number 4, Peleus 452 days (7.3 percent)

Built in 1901 by Workman, Clark & Co. O.N. 113,467, N.R.T. 4,800. Sold to Philippine owners in 1931 and renamed *Perseus.* Sold for scrap in 1933 and broken up in Japan.

Number 5, Tyndareus 385 days (6.2 percent)

Built in 1916 by Scotts' of Greenock. O.N. 137,527, N.R.T. 7,172. Entered service as a troopship. On 6 February 1917 she struck a mine off Cape Agulhas (the southernmost tip of South Africa) but reached port. Entered commercial service in 1920.

During World War II was used as a troopship and supply vessel. Sold for scrap in 1960 and broken up in Hong Kong.

Number 6, Titan 365 days (5.9 percent)

Built in 1906 by D&W Henderson & Co., Glasgow. O.N. 124,015, N.R.T. 5,730. On 4 September 1940, she was torpedoed north west of Rockall. All the crew, 24 Europeans and 66 Chinese, were rescued by HMS *Godetia* and HMCS *Laurent.*

Number 7, Euremedon 355 days (5.7 percent)

Built in 1924 by Caledon Shipbuilding and Engineering Co., Dundee. O.N. 147,291. N.R.T. 3,818. On 25 September 1940, she was torpedoed in the North Atlantic, 370 miles west of Ireland with the loss of 20 crewmembers and nine passengers. The survivors were rescued from the boats by HMCS *Ottawa,* but the master and mate remained on board and were later joined by the survivors of another ship, *Sulairia.* Nothing could be done to save the *Euremedon,* and the *Ottawa* returned on 27 September, to take everyone off shortly before she sank.

Number 8, Protesilaus 274 days (4.4 percent)

Built in 1910 by Hawthorn, Leslie & Co., Newcastle. O.N. 128,014, N.R.T. 6118. On 24 January 1940, she struck a mine in the Bristol Channel near Swansea and was abandoned in a sinking condition. Later, she went aground near the Mumbles lighthouse while under tow. In 1942, she was sold for scrap and broken up at Briton Ferry, which is at the head of Swansea Bay.

Number 9, Ajax 271 days (4.3 percent)

Built in 1900 by Scott & Co., Greenock. O.N. 113,395, N.R.T. 4,477. On 10 October 1915, she was shelled in the Mediterranean but escaped when British warships approached. Sold for scrap in 1930 and broken up in Japan.

Number 10, Oanfa 204 days (3.3 percent)

Built by D. and W. Henderson & Co., Glasgow. O.N. 115,351, N.R.T. 5,809. Sold for scrap in 1931 and broken up in Japan.

Number 11, Perseus 134 days (2.2 percent)

Built in 1923 by the Caledon Shipbuilding and Engineering Co., Dundee. O.N. 147,194, N.R.T. 6,335. On 16 January 1944, she was torpedoed off Madras. All the crew were rescued from the boats later the same day by a Royal Indian Navy corvette.

Number 12, Persander 119 days (1.9 percent)

Built in 1925 by the Caledon Shipbuilding and Engineering Co., Dundee. O.N. 147,304, N.R.T. 3,818. On 17 May 1942, she was torpedoed and sunk in 37°24'N, 65°38'W (in the North Atlantic) but not before all on board had embarked in three lifeboats. Number 4 and 6 were offered rescue on 20 May by the *Baron Sempill,* but on learning that the ship was bound for South Africa, the survivors decided to stay in their boats and arrived at Nantucket Island on 24 May. Number 2 boat was found on 25 May by the U.S. Coast Guard cutter *General Green* and was taken into Newport, Rhode Island.

Number 13, Agapenor 109 days (1.8 percent)

Built in 1914 by Scott & Co. of Greenock. O.N. 135,553, N.R.T. 4,800. She was torpedoed off Freetown (West Africa) on 11 October 1942 and sank with the loss of six lives. The survivors, including survivors from the *Glendene,* which *Agapenor* had picked up the previous day, were rescued a few hours later by HMS *Petunia.*

Number 14, Melampus 71 days (1.2 percent)

Built in 1924 by Palmers' Co., Newcastle for NSM "Oceaan," Alfred Holt's Dutch company. O.N., N.R.T. 6,336. She was transferred to the main company in 1950 and was broken up at Inverkeithing.

Number 15, Stentor 43 days (0.7percent)

Built in 1899 by Workman, Clark & Co. O.N. 149,613, N.R.T. 4,104. Transferred to the NSM "Oceaan" in 1922. Sold to Philippine buyers and renamed *Don José* in 1926. Sold for scrap and broken up at Singapore in 1929.

Number 16, Atreus 35 days (0.6 percent)

Built in 1911 by Scott & Co. of Greenock. O.N. 131,322, N.R.T. 4,290. Sold for scrap in 1949 and broken up at Rosyth.

Number 17, Ping Suey 33 days

Built in 1899 by Workman, Clark & Co. O.N. 110,143, N.R.T. 4,799. On 26 June 1916, she went ashore on Dasseneiland, was later salvaged, sold, and renamed *Atthalifax*.

Ping Suey had left Birkenhead on 31 May. Herbert Holdsworth's Certificate of Discharge records that he arrived in Cape Town on 6 July, and on the same day, joined the *Agapenor*. It, therefore, seems likely that nonessential crew were taken off the *Ping Suey* and joined other Alfred Holt ships as they called at Cape Town.

Herbert Holdsworth's Retirement and Death

The Wall Street crash on 24 October 1929 almost certainly brought an end to Herbert Holdsworth's career at sea. The Alfred Holt Company was severely affected by the subsequent collapse in world trade, and by 1931, profits had been slashed by over three-quarters. Dividend payments were suspended, pay reduced, and many staff were made redundant.

Thus, on 8 May 1932, Herbert Holdsworth stepped off a ship for the last time, and vanished from view. This is not unremarkable. The remarkable thing is that we know so much about his career in the Merchant Navy. Unfortunately, this is not the sort of information that reveals anything about his personal life or his character. Nothing survives that can fill this gap, and all those who knew him, except his daughter-in-law, Gladys Holdsworth, are dead.

Jane Holland Wood never spoke much about her father, but she remembered the absences, the excitement of arrival, and the dreadful good-byes. Seafaring is one of the most unsuitable jobs for a family man. There were also hints about alcohol dependency, a common problem in the Merchant Navy then. Jane would also say of her father, "He was such a nice chap."

At the time of writing this book (2000), the only person still alive who would have actually known Herbert Holdsworth was Gladys, Thomas Herbert's wife, whom he married on 26 July 1936. Gladys met Thomas Herbert at Burslem Art School, where he was studying architecture. (He never qualified.)

She remembers that Herbert and Jane were keeping a public house called the "New Town" at Longton in Staffordshire, a long way from the sea. Jane Holland Wood was helping in the pub, and Mary, at school, helped with food shopping. Gladys also provides vignettes of Herbert and Jane. She describes Herbert as, "A taciturn gentleman who was not very friendly." This is not perhaps all that surprising, having lost his job and been pitchforked into a life that was completely alien. Given Gladys's following description of Jane, he may also have felt that his presence was not really necessary: Jane was, "An autocratic lady who loved her pub and playing dominoes with the men." The author can just remember her, and would use the words "imperious" and "self sufficient," to describe her. It may well have been that Jane, after 22 years of marriage, had learned to manage her life without her husband, given that he had been absent most of that time. At least during those years, his job provided a steady income, but on retirement, he may not even have had a pension. He was probably also suffering from the illness that would eventually kill him.

The only written material that survives from this period is a birthday card and a letter, both of which are addressed to Jane Holland Wood. The card was sent by her parents on Jane's 16th birthday (10 February 1933) and gave their address as Lower Chaplin Road, Stoke-on-Trent, Staffordshire. Whether this implies that Herbert and Jane had left the New Town at Longton or had yet to start living there, we do not know. The card was addressed to "Miss J.H.W. Holdsworth, C/O [care of] Mrs. W. Seale, 56 Keelings Drive, Trent Vale, Stoke-on-Trent." This may suggest that Jane was in domestic service and that the family finances were in a parlous state.

Just over two months after her birthday Jane Holland Wood was in hospital. This is apparent from a letter written by Emma Jane Holdsworth on 27 April 1933. The letter reads as follows:

> My dearest Janey,
>
> I was very very sorry to hear from Daddy that you were going into the Hospital, but I hope it will only be for a short time, and that you will come out feeling better, and stronger than you have ever been.
>
> I am sure everybody will be good and kind to you, they could not help but be so to you, dear. I have asked Daddy to write and give me all news about you. I shall certainly hope to come and see you dear.
>
> Daddy says you are very brave and cheerful, and I am sure you are, and be assured that I shall be thinking about you all the time darling.
>
> My coat, dear, or a coat, will be waiting for you when you get home again, and I have a silk frock that I am going to send you also, and one or two other things. Cheerio dearest, all will be well. I am looking forward to [seeing] you. All my love and thoughts dear.
>
> Auntie Emma.

Jane Holland Wood was suffering from tuberculosis of the small intestine. This is contracted by drinking milk from infected cows. The tuberculin test, which indicates those cows that are infected (so they may be treated), together with the pasteurization of milk, has now eliminated the disease. Prior to these public health measures and the discovery of antibiotics, both the bovine and the human strains were attended by a high mortality rate.

Once in the small intestine the bovine strain of the tubercle bacillus produces a chronic inflammatory process that is debilitating and may cause obstruction. Another manifestation is produced when coils of bowel become stuck to and involved by the inflammation in the primary site(s). This will often result in fistula formation.

Jane Holland Wood survived this terrible disease and was fortunate to do so. Sadly, however, this evidence suggests that in 1933, at least, the Holdsworth family was dogged by poverty and ill health.

Some time after this, Herbert and Jane moved to the Greyhound Inn, Holyhead Road, Okengates (near Wellington) in Shropshire, and a photograph (plate 12) survives showing Herbert Holdsworth (left) standing in front of it with an unknown man. (The Greyhound still survives as a pizza restaurant.)

His tenure was a short one, as he died at 4:25 P.M. on 17 June 1935 at the Royal Salop Infirmary. The house physician who admitted him was Kenneth Howard Wright. He had qualified on 31 July 1934 having been examined by the Conjoint Board of the Colleges of Physicians and Surgeons. Successful candidates became Members of the Royal College of Surgeons and Licentiates of the Royal College of Physicians (M.R.C.S., L.R.C.P.) This qualification was later eclipsed when medical schools became affiliated with universities, which awarded medical degrees. In 1934, however, M.R.C.S and L.R.C.P. were all that were required to practice, and no further training was thought necessary, a situation that is considered unacceptable now.

Dr. Wright reported Herbert Holdsworth's death to the coroner, R. Crawford Clarke:

> I, Kenneth Wright, House Physician at the Royal Salop Infirmary, am reporting the death of Herbert Holdsworth, Greyhound, Holyhead Road, Okengates.

> I saw him on Saturday, 15 instant, at about 4:15 P.M., when he was unconscious and obviously dying. Stimulants were given but he died at 4:25 P.M.

> I carried out a postmortem examination and from the appearance of the various organs I could not definitely exclude poisoning.

The following day Dr. Wright wrote to the Coroner again:

> I, Kenneth Wright, House Physician at the Royal Salop Infirmary, write with further reference to my report of yesterday the death of Herbert Holdsworth, Grey Hound, Holyhead Road, Oakengates.

Plate 12. The Greyhound Inn.

> After further investigations I am now able to state that the above named died
> from natural causes, i.e. pernicious anemia. In this particular case the dis-
> ease manifested itself in such a way that the ordinary postmortem findings of
> pernicious anemia were absent and other intestinal changes not commonly
> present in that disease suggested conditions which lead [*sic*] me to give my
> previous report.
>
> On further chemical tests I have been able to satisfy myself of the presence
> of pernicious anemia.

A death certificate was issued on 18 June 1935. The cause of death was given as, "Pernicious anemia with hemorrhage of the bowel." A note was made that a post mortem had been performed and that death was due to natural causes.

Pernicious anemia was first described by Thomas Addison (1793–1860) in 1855. The basic lesion is atrophy of the stomach, which results in a failure to secrete a substance called "intrinsic factor." This is essential for the absorption of vitamin B_{12} and a lack of this vitamin results in the production of abnormal red blood cells, which cannot carry oxygen thus causing anemia. Other symptoms are glossitis and damage to nerves and the spinal cord. Hemorrhage from the gut is *not* a recognized complication.

Dr. Wright's brief reports are incomprehensible, particularly as the post mortem findings on which they are based cannot be found. The Royal Salop Infirmary closed in 1977, when it moved to Copthorne and was renamed the Royal Shrewsbury Hospital. The Department of Pathology and all its records had moved in 1970, but no post mortem records prior to 1941 survive.

There are three points that are inexplicable:

- "The disease manifested itself in such a way that *the ordinary postmortem findings of Pernicious Anemia were absent*";

The sine qua non for diagnosis of the disease at autopsy is gastric atrophy, yet Dr. Wright implies that this was not present; and

- "*other intestinal changes not commonly present in that disease suggested conditions which led me to give my previous report.*" That is to say that death was due to poisoning.

There are no intestinal changes (visible to the naked eye) in pernicious anemia.

- It is difficult to imagine what post mortem *biochemical tests* were available in 1935 that would prove a diagnosis of pernicious anemia.

The only certain conclusions that may be drawn from Dr. Wright's observations are that Herbert Holdsworth was admitted to hospital moribund due to haematemesis (vomiting blood).

Anecdotal evidence suggests that he had an alcohol problem and was jaundiced for some months before death. The disease that would link these various symptoms is cirrhosis of the liver. In that disease, varicose veins may form at the lower end of the esophagus due to obstruction of the venous return. An extremely dangerous complication is rupture of the varices resulting in torrential hemorrhage.

A possible explanation of Dr. Wright's diagnosis of poisoning is that he meant alcohol poisoning. If this were given as a cause of death, however, an inquest would have to be held. This requirement has only recently been abolished, and prior to this, efforts were always made to avoid it due to the implied slur on the deceased's character and the distress this caused relatives.

Jane Holland Wood was told that the reason for the coroner's involvement was that because Herbert Holdsworth had been abroad for much of his adult life, he may have had a tropical disease, and the cause of death was obscure. This suggests a degree of obfuscation. It is possible that an (incorrect) ante mortem diagnosis of pernicious anemia, based on confusing the lemon-yellow tinge that occurs in that disease with the jaundice of liver failure, enabled Dr. Wright to persuade himself that this was the cause of death.

Herbert Holdsworth's Will

This was drawn up on 8 April 1921 when Herbert and Jane were living at 35 Bankburn Road, Tue Brook, Liverpool. The witnesses were William Ashbrook Roberts, clerk, and his wife Rozel Sarah who lived at 41 Bankburn Road. The will stated: "I give and bequeath to my wife Jane all personal belongings, household effects and all monies due to me from salary, life insurance and other sources."

When probate was granted, Herbert Holdsworth's estate amounted to £197:10s (£6,233 in 1999 values.) His wages on S.S. *Perseus*, on his last voyage, had been £252:00s a year.

Jane Holdsworth

Jane was a widow for 16 years. She moved from the Greyhound inn at an unknown date to become landlady of the Barley Mow pub at Hadley near Wellington in Shropshire. That pub was subsequently demolished to make way for a new road.

Jane died on 26 January 1951 at the age of 63. She had been suffering with Crohn's disease for some time. The disease is characterized by a chronic inflammatory process, which mainly involves the small intestine. The appearances are similar to tuberculosis, but the tubercle bacillus has never been isolated, and the etiology remains enigmatic.

Chapter 3

Colin Hannah, 1866–1948

At the age of 15, Colin Hannah was an agricultural laborer in southwest Scotland. But as well as agriculture, there was also a tradition of seafaring in the area, and this provided a means of escape and an opportunity to better oneself. Colin Hannah seized his opportunity and made a successful career for himself in both square rig and steam.

Family Background

Colin Hannah was born at 2:30 A.M. on 6 March 1866 at Port William, Parish of Mochrum, in Dumfries and Galloway, Scotland. He would have attended school, but it is not known at what age he left. At the time of the 1881 census, when he was fifteen, he was working as an agricultural laborer, and must have realized that his prospects were nonexistent if he remained in Scotland.

The address of the Hannah family at this time was Southside, Mochrum, Wigtown, Dumfries and Galloway. The village consists of a street of the single storey cottages that are typical of many parts of Scotland, and cannot have altered much since Colin Hannah lived there. It has not been possible to discover if Southside was an area, or the name of a cottage, no one in Mochrum, or its environs, recognizes the name at the present time.

Other members of the family present at the address on census day were recorded as follows: Thomas Hannah, 52, master tailor, is listed as head of the household. He was born in 1829 at Glasserton, which is ten miles southeast of Port William. He married in 1856, when he was 25. Mary Hannah, his wife, was 47 and married when she was 22. She had been born in Ireland, in 1834 and, given the proximity of the Irish ferry terminal at Stranraer, this is not surprising. Fanny, daughter, 24, was born in 1857 at Glasserton. All subsequent children were born at Mochrum:

Henry, son, 17, born 1864, occupation: tailor;
Colin;
Elizabeth, daughter, 13, born 1868, scholar (that is, still at school);

John, son, 8, born 1873, scholar;

Janet, daughter, 5, born 1876; and

Catherine White, mother in law, 70, born in Ireland, 1811, annuitant.

Colin's older brother, William, must have been elsewhere when the census was held, as he is not mentioned. He had been born in 1861, and was therefore five years older than Colin. He was also a tailor.

When he was 17, Colin must have decided that his future lay at sea, and he appears in Liverpool in September 1883. As well as being one of the largest ports in the world, it would have been an easy place to get to from Dumfries and Galloway, as paddle steamers provided a ferry service from Wigtown.

Once Colin Hannah embarked on his new career, one attribute, which distinguished him from his fellows, was his constancy. Once he joined a ship, he stayed with it for as long as possible, so that he only left, either when disaster struck, or an important career change dictated the move.

Colin Hannah's First Ship: *Penthesilea*

Colin Hannah first appears in an Agreement and Account of Crew of a Foreign-Going Ship on 8 September 1883, in the sailing ship *Penthesilea,* O.N. 63,167 registered in Liverpool in 1869, and owned by N.D. Reid of 169 Parliament Street, Liverpool. G.R.T. 1,706 (1,998) N.R.T. 1,667 (1,942). Figures for *Ladakh* in brackets. *Penthesilea* thus had 14 percent less space than *Ladakh* for carrying cargo.

Crew Agreement—First Voyage in Square Rig

6 September 1883–14 August 1884, Liverpool–Bombay–Rangoon–Liverpool

Total number signing: 37
Failed to join: 1
Left behind in prison: 1

£1 in 1884 was equivalent to £46.89 as at March 1999.

A total of 33 signed the agreement in Liverpool:

H. Murdoch   42   Sussex   Master

He had been master on the previous voyage.

H. Patterson   27   Whithorn   First Mate   £8 :00s

This is close to Port William where Colin Hannah was born, and this may explain why he joined the *Penthesilea.* An able seaman also came from here.

R. Murray-Menzies	28	Sheiling	Second Mate	£5:10s
William Davidson	35	Dundee	Carpenter	£6:10s
John Hamilton	37	Liverpool	Bosun	£5:00s
William Quayle	42	Liverpool	Sailmaker	£6:00s

Both the bosun and sailmaker had served in *Penthesilea* on the previous voyage. Together with the steward and the cook, 20 able seamen signed the agreement. Their average age was 28. The oldest was 47 and the youngest 19. Their wages were £2:15s per month. One of them, George Robbs, 21, gave his place of birth as Whithorn. Three ordinary seamen were on board (one had failed to join); two were 19 and one was 20. They were each paid £2:00s

Colin Hannah signed the agreement last with the rank of boy. He was paid 15 shillings per month. He was not entirely truthful about his age, saying that he was born in 1865, when in fact, it should have been 1866. He was therefore 17 years old, and the youngest person on board.

The nationalities of those on board were as follows:

English	10
Scottish	5
Southern Irish	1
Austrian	1
Ceylonese	1
Danish	1
Finnish	4
Norwegian	2
Italian	1
Swedish	1
Illegible	4

Penthesilea sailed for Bombay on 8 September 1883, arriving on 28 December, 111 days out, 10,750 miles, 97 miles per day at 4.0 knots. She left for Rangoon on 16 January 1884, and arrived on 6 March, 49 days out, 2,117 miles, 43 miles per day at 1.8 knots. Three of the crew left the ship by mutual agreement, and one was left behind in prison. He was Alfred McDermott, 24, who gave his place of birth as Cheshire. His crime is not recorded. Five joined the ship, including two boys who were 16 and 17, so Colin Hannah was no longer the youngest on board.

Penthesilea sailed for Liverpool on 3 April, arriving on 13 August 1884, 132 days out, 11,660 miles, 88 miles per day at 3.7 knots. *Lloyd's List* reported:

Liverpool, 13 August, 11.25 A.M. The *Penthesilea* arrived here from Rangoon and *Wallington* (steam ship) Baltimore for Antwerp, were in collision 7 inst., in 48°N, 24°W. Former had jib boom figurehead and some head–gear carried away. Damage to latter, if any, not known. The *Wallington* has since passed Prawle Point.

Crew Agreement — Second Voyage in Square Rig

20 September 1884–7 September 1885, Liverpool–Rangoon–Liverpool

Captain Murdoch remained as master, and Alexander Patterson as first mate. The carpenter and sailmaker also stayed with the ship. Of the seamen, only Colin Hannah and an able seaman remained from the previous voyage. Colin Hannah was promoted to ordinary seaman with wages of £1:15s. George Roberts, the able seaman from Whithorn, was one of two who failed to join. A total of 17 able seamen signed the agreement. Two of them were first voyagers who were signed on by Captain Murdoch, as last minute substitutes, for the two who failed to join. Perhaps it was an inducement, together with the fact that they were 28 and 31 years old, that resulted in their being given rank and wages (at £2:15s) beyond their experience. As well as Colin Hannah, there was one other ordinary seaman, and two boys who were first voyagers.

Penthesilea sailed for Rangoon on 20 September 1884 and arrived on 22 January 1885, 124 days out, 11,660 miles, 94.0 miles per day at 3.9 knots. The second mate and an able seaman were discharged by mutual consent and another able seaman deserted. The latter was not replaced. *Penthesilea* left Rangoon, for Liverpool, on 23 March 1885. The following day a 16 year-old stowaway was discovered. *Penthesilea* arrived in Liverpool on 6 September, 167 days out, 11,660 miles, 69.8 miles per day at 2.9 knots.

Crew Agreement — Third Voyage in Square Rig

9 October 1885–9 September 1886, Liverpool–Bombay–Liverpool

H. Murdoch remained as master. The first mate was A.J. Davis, 26, and the second mate was J.E. Blackburn, 22. Both the carpenter and sailmaker remained, as did the bosun, although he left the ship in Bombay by mutual consent. Colin Hannah continued as an ordinary seaman, with wages of £1:15s per month.

Penthesilea left Liverpool on 9 October 1885 and arrived at Bombay on 11 February 1886, 125 days out, 10,750 miles, 86 miles per day at 3.6 knots. She left for Liverpool on 8 May and arrived on 9 September 1886, 124 days out, 10,750 miles, 86.7 miles per day at 3.6 knots.

A home trade agreement was drawn up, and *Penthesilea* left Liverpool on 1 October for Penarth, South Wales, arriving on 3 October. A new master was appointed, William Fortay, 41, from Wigtown, which is close to Port William. He was the second person to serve in the *Penthesilea* who came from this area. (The other was H. Patterson, the first mate in the 6 September 1883 agreement described above.) Colin Hannah was briefly promoted to able seaman for this short trip, although his wages were £2:00s, whereas the others received £2:10s.

Crew Agreement—Fourth Voyage in Square Rig

21 October 1886–26 October 1887, Penarth–Bombay–Rangoon–Liverpool

This would be Colin Hannah's last voyage before the mast. William Fortay remained as master, A.J. Davis as first mate, and W. Davidson as carpenter. The third mate was S. Gahen, 26, of Liverpool, and the sailmaker was John Jones, 49, also of Liverpool. The bosun was Allen Shuker, 24, of Shrewsbury. There were 18 able seamen who were paid £2:10s. Two ordinary seamen signed the agreement. One was Colin Hannah, who was paid £2:00s, whereas the other's wages were £1:00s. Two boys were paid £0:15s. The agreement was unusual in that there were no changes during its entire course.

Penthesilea left Penarth, presumably laden with coal, on 21 October 1886, and arrived in Bombay on 19 February 1887, 121 days out, 10,563 miles, 87.3 miles per day at 3.6 knots. She sailed for Rangoon on 1 April, arriving 36 days later on 6 May, 2,117 miles, 59 miles per day at 2.5 knots. Her passage back to Liverpool, leaving on 28 May, was a long one, 151 days, 10,750 miles, 71.2 miles per day at 3.0 knots. She finally arrived back on 26 October 1887, having been away for just over one year.

Colin Hannah is Promoted to Third Mate

For her usual trip back to Penarth on 9 November 1887, Colin Hannah was appointed third mate at the age of 21. He had never served as an able seaman and had been with the *Penthesilea* for four years and three months. This is the duration of an apprenticeship, but Colin Hannah had, of course, started with the rank of boy. The second mate was also remarkable as he was only 20.

Crew Agreement—Fifth Voyage in Square Rig

18 November 1887–31 October 1888, Penarth–Bombay–Rangoon–Liverpool

Total number signing:	33			
Failed to join:	1			
Deserted:	2			
Sick:	1			
William Fortay	42	Wigton	Master	
G. Fairweather	39	Johnston, New Brunswick	First mate	£7:10s
J. Hughes	20	Ardglass	Second mate	£5:00s
Colin Hannah	21	Port William	Third mate	£3:05s

Colin Hannah's wages were now at the level of an agricultural laborer.

W. Davidson	37	Dundee	Carpenter	£6:10s
John Jones	51	Liverpool	Sailmaker	£5:00s
Fred. Donnelly	41	County Down	Steward	£4:00s
Patrick Mulrenay	50	Londonderry	Cook	£4:00s

All remained with the ship until the termination of the agreement, except the steward, who left at Bombay. Seventeen able seamen signed the agreement in Penarth. Their wages were £2:10s. Three ordinary seamen were paid £1:10s, and a boy was paid £0:15s.

Penthesilea sailed for Bombay on 18 November 1887, arriving on 15 March 1888, 117 days out, 10,563 miles, 90.3 miles per day at 3.8 knots. The steward was discharged by mutual consent and was replaced. An able seaman deserted. *Penthesilea* left for Rangoon on 10 April and arrived on 10 May, 30 days out, 2,117 miles, 70.6 miles per day at 2.9 knots. An able seaman was left behind sick when the ship departed for Liverpool on 1 June 1888. She made port on 31 October, 153 days out, 10,750 miles, 70.3 miles per day at 2.9 knots.

Second Mate

On 9 November 1888, Colin Hannah submitted his application to be examined for the certificate of competency as second mate, in square rig, and paid the fee of £1:00s. He gave his permanent address as Port William and his present address as 14 Aughton Street, Liverpool. Colin Hannah was lodging here, the home of Police Sergeant and Mrs. McDowall, the parents of his future wife, Catherine. He also rehearsed his experience to date, which consisted of his service in the *Penthesilea* since 8 September 1883. On 12 November, the examiner passed him in all three parts of the examination: navigation, seamanship, and the color test, which was to exclude color blindness. On 15 November, he was issued with his certificate of competency, and two days later its' number: 020322. He had been at sea for five years and two months. There was not much time to celebrate his success, as four days later he was at sea again.

Crew Agreement—Sixth Voyage in Square Rig

21 November 1888–23 November 1889, Liverpool–Rangoon–Amsterdam

Total number signing:	35
Deserted:	4
Sick:	1
Injured:	1

A total of 30 signed the agreement in Liverpool.

Frederick Wilson	38	Birmingham	Master	
John Dyer	32	Mevagissey	First mate	£7:10s
Colin Hannah	22	Port William	Second mate	£5:00s

These wages are what a skilled worker on land could command.

William Davidson	39	Dundee	Carpenter	£6:10s
William Greenfield	46	Liverpool	Sailmaker	£6:00s
John Morrison	46	Inverness	Bosun	£4:04s
G. Cambridge	30	Nassau	Steward and cook	£5:00s
Robert Smith	35	Tobago	Assistant cook	£3:00s

Eighteen able seamen signed the agreement and were paid £2:15s. Two ordinary seamens' wages were £2:00s and £1:15s, and two boys were paid £0:15s.

Penthesilea sailed for Rangoon on 21 November 1888, and arrived on 1 April 1889, 130 days out, 11,660 miles, 90 miles per day at 3.7 knots. Four men deserted and one was left behind sick. Another crewmember, Andro Bergman, a Finn, had been injured, and the superintendent of the mercantile marine office recorded in the agreement:

> I certify that A Bergman was left behind at this port, on the ground of inability to proceed to sea through injury sustained to his hip in the service of the ship, that he refused to sign the account of wages on the ground that he was entitled to compensation for such injury, and that under the circumstances, his balance of wages have been paid into this office and his effects handed to him at the hospital.

Five replacement able seamen signed the agreement, one of whom failed to join. *Penthesilea,* loaded with rice, left Rangoon on 27 April 1889 for orders at Queenstown. She had to put into Saint Helena on 31 August to land two able seamen who were sick. Both had served in the *Gulf Stream* prior to joining at Rangoon. *Penthesilea* arrived off Queenstown on 22 October, and was directed to Amsterdam, where she arrived on 1 November 1889, 156 days out, 11,795 miles, 76 miles per day at 3.2 knots.

Lloyd's List reported:

> Amsterdam, 31 October 3.50 P.M. *Penthesilea* from Rangoon, got ashore in entering Ymuiden [Ijmuiden] but afterwards floated and arrived.

The agreement terminated at Amsterdam, and the crew was discharged including Colin Hannah. The master and second mate, plus a boy who had been a first voyager, remained with the ship for the trip back to Liverpool, under tow. Sixteen able seamen were engaged, one of whom failed to join. *Penthesilea* was back in Liverpool on 23 November 1889, and on 12 December, another crew was signed on to move her to Newport, South Wales, where she arrived two days later. Included in this crew were Colin Hannah and two able seamen, who had been discharged in Amsterdam. It is not known why they did not stay with the ship all the time.

Crew Agreement—Seventh Voyage in Square Rig

Disaster in Bideford Bay

With Frederick Wilson remaining as master, and Colin Hannah as second mate, a new first mate, one Sherwood Forrest, 34, was appointed, and *Penthesilea* set sail from Newport for Mauritius on 9 January 1890. This latter date may, or may not be, correct, because a week later, on 16 January, *Lloyd's List* reported under "Ships Spoken" that *Penthesilea* was only ten miles north west of Lundy, about 80 miles from Newport. A series of reports then followed:

> 20 January. Braunton [in Bideford Bay] 9:09 A.M. *Penthesilea*, ship, Newport for Mauritius, coal laden, ashore Saunton Sands. Crew saved.

Historic weather records at the National Meteorological Archive, Bracknell record:

> The period of 16–20 January 1890 was characterized by a mild and windy spell of weather. Wind speeds recorded at Falmouth show that there were frequent periods when the speed was near gale force 7 (28–33 knots). The strongest winds occurred late evening on 17 January: severe gale force 9 (41–47 knots) and early evening on 18 January: gale force 8 (34–40 knots). The direction of the wind was generally from the south or southwest.

In the open ocean these winds would not have been a problem, but, caught without sea room, a sailing ship that could not beat to windward would be in great danger. *Lloyd's List* continues:

> Liverpool, 20 January 3:22 P.M. Following telegram received by owners states: *Penthesilea* ashore Saunton Sand, deck clean swept, vessel full of water, don't think at present any chance of getting ship off. Sandy bottom.

> London, 21 January. The Liverpool Salvage Association reports under date Liverpool, 21 January 10:32 A.M. as follows: *Penthesilea* lies end–on on the sands, about one mile south of Baggy [Point].

> Liverpool, 21 January 6:53 P.M. Liverpool Salvage Association reports: *Penthesilea* dries half tide, stern out, embedded five feet, slight list, bilge butts and "landing" leaking badly, other butts strained, keel broken and large hole there aft, rudder gone, mainmast up two inches, part port bulwark gone, deck houses gutted. Engaged sending down hamper [That is top hamper, the masts and rigging] and arranging to run out spare anchor. Other anchors lost.

London, 21 January. The salvage association had received the following telegram from Captain Gillon, dated Braunton, 21 January: *Penthesilea* stranded three miles North and East from Braunton Lighthouse, head to land, dry at half tide, rudder gone, sternpost and keel twisted to starboard, starboard bilge landing and butts started, water falls in hold through bottom, mainmast set up, deck houses gutted, both anchors with part cable gone. Now dismantling top gear, probably to lower masthead. Part cargo must be disposed of. Will report further as to prospects.

Liverpool, 22 January 6:48 P.M. Liverpool Salvage Association reports: *Penthesilea*. More damage to poop houses by last nights gale, little more list, but otherwise position unchanged.

Liverpool, 27 January 12:05 P.M. Following telegram received this morning from Braunton,

9:55 A.M. *Penthesilea:* heavy gale last night and yesterday. More settled today. No alteration.

Liverpool, 30 January 12:29 P.M. Liverpool Salvage Association reports: *Penthesilea*. Discharging commenced onto beach. Weather finer, but tides scarcely leave the vessel. Fear may not be ready by next springs [tides] unless quantity of cargo jettisoned.

Liverpool, 18 February 6:03 P.M. Liverpool Salvage Association report that *Penthesilea* was floated this afternoon.

Bideford, 19 February 11:22 A.M. *Penthesilea* was safely towed into Appledore last evening.

Appledore was (and still is) an important center for both shipbuilding, and repairing, with facilities that include a dry dock, which is 330 feet long. *Penthesilea* returned to Liverpool on 24 May, where more work may have been done on her, as it was not until 20 October that she was fully back in service, on which date she sailed for San Francisco. Colin Hannah, however, was not on board.

First Mate

The voyage to Mauritius having come to an untimely end, Colin Hannah seized the moment and, on 14 February 1890, applied to be examined for the certificate of competency as first mate. He now gave his permanent address as 14 Aughton Street, Liverpool, that is to say, the house of Sergeant and Mrs. McDowall. It was under one year and three months since he had sat for the examination for second mate, and six years and five months since he started in deep water sail. He was examined on 19 February, and passed all three parts of the examination. His certificate was issued on 20 February and its number, 090322, the following day. On 1 March, he joined the *Caroline Morris* as first mate.

The *Caroline Morris*

The *Caroline Morris* was owned by Thomas Beynon of Newport, Monmouthshire, South Wales. She had been built in 1877 and was registered in Newport. G.R.T. 960 (1,998), N.R.T. 922 (1,942). Figures in brackets for *Ladakh*. Her capacity to carry cargo was thus just under half that of *Ladakh*. She was the smallest ship that Colin Hannah sailed in.

Crew Agreement—Eighth Voyage in Square Rig

1 March 1890–22 December 1890, Newport–Valparaiso–Pisagua (Chile)–London

| Total number signing | 15 | | | |
| Apprentices | | 4 (one deserted) | | |

| W.H. Bridle | 38 | Miltown (Cork) | Master | |
| Colin Hannah | 23 | Port William | First mate | £6:15s |

This is less than the £8:00s he might have expected to earn in a larger ship, but significantly more than a skilled worker earned ashore.

Theodore Affolter	21	Liverpool	Second mate	£4:10s
William Bennett	50	Padstow	Carpenter	£7:10s
James Collins	25	Newport	Sailmaker	£5:00s
Peter Hanfin	38	Copenhagen	Steward	£5:00s
J. Hammonds	23	Kings Lynn	Cook	£4:00s

Eight able seamen signed the agreement with wages of £3:10s per month. Their average age was 32, and their nationalities were:

English	5 (including 3 from Newport)
Swedish	2
Southern Irish	1

Also on board were four apprentices their ages were 14, 15, 17, and 18.

Caroline Morris left Newport for Valparaiso (Chile), presumably laden with coal, on 4 March 1890, and arrived in 12 June, 101 days out, 8,787miles, 87 miles per day at 3.6 knots. She left Valparaiso on 18 June, and arrived at Pisagua, 800 miles north, on 4 August, 47 days out, 17 miles per day at 0.7 knots. (See map 3.)

It is probable that *Caroline Morris* was involved in the Chilean nitrate trade. Nitrates were (and still are) extracted from opencast mines in the Atacama Desert, and are used, inter alia, in the production of glass, explosives, and fertilizer. Thus coal was carried out to Chile, and nitrates back. In his book *The Cape Horn Breed,*

Map 3. South America.

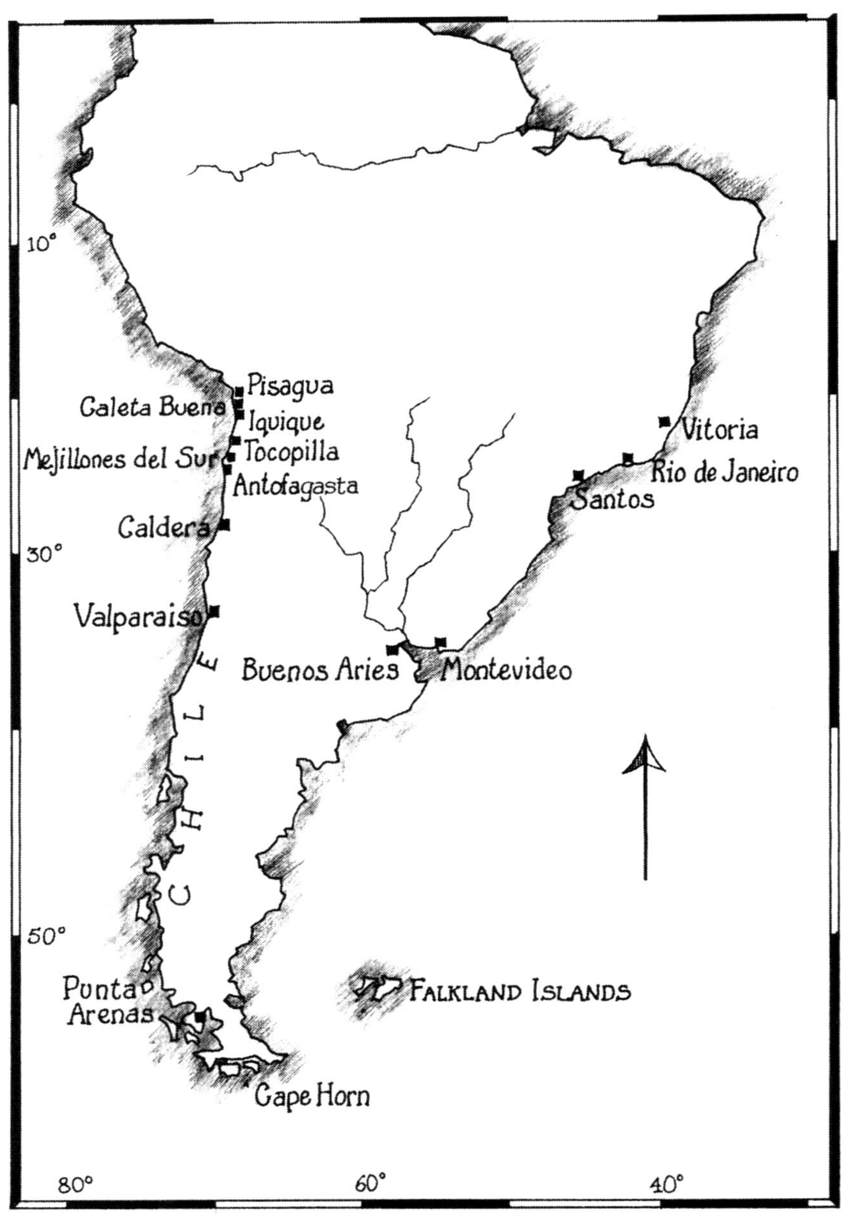

Captain W.H.S. Jones records, that in 1905, coal was purchased for £0:10s:06d per ton at the South Wales coalfields and could be sold in Chilean ports for £4:10s:00d. He describes Pisagua thus:

> The "Town"–if it could be called such–consisted of a collection of white-washed *adobe*, or mud, huts and straggling dilapidated timber houses with galvanized-iron roofs, the exteriors stripped of any paint they once may have boasted by strong nitrate of soda dust which filled the air when a breeze was blowing. There were wine saloons, and other less respectable business premises, conveniently situated among the dwellings of the port workers and officials. The offices and dwellings of the merchants and nitrate exporters were somewhat larger than the other houses, but in no sense edifices of architectural splendor.
>
> There were no gardens or trees. The street was unpaved, and its surface deep in dust, stirred up by the hooves of mules and donkeys. Black clouds of flies hummed around the butchers' shops and the heaps of garbage, stinking in the hot and stagnant air. Mongrel dogs, infected with fleas, roamed ownerless, searching for scraps of nourishment in the garbage. The houses, we were told, swarmed with bugs, fleas, lice, cockroaches and other vermin. The inhabitants seemed to spend most of their time drowsing in the shade while brushing away flies from their eyes.

While in Pisagua, the 15 year old apprentice, Edgar George Edwards, deserted. His indentures had been registered on the day *Caroline Morris* sailed from Newport, and she was presumably his first ship. It would be interesting to know what became of him, adrift in an obscure port, on the other side of the world.

Caroline Morris left Pisagua on 13 September, and arrived in London on 22 December 1890, 100 days out, 9,890 miles, 98.9 miles per day at 4.1 knots.

Crew Agreement—Ninth Voyage in Square Rig

2 February 1891–23 November 1891, London–Valparaiso–South Shields (England)

The officers, carpenter, and crew were the same as those on the previous voyage. The only change was that there was no dedicated sailmaker, he was replaced by a sailmaker/able seaman, who was paid £3:15s, only five shillings more than the other able seamen and £1:05s less than the sailmaker on the previous voyage. Two apprentices remained from the previous voyage: A.E. Jackson and W.J. Goodyear. Two new ones joined: Lionel Hurlow Williams, 16, and Willie Allingham, 15.

Caroline Morris sailed for Valparaiso on 2 February 1891 and arrived on 18 May, 105 days out, 9,090 miles, 86.6 miles per day at 3.6 knots. She remained in Valparaiso for 71 days, leaving on 28 July, arriving in South Shields on 21 November 1891, 116 days out, 9,215 miles, 79 miles per day at 3.3 knots.

Colin Hannah Obtains His Master's Certificate

On 11 December 1891, Colin Hannah applied to be examined for a certificate of competency as master. His age was 25 years and 9 months, and it was just over eight years since he had joined the *Penthesilea* as a boy, on 8 September 1883. The examination took place on 18 December and he passed the three parts—navigation, seamanship, and the color test. On 19 December he received his certificate from the Lords of the Committee of Privy Council for Trade, and the following day the number, 020322, was issued. Colin Hannah gave his address as 38 Northumberland Terrace, Liverpool, the same address as Sergeant and Mrs. McDowall. Although he now had his master's ticket it would be another five years before he obtained a command, years that would be spent as first mate in the *Sierra Parima*.

The *Sierra Parima*

Built of iron in 1882 by J. Reid & Co. of Port Glasgow for the Sierra Shipping Company, and managed by Thompson, Anderson & Co. of Fenwick Chambers, Fenwick Street, Liverpool. She was registered in Liverpool, official number 86,212. G.R.T. 1,583 (1,998), N.R.T. 1,480 (1,942). (Figures in brackets for *Ladakh*.) *Sierra Parima* (plate 13) was thus 36 percent smaller than *Ladakh*. Her length = 239.8 ft. (269.0), breadth = 38.2 ft. (39.5), and Draft = 23.1 ft. (24.2)

Crew Agreement—Tenth Voyage in Square Rig

6 February 1892–22 November 1892, Penarth (South Wales)–Mauritius–Rangoon–Liverpool

Total number signing: 26
Deserted: 1

£1 in 1892 was equivalent to £51:28 as at March 1999.

| T. Wishart | 39 | Forfar | Master | |
| C. Hannah | 25 | Wigtown | First mate | £8:00s |

These wages were 60 percent more than a skilled worker could expect to earn on land.

| Edward Atkinson | 22 | Dublin | Second mate | £5:10s |

He was mentioned in Colin Hannah's will (see page 138)

| A.G. Peterson | 34 | Illegible | Carpenter | £6:00s |
| William Leather | 53 | Illegible | Sailmaker | £5:05s |

Plate 13. S.S. *Sierra Parima*.

R. Anthony	29	Holyhead	Steward	£4:10s
A.E. Thurston	26	Holyhead	Cook	£4:10s
L. Finn	33	Folkstone	Bosun	£3:10s

All remained with the ship until the agreement expired in Liverpool on 22 November 1892.

Seven Apprentices were due to join the ship; five had been on the previous voyage but of the two new ones, a 15 year old did not join, and the other, who was 17, "Did not wish to go to sea." Fifteen able seamen signed the agreement in Penarth. Their wages were the same as the bosun, £3:10s.

Sierra Parima sailed from Penarth, with a cargo of coal, on 9 February 1892, arriving at Mauritius on 27 April, 77 days out, 8,228 miles, 107 miles per day at 4.5 knots. On 7 May 1892 *Lloyd's List* reported as follows:

> Hurricane at Mauritius.
>
> We had a severe hurricane on 29 April, causing much damage to shipping, canes [i.e., sugar cane.] The hurricane was one of the most severe on record, and the damage done is enormous. All business is interrupted; 50 percent of the crop is damaged.
>
> Also: by Telegraph via Colombo.
>
> Port Louis, Mauritius. Disastrous hurricane on April 29,
>
> Unprecedented force and destruction of property. Very much damage done shipping in harbor; majority (of vessels) stranded. Western half of Port Louis devastated. Crop very much damaged, estimated reduction 50 percent. Mortality, casualties, distress appalling.
>
> *Strathspey, Leander, Aconcagua, Queen of Scots, Eurydice, Sierra Parima, Amaranth,* and *Gladiator* still aground.
>
> [On 12 May, a fuller report appeared:] One of the most severe hurricanes on record passed over this Island on 29 April, which did immense damage in the harbor and to the island generally, the destruction to property and canes being enormous. The storm commenced at about 10:00 A.M. and blew heavily from the NE until about 1:25 P.M. when it fell calm: the center passed immediately over us, and the barometer fell to 27.96 inches, which is the lowest ever recorded here. The calm continued until 3:00 P.M. when it blew with redoubled force from WSW. The wind exceeded the rate of 120 miles per hour and in the space of about 2 hours nearly every vessel in the harbor was aground and the upper part of Port Louis was completely wrecked. Over 600 deaths have been declared in Port Louis alone. Several thousand persons have been wounded, and out of a total of 9000 houses, 3000 have been destroyed. The dry docks have been partly disabled, only one dock being at present serviceable, and owing to both of the Government tugs having been

run on the Port Office quay, and to the majority of the lighters having been either sunk or driven ashore, the work in the harbor has been almost at a standstill. Every effort is being made, but there must be great delay in getting stranded vessels afloat and repairs effected. The reports from the country districts are very meagre, but there is no doubt that there has been much loss of life and property, several sugarhouses being completely destroyed and a large number more or less damaged. It is estimated that there will be a reduction of about 50 percent in the coming crop, but very much will depend upon the weather we have during the next four months, and the above estimate may have to be modified later on.

P.S. One of the Government tugs has been floated and is at work.

[There then follows information about the various ships that had been damaged including the *Sierra Parima*.] *Sierra Parima* ship of Liverpool, Wishart, arrived from Cardiff with coals on 27 April. During the hurricane the vessel dragged her moorings and went ashore on the east side of the harbor, on a muddy bottom. The *Leander* drifted and fell across her bows, damaging her headgear. The hull is apparently intact, and the vessel is making no water, but she has sustained considerable damage to bulwarks and is now lying in about nine feet of water and will no doubt come off when her cargo is discharged.

[On 30 May it was reported:]

Sierra Parima came off without assistance and will leave in ballast without going into dock.

She finally left for Rangoon on 21 June, arriving on 11 July, 20 days out, 3,215 miles, 161 miles per day at 6.7 knots. One crewmember had deserted in Mauritius, he was replaced, and a further two men joined in Rangoon. *Sierra Parima* left Rangoon on 27 July 1892 carrying rice. She arrived back in Liverpool on 23 November, 119 days out, 11,660 miles, 97.9 miles per day at 4.1 knots. Five days later Colin Hannah and Catherine McDowall were married.

Marriage

Colin Hannah and Catherine McDowall were married on 28 November 1892 at Saint George's Church, Liverpool, registration district of West Derby. Colin was 26 and Catherine 25, although she stated she was 24 on the certificate. They gave their address as 38 Northumberland Terrace, Catherine's parents' house. Colin's father was given as Thomas Hannah, tailor, and Catherine's as Thomas McDowall, policeman. The witnesses were James Killop and Mary Ann Carbranagh. The union would be without issue.

Forty days after the wedding, Colin Hannah left on his next voyage; whether Catherine went with him we do not know.

Crew Agreement—Eleventh Voyage in Square Rig

7 January 1893–9 October 1893, Liverpool–San Francisco–South Shields

Total number signing: 33
Deserted   6
Apprentices   6
Sick   1
   (one of the apprentices)

£1 in 1893 was equivalent to £52.94 as at March 1999.

J.T. Wishart	40	Forfar	Master	
C. Hannah	26	Wigtown	First mate	£8:00s
Edward Atkinson	23	Dublin	Second mate	£5:10s
J. Travis	21	Liverpool	Third mate	£3:10s
John Blacklam	47	Aberdeen	Carpenter	£6:00s
William Pengelly	30	Devonport	Bosun	£4:00s
William Leather	54	Liverpool	Sailmaker	£6:00s
R. Anthony	30	Holyhead	Steward	£5:05s
Illegible	44	Devon	Cook	£4:00s

All remained with the ship until the agreement expired on 9 October 1893.

One of the apprentices was Adam McDowall, 17, but it has not been possible to discover if he was a relative of Catherine's. Fifteen able seamen signed the agreement in Liverpool, their wages were £3:00s per month.

Sierra Parima left Liverpool on 7 January 1893, and arrived in San Francisco on 22 April, 105 days out, 13,667 miles, 130 miles per day at 5.4 knots. She remained in port for 54 days loading wheat, during which time, six crew deserted and an apprentice was left behind sick. They were replaced by nine men.

Sierra Parima sailed for Queenstown for orders on 15 June 1893 and arrived on 28 September, 105 days out, 13,412 miles, 127 miles per day at 5.3 knots. From here she was directed to South Shields, leaving on 4 October, arriving on 9 October, 720 miles, 144 miles per day at 6 knots.

Sierra Parima was moved to Swansea on 21 November 1893 with a scratch crew of ten able seamen engaged by Colin Hannah. Each was paid £4:00s "for the run." As the trip only took four days these were very generous terms. J. Travis was promoted to second mate, E. Vooght joined as third mate, R. Anthony remained as steward, and a new carpenter, C. Fraser, also joined. The five apprentices stayed with the ship. No sailmaker was on board.

Crew Agreement—Twelfth Voyage in Square Rig

22 December 1893–10 December, Swansea (South Wales)– San Francisco–Liverpool

Total number signing: 41
Failed to join: 3
Deserted: 14

£1 in 1894 was equivalent to £54.70 as at March 1999.

J.T. Wishart	41	Forfar	Master	
Colin Hannah	27	Wigtown	First mate	£8:00s
J. Travis	22	Liverpool	Second mate	£5:00s
E. Vooght	21	Liverpool	Third mate	£3:10s
C. Fraser	30	Glasgow	Carpenter	£6:00s
William Leather	58	Liverpool	Sailmaker	£6:00s
R. Anthony	30	Holyhead	Steward	£5:05s
Illegible	36	Bremen	Cook	£4:00s

All remained with the ship until the agreement expired.

Six apprentices were also on board, one of whom died on the voyage. Eighteen able seamen signed the agreement in Swansea and were paid £3:00s per month. *Sierra Parima* left Swansea for San Francisco on 29 December 1893. She arrived on 24 April 1894, 116 days out, 13,540 miles, 116 miles per day at 4.9 knots.

Three days before arriving at San Francisco on 21 April 1894—In 37°20'N, 130°45'W—Adam McDowall, one of the apprentices, fell to his death from the main yard. Born in 1875, he joined the *Sierra Parima* on 6 February 1892, and his indentures had been registered three days previously. He, therefore, served in the ship for over two years. Although we know he was not Catherine's brother, it has not been possible to discover if he was some other relative.

While in San Francisco, 13 of the crew deserted and were replaced by 14 others, one of whom did not join. *Sierra Parima*, loaded with wheat, sailed for Queenstown on 6 August 1894. Two days later, one of the apprentices, J. Waterhouse, 21, completed his articles and was appointed fourth mate, his wages being £3:05s. On 26 August, H. Maddocks, 21, also finished his apprenticeship, but had to be content with the rank of able seaman and £3:00s per month. *Sierra Parima* was off Queenstown on 7 December 1894, and arrived in Liverpool the next day, 124 days out, 13,667miles, 110 miles per day at 4.6 knots.

Crew Agreement—Thirteenth Voyage in Square Rig

14 February 1895–24 December 1895, Liverpool–Astoria (Oregon)–Portland–Liverpool

Total number signing: 38
Did not join   1
Deserted   9
Drowned   4

J.T. Wishart	42	Forfar	Master	
Colin Hannah	29	Wigtown	First mate	£8:00s
John Travis	23	Liverpool	Second mate	£5:05s
Edward Jones	40	Liverpool	Carpenter	£5:00s
James Falconer	31	Liverpool	Bosun	£4:05s
Thomas Hughes	47	Liverpool	Sailmaker	£5:00s
R. Anthony	32	Holyhead	Steward	£5:05s
C.M. Gleeson	50	Illegible	Cook	£4:00s

Fifteen able and two ordinary seamen joined in Liverpool. Five apprentices were also on board. *Sierra Parima* sailed for Astoria on 14 February 1895. Two days later, she had only got as far as Milford Haven when *Lloyd's List* reported as follows:

> Milford Haven, 16 February 2:52 P.M.
>
> Ship *Sierra Parima* Liverpool for Portland, Oregon, general cargo, put in this morning having smashed lifeboat and lost four men off Bardsey Island.

It would appear that a large wave had swept over *Sierra Parima*, smashing a lifeboat, and carrying four men overboard. This is suggestive of a severe winter storm, but historic weather records do not bear this out. The National Meteorological Archive at Bracknell records:

> Around 16 February 1895 it was certainly windy over Southwest Wales, although not exceptionally so. The strongest winds were during the evening of the 14 February, when Saint Anne's head [at the entrance to Milford Haven] reported force 7 from the southeast. During the 15th the wind remained at force 6, but on the morning of the 16th it had dropped to force 4.

A wind strength of force 7 (28–33 knots) would not have been a problem for *Sierra Parima*, but perhaps, with wind against tide, on a shoal off Bardsey Island, an abnormal wave may have been generated, and this had swept over the ship. Unfortunately, the logbook has been lost, and so no definite evidence survives to tell us what really happened. The men who had died were as follows:

James Falconer	31	Bosun
Joseph Dennison	44	Able seaman
Frederick Newell	20	Apprentice
Arthur Coates	20	Apprentice

They were replaced by three able seamen who joined at Milford Haven on 18 February 1895.

Sierra Parima arrived at Astoria (the entrance to the Columbia River) on 23 June, 125 days out, 14,237 miles, 114 miles per day, 4.7 knots. On 25 June, she proceeded up the river, and arrived at Portland the following day, where seven able seamen and an apprentice, aged 17, deserted. They were replaced by a bosun (a substitute for the one who had drowned), five able seamen, and a boy aged 19. *Sierra Parima* left Portland on 29 July, arriving back at Astoria on 30 July. She remained here until 17 August, during which time another able seaman deserted, who was also replaced. What was Colin Hannah's last voyage in *Sierra Parima,* ended at Liverpool on 23 December 1895, 128 days out, 14,237 miles, 111 miles per day at 4.6 knots.

Fifty-two days later, on 13 February 1896, Colin Hannah would become master of the *Cabul.*

Colin Hannah's First Command: *Cabul*

Although Colin Hannah achieved his master's ticket on 14 December 1891, he had to wait four years and two months before attaining his first command. This was the ship *Cabul* owned by Edward Bates & Sons and registered in Liverpool, official number 76,516. G.R.T. 1,441 (1,998.), N.R.T. 1,397 (1,908). Figures in brackets for Ladakh. *Cabul* thus carried 27 percent less cargo than *Ladakh.* Her length=223.2 ft. (269), breadth=37.3 ft. (39.5), and depth=22.7 ft. (24.2). She was built of iron by Oswald, Mordaunt & Co., Southampton, in 1877.

Her voyage prior to Colin Hannah joining had been problematic. *Lloyd's List* reported on 1 January 1896:

> The ship *Cabul,* from Rangoon, rice, arrived at Queenstown yesterday after a prolonged voyage of 203 days. She left Rangoon on 11 June 1895, and 35 days ago all the provisions had been consumed, and since then the crew had been living on rice alone. On 23 December a hurricane was encountered and much damage was done to the vessel.

Rangoon–Queenstown, 11,480 miles, 56.6 miles per day at 2.4 knots. On 2 January *Lloyd's List* reported again:

> Liverpool 1 January, 3:22 P.M. Telegram received by owners of *Cabul* from their Queenstown agents states: Captain does not apprehend damage to cargo; damage to ship very trifling. Report as to much damage erroneous.

On the voyage out to Rangoon the cook, an American aged 56, had died although the cause of death is not recorded. Alfred Edmund Bridger, 17, had joined *Cabul* on 19 October 1894 as an apprentice. He would remain with the ship for her next voyage and complete his apprenticeship in *Ladakh.*

Cabul arrived at Antwerp on 15 January 1896. The master, John Urquart, left, and on 13 February a new master, J.G. Lewin, 59, signed the new agreement. He had been master of the Edward Bates & Sons' *Kelat.* However, on the same day he, in turn, was replaced by Colin Hannah, and against Captain Lewin's name in the agreement was written "Suspended."

Crew Agreement—Fourteenth Voyage in Square Rig

14 February 1896–3 May 1897, Antwerp–Cardiff–Mauritius–Astoria–Portland–Hull (England)

Total number signing:	47
Failed to join	2
Total sailing	45
Deserted	9
Died	2

Eighteen men signed the agreement in Antwerp on 13 February 1896.

| Colin Hannah | 29 | Port William | Master | |
| C.G. Henny | 24 | Lewes | First mate | £8:00s |

He had sailed with captain Urquart on the previous voyage.

| A. Dyke | 23 | Liverpool | Second mate | £5:00s |

His previous ship had been *Yarkand* also owned by Edward Bates & Sons.

| J. Brown | 40 | Montreal | Bosun | £3:05s |
| A. Jameson | 29 | New Brunswick | Steward/cook | £4:00s |

Thirteen able seamen also signed.

Cabul left Antwerp on 14 February 1896, towed by the tug *John Bull.* She arrived at Cardiff on 20 February, presumably to load coal. On the front of the agreement was written: "The master has the option of discharging any or all members of the crew on ship's arrival at Cardiff." In the event, the first mate left the ship, and was replaced by W.H. Bond, 36. He had served in *Cabul* before, with Captain Doyle, and then in *Ladakh,* during the voyage from New York to Hong Kong, which had resulted in both he, and Captain Doyle, being injured, forcing *Ladakh* to put into the Cape Verde Islands on 25 February 1895 (see p. 163). *Cabul* was his first ship since the accident, so he had not been to sea for almost a year. W.H. Bond was left behind due to a broken leg.

W. Thomas Hughs   21   Carpenter   £4:15s

He had been born in Dundalk and in the agreement where he had to record his last ship he wrote: "Not at sea." It is not clear whether this means that *Cabul* was his first ship.

A. Olsen   34   Norway   Sailmaker   £4:10s
George H. Crouch   19   Burnley   Steward   £4:10s

Ten able seamen joined the ship and were paid £2:15s. Their average age was 26. Their nationalities were:

English	4
Welsh	2
Scottish	1
Southern Irish	1
Dutch	1
Swedish	1

Cabul sailed for Mauritius on 27 February 1896, which meant that she only took a week to load. She arrived on 27 May, 89 days out, 8,228 miles, 92.4 miles per day at 3.9 knots. Two Englishmen and the Irishman deserted. A Norwegian, C. Johanson, 24, died of dysentery in the hospital. His death caused Colin Hannah some bureaucratic trouble when the voyage terminated in Hull in May 1897. The deceased's balance of wages due was recorded in the appropriate column in the agreement, but not in the official log, and the date of death was recorded differently in the agreement, and the log. Colin Hannah was called upon to explain by the Registrar General of Seamen and wrote in the agreement:

Sir

I beg to state the reason why I made no entry in the Official Log of the particulars of the wages in detail of Johanson Dec'd, is because I thought an entry of the balance due would be sufficient. As regards the difference in the dates of the death of Johanson in the tabulated statement and the entry on page 22 of the Offl. Log, I may state that the latter is the correct day viz: the 18 June /96.

I am Sir

Your Obdt.Servant

[Signed] Colin Hannah.

[This statement was endorsed]:

The attention of the master has been fully called to the requirement of the Law as regards the Official Log.

Three able seamen joined the ship in Mauritius with wages of £3:00s and an ordinary seaman who was paid £1:15s. *Cabul* sailed for Astoria on 30 June 1896, and arrived on 4 November, 127 days out, 12,763 miles, 100.5 miles per day at 4.2 knots.

Astoria is situated on the southern bank of the Columbia River, which is the boundary between the states of Washington (to the north) and Oregon (to the south), on the northwestern seaboard of America. Portland, *Cabul*'s ultimate destination, is sixty miles inland. Opposite Astoria, on the northern entrance of the river, are Cape Disappointment and Ilwaco. The latter is where the captains of the United States Coast Guard lifeboats are trained to cope with the treacherous seas that may occur on this coast. The entrance to the Columbia River is particularly difficult, due to its bar. Here the huge Pacific rollers meet the fast flowing river, and when tidal streams and the wind also exert their effects, the results can be extremely dangerous.

Conditions were probably good, however, when *Cabul* arrived off the entrance on 4 November 1896, for she immediately set off for Portland, and arrived on the 6 November 1896. Here the death of an able seaman, John Donovan, 48, of Bandon in County Cork was reported. He had died on 23 September in 22°N, 129°W. The cause of death was given as "jaundice and heart failure." George Crouch, the steward, was discharged by mutual consent and was replaced by an able seaman Henry Harding, aged 48. Five of the other able seamen deserted. Of the ten who signed the agreement in Cardiff, and excluding Henry Harding, only two would stay with the ship until the end of the voyage. Seven able seamen and an ordinary seaman now joined *Cabul*. Their wages were £4:00s and £2:10s, respectively, and their average age was 25.

Their nationalities were:

English	1
Scottish	1
American	3
Canadian	1
Danish	1
Honolulu	1

Cabul sailed for Hull, via Queenstown, on 5 December 1896, and arrived on 3 May 1897, 149 days out, 14,480 miles, 97.2 miles per day at 4.0 knots.

This voyage completed Colin Hannah's service in *Cabul*, and on 14 August 1897, he took command of *Ladakh* and made four voyages in her. This brought to 18 his total voyages in square rig. It was just over 19 years since he had joined the *Penthesilea* and during that time he had actually been at sea for 13 years (68 percent of the time). Of the six years spent in port, two had been spent in British ports. Therefore, he had spent 11 percent of the nineteen years at home. The total, nominal, nautical mileage for Colin Hannah's career in square rig was 456,995.

Colin Hannah's Career after *Ladakh*

When Colin Hannah left *Ladakh* on 7 November 1902, following her sale to Italian owners, he never served in a sailing ship again. This must have been a difficult time for him because, when he joined the Edward Bates and Sons' steam ship *Imaum* on 3 December, it was as second mate with wages of £8:00s per month, the same amount as the fourth engineer. The chief engineer earned £18:00s per month. As he had gained his master's certificate in square rig, perhaps this apparent demotion was necessary to gain experience in steam.

S.S. *Imaum*

The *Imaum* was built in 1890, and registered in Liverpool, official number 97,786. Gross tonnage: 4,128 (1,998), net tonnage: 2,705 (1,883). Figures in brackets for *Ladakh*. Thus, 65.5 percent (94.2) of the ship's volume was available to carry cargo. This volume was 30 percent greater than that of *Ladakh*. Nominal horsepower of engines: 450. Horsepower per net ton: 6.0

Crew Agreement

2 December 1902–30 January 1903, Avonmouth (England)–Galveston– Havre (France)–Newport (South Wales)

£1 in 1903 = £51.28 as at March 1999. The preamble to the agreement states: "The several persons whose names are here subscribed, and whose descriptions are contained herein, and of whom *Lascars* are engaged as sailors . . . ."

In fact the Lascars signed a separate agreement, which has not survived, and only the officers, together with the steward and the quartermasters, signed the main agreement. With exceptions, detailed below, the agreement was signed in Avonmouth.

S.G. Penberthy	52	Saint Ives	Master	
R. Entwistle	41	Liverpool	First mate	£11:00s
John (Illegible)	34	Dundalk	Second mate	£8:00s

This second mate signed the agreement in Avonmouth on 1 December 1902, and was discharged the same day at Newport. Colin Hannah replaced him on 3 December.

| M. Gobby | 28 | London | Third mate | £6:00s |

He was also replaced in Newport on 3 December by P.J. Thomas, aged 26 who gave his place of birth as Williamstown, Victoria, Australia. His current address however, was 35, Cambridge Road, Seaforth, Liverpool.

A. Haggstrum	32	Sweden	Carpenter	£6:05s
M. Corke	50	Isle of Wight	Steward	£6:00s
B. Jensen	39	Norway	Quartermaster	£4:05s

The quartermasters were primarily helmsmen.

A. Gustafson	28	Illegible	Quartermaster	£4:05s
A. Jensen	37	Norway	Quartermaster	£4:05s
W. Bowden	44	Ardrossan	Quartermaster	£4:05s
David Boughton	34	Cardiff	First engineer	£18:00s
William Caruduff	29	Belfast	Second engineer	£13:00s
Harold Hunter	25	Birkenhead	Third engineer	£10:00s
W.T. Harris	22	Illegible	Fourth engineer	£8:00s

All had served in *Imaum* on the previous voyage except Colin Hannah, the replacement third mate, and the steward.

The voyage that *Imaum* now undertook was as follows:

5 December 1902: departed Newport for Galveston (Texas) arriving on 23 December, 18 days, 4,820 miles, 268 miles per day at 11 knots. This is almost three times faster than *Ladakh*'s speed made good.

1 January 1903: departed Galveston for Havre, arriving on 20 January, 19 days, 4,880 miles, 256 miles per day at 10.7 knots.

27 January: departed Havre for Newport (South Wales) 450 miles. *Lloyd's List* reported: "Newport, 2 February. The steamer *Imaum*, when coming up the river here, 31 January [*sic*] collided with the ketch *Verbena* of Milford, carrying away her bowsprit." On 30 January 1903, the voyage and agreement terminated.

Crew Agreement

3 February 1903–21 April 1903, Newport–Bombay–Plymouth (England)–Antwerp–Cardiff

The crew remained the same, except for the third mate, a quartermaster, and a fourth engineer. Colin Hannah gave his address as 23 Second Avenue, Fazakerley, Liverpool. This signaled an absence of 16 months from his usual address, 38 Northumberland Terrace. The reason for this is unknown.

This voyage is unusual because the official logbook survives. It does not contain navigational information but records events that involved the crew in what would now be called personnel management; in particular, a case of sickness, which had consequences for Colin Hannah.

Imaum left Newport on 4 February 1903. On 16 February she was at Port Said. Passing through the Suez Canal the following day, she arrived at Bombay on 1 March, 24 days out, 6,110 miles, 255 miles per day at 10.6 knots. She left Bombay on 18 March, and it is now that the entries in the logbook begin. B. Jensen, one of the quartermasters, was sick with a diarrheal illness, but this had cleared up by 25 March. On 23 March, the following entry was made in the logbook:

12°50'N, 49°00'W. 11:00 A.M.

This is to certify that one Ebromk Bapook (fireman) did at the aforesaid time and place leave the stokehold to fetch water for the men, and was never seen after. When it became known that the said fireman was missing, a thorough search was made both below and on deck. The only things that were found belonging to the missing man were his slippers and belt on the after deck. I instituted the second and third searches but to no avail, for said fireman was never seen after leaving the stokehold at the aforesaid time and date, so that we came to the conclusion that the fireman Ebromk Bapook either willfully, or accidentally got over the steamer's side into the water and was drowned. There were no wages due to said fireman.

[Signed] S. Penberthy

Colin Hannah.

On the same day, 23 March, the first mate, Robert Entwistle, became ill. The entries in the logbook were as follows:

23 March. This is to certify that Robert Entwistle is sick and off duty suffering from a severe bilious attack. Gave castor oil, vomiting followed.

> Temp. 102   Pulse 98 morning
> 103   99 evening

24 March. Robert Entwistle is still off duty suffering from pains in the limbs and fever. Bowels freely moved. Tongue foul.

> Temp. 103   Pulse 99 morning
> 104   99 evening

Diet consisting of arrowroot, porridge, milk and beef tea with weak brandy and water, also limejuice. Isolation strictly carried out.

25 March. Skin eruption on body. Tongue very foul.

Every precaution taken. All utensils, cabin effects and hospital fumigated, and disinfectant freely used.

> Temp. 100   Pulse 80 morning
> 98   84 evening

The patient is still isolated with one man in attendance.

26 March. Robt. Entwistle says that he feels much better today but weak.

> Temp. 98   Pulse 84 morning
> 101   90 evening

Eruption on body similar to yesterday. Treatment as above.

28 March. This is to certify that there is no change in the patient since my last report. Isolation is strictly carried out and all possible means used to prevent the spread of disease.

29 March. 3:00 P.M. Suez.

This is to certify that Robert Entwistle, Chief Officer has this day at the aforesaid time been landed and put to hospital suffering from small pox, or said to be. All his effects went with him and the boy [his name has been scratched out several times, as the Captain had difficulty spelling it, and it is therefore illegible, but the boy was obviously a Lascar] with his effects, bed and bedding, towels, and everything that was used or come in contact with the patient was destroyed [but presumably not the boy.]

31 March. Port Said

This is to certify that I this day promote Colin Hannah from second mate to chief mate and J. McKee from third mate to second mate with wages accordingly.

Colin Hannah's wages were thus increased to £11:00s per month.

Imaum now sailed for Plymouth arriving on 11 April at 10:30 A.M. and left the same day for Antwerp, arriving two days later, 26 days, 6,360 miles, 245 miles per day at 10.2 knots.

The final voyage on this agreement was from Antwerp, departed, 19 April, to Cardiff where she arrived on 21 April 1903, 2 days, 570 miles. *Lloyd's List* reported: "Cardiff, 21 April 4:49 P.M. Steamer *Imaum* docked Roath dock this tide with after tank leaky."

Colin Hannah did not go to sea again until October, but when he did so, it was again as master.

In Command Once More: S.S. *Sierra Morena*

Colin Hannah joined the *Sierra Morena,* as master, on 13 October 1903, and remained with her until 14 October 1911, during which time he made 16 voyages. In October 1910, he nearly lost his life in her off the Rebecca light in Florida. Following this disaster, *Sierra Morena* was sold to new owners in 1911, and renamed *Graciana.* Colin Hannah made a further six voyages in her, the last of which was completed on 30 June 1913.

Sierra Morena was built in 1903 by C. Connell & Co. of Scotstoun, on the Clyde. She was registered in Liverpool, Official number 118,054, and was owned by the Sierra Shipping Company of Fenwick Chambers, Liverpool. This was the same company that owned *Sierra Parima* in which Colin Hannah had served as first mate.

G.R.T. 3,535 (1,998), N.R.T. 2,282 (1,908.) Figures in brackets for *Ladakh,* which indicate that *Sierra Morena* carried 16 percent more cargo. Nominal horsepower of engines: 222.

Crew Agreement

13 October 1903–25 December 1903, Glasgow–Galveston–Havre–Hull (England)

Total number signing: 36
Deserted: 4

£1 in 1903 = £51.28 as at March 1999.

As *Sierra Morena* was Colin Hannah's first command in a steamship, the whole crew will described to provide an idea of what that command entailed.

Colin Hannah   37   Master

It is possible, for the first time, to obtain some idea of Colin Hannah's salary. The master would have outranked the first engineer, and as the latter earned £16:00s per month, £192:00s a year, it is likely that Colin Hannah earned more. In 1906, the highest paid industrial worker was a coal miner who earned £76:00s a year, so that the master of a steam ship may well have been earning three times more.

Colin Hannah had yet to return to Northumberland Terrace and was still recording his address as 23 Second Avenue, Fazakerley, Liverpool.

R. Compton	31	Cork	First mate	£10:00s
R. Oakey	31	Hull	Second mate	£8:00s
Alfred Bramman	37	London	Third mate	£5:00s
John Morrison	24	Lewes	Carpenter	£5:00s
D. Mason	39	Liverpool	Steward	£7:00s
A. Craig	19	Isle of Man	Assistant steward	£2:00s

Sierra Morena was his first ship

E. Lenner	17	Glasgow	Mess steward	£1:10s
John Knight	36	Jersey	Cook	£7:10s
John Swindersen	33	Norway	Bosun and lamps	£4:15s
O. Jakobsen	28	Norway	Able seaman	£4:00s
J.S. Robertson	48	Stirling	Able seaman	£4:00s
Illegible	29	Norway	Able seaman	£4:00s
H. Brasker	21	Hamburg	Able seaman	£4:00s
Otto Elmlund	23	Sweden	Able seaman	£4:00s
William Jones	27	America	Ordinary seaman	£2:05s
Maurice foster	19	Ottawa	Ordinary seaman	£2:00s

James Watt	44	Isle of Arran	Chief engineer	£16:00s
James Dixon	28	Liverpool	Second engineer	£11:10s
Harold Hunter	25	Birkenhead	Third engineer	£9:00s
J.A. Stewart	27	Liverpool	Fourth engineer	£7:00s
John Stalker	40	Stirling	Donkyman	£5:00s
Thomas Venables	26	Glasgow	Fireman and trimmer	

All the firemen and trimmers were paid £4:00s

Robert Semple	31	Carrickfergus	Fireman and trimmer
William Proctor	33	Dundee	Fireman and trimmer
Andrew Morse	29	Glasgow	Fireman and trimmer
John McGlynn	31	Glasgow	Fireman and trimmer
Hugh McLean	27	Glasgow	Fireman and trimmer
John Keaney	31	Belfast	Fireman and trimmer
Thomas Gillen	29	Belfast	Fireman and trimmer
Samuel Herd	35	Tyrone	Fireman and trimmer

The last person to sign the agreement was Ernest Mottram, 19, of Nottingham who was a midshipman. His pay was one shilling per month, obviously a token payment.

Sierra Morena left Glasgow on 13 October 1903, and arrived in Galveston on 7 November, 25 days out, 5,045 miles, 202 miles per day at 8.4 knots. Three able seamen deserted: William Jones, the American; Otto Elmlund, the Swede; and the Norwegian, aged 29, whose name was illegible. They were replaced by two able seamen:

| Jahn W. Ericson | 29 | Swedish |
| Vincent Scarperi | 31 | Austrian |

And one ordinary seaman:

| Angus McDonald | 19 | North Uist |

Sierra Morena remained in Galveston for 16 days before sailing for Havre on 25 November, a voyage of 4,880 miles. Unfortunately, it is not possible to decipher the date of arrival but it was in December 1903. Vincent Scarperi deserted before the ship left for Hull (date of sailing illegible), where she arrived on Christmas Day, a voyage of 260 miles.

Summary of Voyages in Sierra Morena

Number 2

Departed Hull 4 January 1904 and arrived Savannah (Georgia) on 27 January, 3,975 miles, 23 days, 172 miles per day at 7.2 knots. *Sierra Morena* then departed Savannah on 13 February and arrived Liverpool on 29 February, 3,715 miles, 16 days, 232 miles per day at 9.8 knots.

Number 3

This agreement is of interest, because the last person to sign it was Catharine Hannah, who was engaged, ostensibly, as a stewardess, with wages of one shilling per month, a token payment. In the column headed "Ship in which he [*sic*] last served" is written "First." Catherine had obviously been to sea before, but this was the first occasion when it was necessary to appear on the agreement. Why this was so is impossible to discover at this remove, but perhaps the owners were reluctant to allow wives to accompany their husbands, and this was a way of stretching the rules. The entry is in Colin Hannah's handwriting, and he has given her name as "Cath Hannah," so that it is possible that "Cath" was the name by which she was known. At the end of the voyage, she did not sign the column releasing the ship and its owners from any further claims with regard to wages etcetera. Colin Hannah gave his wife's age as 30, when she was, in reality, 36. Also signing the agreement for the first, and last, time is a purser. Alan Villers, in *At War with Cape Horn*, states that passengers were usually disguised as pursers, or stewardessess if female.

Voyage number 3 departed Liverpool and arrived in Cardiff on 7 March 1904. The ship then departed on 21 March and arrived Colombo (Ceylon) on 18 April.

Thus the voyage took 28 days. The distance is 10,328 miles via the Cape of Good Hope, which would give a daily average of 366 miles, and a speed of 15 knots. Via the Suez Canal, the distance is 6,538 miles, 234 miles per day, 9.7 knots. Therefore, although there is no mention in the agreement of stopping at Suez or Port Said, *Sierra Morena* probably used the Canal to reach Colombo.

Departed Colombo (Ceylon)	26 April 1904
Arrived Negapatam (Near Madras, India)	29 April
240 miles.	
Departed Negapatam	8 May
Arrived Cuddalore	9 May
60 miles.	
Departed Cuddalore	12 May
Arrived Marseille	10 June
6,105 miles, 29 days, 211 miles per day at 8.8 knots.	
Departed Marseille	16 June
Arrived Barry	25 June 1904
472 miles.	

As this voyage took 9 days, *Sierra Morena* may have called at another port en route for South Wales.

Number 4

Catharine Hannah did not appear on this agreement. The Hannahs were again living at 39 Northumberland Terrace.

Departed Barry	30 June 1904
Arrived Rangoon	Date not recorded in the agreement.
7,750 miles.	

Departed Rangoon	?5 September
Arrived Malta	10 October
5,710 miles.	

Departed Malta	15 October
Arrived Hamburg	1 November
2,625 miles, 15 days, 175 miles per day at 7.3 knots.	

Departed Hamburg	17 November
Arrived North Shields	21 November 1904
407 miles.	

Number 5

Catharine Hannah signed this agreement.

Departed North Shields (England)	22 January 1905
Arrived Mobile (Alabama)	15 February
4,970 miles, 24 days, 207 miles per day at 8.6 knots.	

Departed Mobile	18 March
Arrived Havre	6 April
4,640 miles, 19 days, 244 miles per day at 10.2 knots.	

Departed Havre	Not recorded.
Arrived Dunkirk	13 April
143 miles.	

Departed Dunkirk	15 April
Arrived Cardiff	15 April [*sic*] 1905
538 miles.	

Number 6

Catharine Hannah did not sign this agreement.

Departed Cardiff	3 May 1905
Arrived Sourabaya (Java)	1 July

This is a voyage of 58 days. Via the Suez Canal the distance is 8,748 miles, so the average speed would have been 6.3 knots. Via the Cape, the distance is 11,493 miles, giving an average speed of 8.3 knots. It is not known which route *Sierra Morena* took.

Departed Sourabaya	1 August 1905
Arrived New York	11 October

Via the Suez Canal the distance is 10,809 miles, and as the voyage took 72 days, this would give an average speed of 6.3 knots. Via the Cape, the distance is 12,360 giving an average speed of 7.2 knots.

Departed New York — 25 October 1905
Arrived Fernandina (Florida) — 30 October
790 miles, 5 days, 6.6 knots.

Departed Ferdandina — 3 November
Arrived Savannah (Georgia) — 4 November
148 miles.

Departed Savannah — 11 November
Arrived Norfolk (Virginia) — 18 November
450 miles.

Departed Norfolk — 18 November
Arrived Bremerhaven — 6 December 1905
3,680 miles, 18 days, 204 miles per day at 8.5 knots.

Departed Bremerhaven — 11 December for Barry (South Wales) via London.
Arrived Barry — 25 December 1905
(1000 miles in total).

Number 7

Catherine Hannah did not sign this agreement.

The first direct evidence that *Sierra Morena* was carrying coal from South Wales comes in a warning stamped on the front of the agreement:

> The crews of vessels laden with coal are warned that taking naked lights into, or striking matches in holds or places below deck, is attended by very great danger.

Departed Barry   28 December 1905
Arrived Mobile (Alabama)   20 January 1906
4,480 miles, 23 days, 195 miles per day at 8.1 knots.

Departed Mobile   7 February
Arrived Havre   28 February
4,640 miles, 21 days, 221 miles per day at 9.2 knots.

Departed Havre   3 March
Arrived Bremerhaven   7 March 1906
540 miles.

Number 8

Catherine Hannah did not sign this agreement. David Morrison, 41, from Ardrossan, which is 25 miles south west of Glasgow, joined the ship as chief engineer. He would remain with her until 4 October 1911. The agreement carried the warning about naked lights.

Departed Cardiff   31 March 1906
Arrived Batavia (Jakarta)   25 May
55 days. Via the Suez Canal the distance is 8,350 miles,
152 miles per day at 6.3 knots. Via the Cape, 11,123 miles,
202 miles per day at 8.4 knots.

Departed Batavia   5 June
Arrived Sourabaya (Java)   7 June
386 miles.

Departed Sourabaya   15 June
Arrived Hong Kong   2 July
1,939 miles, 13 days, 149 miles per day at 6.2 knots.

Departed Hong Kong   9 July
Arrived Sourabaya   25 July
1,939 miles, 16 days, 121 miles per day at 5 knots.

Departed Sourabaya   30 July
Arrived Hong Kong   11 August
1,939 miles, 19 days, 102 miles per day at 4.3 knots.

Departed Hong Kong   15 August
Arrived Sourabaya   27 August
1,939 miles, 12 days, 162 miles per day at 6.7 knots.

Departed Sourabaya   1 September
Arrived Samarang (Java)   7 September
360 miles.

Depasted Samarang   8 September
Arrived Hong Kong   17 September
2,300 miles, 9 days, 256 miles per day at 10.6 knots.

Departed Hong Kong   26 September
Arrived Samarang   15 October
2,300 miles, 11 days, 209 miles per day at 8.7 knots.

Departed Samarang   18 October
Arrived Hong Kong   31 October
2,300 miles, 13 days, 177 miles per day at 7.4 knots.

Departed Hong Kong   8 November
Arrived Sourabaya   19 November
1,939 miles, 11 days, 176 miles per day at 7.3 knots.

Departed Sourabaya   24 November
Arrived Hong Kong   10 December
1,939 miles, 14 days, 139 miles per day at 5.8 knots.

Departed Hong Kong   15 December
Arrived Batavia   27 December 1906
1,789 miles, 12 days, 149 miles per day at 6.2 knots.

Deparzed Batavia   14 January 1907
Arrived Philadelphia   15 March
60 days out, 10,579 miles via the Suez Canal, 176 miles per
day at 7.3 knots. 12,065 miles via the Cape, 201 miles per
day at 8.3 knots.

Departed Philadelphia   28 March
Arrived Savannah   2 April
676 miles.

Departed Savannah   29 April
Arrived Havre   19 May
3,530 miles, 20 days, 177 miles per day at 7.4 knots.

Departed Havre   21 May
Arrived Hamburg   27 May 1907
560 miles.

Number 9

Catherine Hannah did not sign the agreement. It carried the warning about the
danger of naked lights in vessels carrying coal.

Departed Barry   29 June 1907
Arrived Punta Arenas (Chile)   1 August
7,163 miles, 32 days, 224 miles per day at 9.3 knots.

Departed Punta Arenas   9 August
Arrived Pisagua (Chile)   19 August
2,240 miles, 10 days, 224 miles per day at 9.3 knots.

Departed Pisagua   21 September
Arrived Sydney (Australia)   24 October
6,820 miles, 33 days, 207 miles per day at 8.6 knots.

Departed Sydney   14 November
Arrived Antofagasta (Chile)   18 December
6,717 miles, 34 days, 198 miles per day at 8.2 knots.

Departed Antofagasta   23 December

Sierra Morena must have been calling at ports where there was no British Consul, as the next entry is:

Arrived Antofagasta   28 January 1908
Departed Antofagasta   6 February
Arrived Caldera   8 February
200 miles.

Departed Caldera   6 March
Arrived Puntas Arenas   16 March
1,780 miles, 10 days, 178 miles per day at 7.4 knots.

Departed Puntas Arenas   31 March

The next endorsement is dated 14 May at Tilbury. 7,326 miles. The 14th is probably the day that *Sierra Morena* departed for Antwerp as she arrived here on 16 May 1908, 193 miles. She was back in Swansea on   23 May, 525 miles.

Departed Swansea   29 May
Arrived Liverpool   31 May
236 miles.

Number 10

Sierra Morena departed Liverpool for Newport on 13 August 1908. Catherine Hannah signed the agreement in Newport, as stewardess, on 26 August. Her wages were recorded as £2:00s per month, again, a nominal sum. She was the penultimate person in the agreement. The last to sign was an able seaman who did so "Off Lundy" on 27 August. He would desert in Buenos Aires.

Arrived La Plata (Argentina)   25 September
6,100 miles, 30 days, 203 miles per day at 8.5 knots.

Departed La Plata   6 October
Arrived Buenos Aires   8 October
25 miles.

Departed Buenos Aires   22 October
Arrived Bahia (Blanca)   1 November
540 miles.

Departed Bahia Blanca   3 November
Arrived Liverpool   27 November
6,520 miles, 24 days, 272 miles per day at 11.3 knots.

Number 11

Sierra Morena was probably now engaged in the nitrate trade. Colin Hannah had last visited the Chilean nitrate ports when he served in *Caroline Morris*. Catherine Hannah did not sign this agreement. *Sierra Morena* probably left Liverpool on 11 December 1908, and was in North Shields on 22 December, and may have left on this date.

Arrived Valparaiso (Chile)   4 February 1909
7,450 miles, 44 days, 169 miles per day at 7.1 knots.

Departed Valparaiso   the same day
Arrived Iquique   9 March
783 miles.

Departed Iquique   15 March
Arrived Pisagua   16 March
40 miles.

Departed Pisagua   20 March
Arrived Hamburg   13 May
10,030 miles, 54 days, 186 miles per day at 7.7 knots.

Number 12

Catherine Hannah did not sign this agreement.

Departed Hamburg for Barry   11 June
900 miles.

Departed Barry   24 June
Arrived Santos (Brazil)   19 July

5,180 miles, 25 days, 207 miles per day at 8.6 knots.

| Departed Santos | 30 July |
| Arrived Iquique (Chile) | 22 August |

4,262 miles, 23 days, 185 miles per day at 7.7 knots.

| Departed Iquique | 6 September |
| Arrived Fiume (now Rijeka, Croatia) | 1 November |

8,050 miles, 55 days, 146 miles per day at 6.1 knots.

| Departed Fiume | 15 November |
| Arrived South Shields | 2 December |

3,200 miles, 17 days, 188 miles per day at 7.8 knots.

Number 13

Catherine Hannah signed this agreement.

| Departed North Shields | 10 December 1909 |
| Arrived Iquique | 27 January 1910 |

9,930 miles, 48 days, 207 miles per day at 8.6 knots.

Departed Iquique	19 February
Arrived Tocopilla (Chile)	20 February
130 miles.	

| Departed Tocopilla | 1 March |
| Arrived Hamburg | 20 April |

7,123 miles, 51 days, 140 miles per day at 5.8 knots.

| Departed Hamburg | 29 April |
| Arrived Barry | 3 May |

900 miles, 4 days, 225 miles per day at 9.4 knots.

These 13 voyages extended over a period of six years and six months. Catherine Hannah was on board for one year and two months, 17 percent of the time.

Disaster off the Rebecca Light

On 13 May 1910 *Sierra Morena* left Barry on her 14th voyage, which ended in disaster off the coast of Florida five months later. Mercifully, Catherine Hannah was not on board.

Before the accident *Sierra Morena* called at a number of ports. As usual, there is no record of cargoes, but there is a section in the log that indicates when the ship was in ballast, and when loaded. This section is headed: "Date of arrival at, and departure from, each port touched at, with the free-board and draught of water upon every occasion of the ship proceeding to sea." The ship was fully loaded in all of the voyages below, except where indicated. The fact that it was unusual for *Sierra Morena* to be in ballast, suggests that the owners were running a commercially successful operation.

Arrived Saint Vincent (Cape Verde Isles)   24 May 1910
2,330 miles, 11 days, 212 miles per day, 8.8 knots.

Departed Saint Vincent   24 May
Arrived Bahia Blanca (Argentina)   9 June
4,065 miles, 16 days, 254 miles per day at 10.6 knots.

Departed Bahia (in ballast)   29 June
Arrived Valparaiso (Chile)   13 July
2,433 miles, 14 days, 174 miles per day at 7.2 knots.

Departed Valparaiso (in ballast)   13 July
Arrived Caleta Buena (Chile)   16 July
800 miles, 3 days, 267 miles per day at 11 knots.

Departed Caleta Buena   31 July
Arrived Mejillones (Chile)   1 August
140 miles.

Departed Mejillones   3 August
Arrived Montevideo (Uruguay)   19 August
3,350 miles, 16 days, 209 miles per day, at 8.7 knots.

Departed Montevideo   20 August
Arrived Saint Lucia (West Indies)   7 September
4,224 miles, 18 days, 235 miles per day at 9.8 knots.

Departed Saint Lucia   8 September
Arrived Philadelphia   16 September
1,500 miles, 8 days, 188 miles per day at 7.8 knots.

Departed Philadelphia (in ballast)   1 October
Arrived Tampa   7 October
1,347 miles, 7 days, 192 miles per day at 8.0 knots.

Tampa is a port on the West coast of Florida. *Sierra Morena* loaded here and departed, on 11 October 1910, bound for Savannah, Georgia. Had she been in ballast, the outcome of the disaster may well have been different. In order to reach Savannah, she had to steam around the south of Florida, and then turn north. The southern end of Florida is a difficult passage for the mariner, as a string of islands and shoals extend southwest from its southeast tip. These are called the Florida Keys, and beyond them are the Marquesas Keys, and the Dry Tortugas.

Between the latter two is a passage eight miles wide, providing a useful shortcut through the barrier, and bounded on its eastern side by the Rebecca and New Ground shoals. The distance from Tampa to the passage is 180 miles, and the direct course, uncorrected for tidal stream and currents, is 174° true. Because magnetic north is not true north, it is important to state which north is being used. The difference between the two is called the variation, and this changes both in time, and geographically. The variation is noted on the chart (map 4), and it is a simple task to convert one to the other. This account of how the *Sierra Morena* went ashore was written in the official log by Colin Hannah. All entries are signed by Colin Hannah and the first mate Frederick Ingram. The quadrantal system of compass notation is used in the log; the modern 360 degree notation is added in brackets.

11 October 1910. Newground Shoal.

This is to certify that we left the dock at Port Tampa about 9am and proceeded to sea, discharging Pilot about 1:17P.M. 1 mile off whistle buoy.

Set course west true [270°] and ran 3 miles, current setting strong to the westward.

1:53P.M. a/c [altered course] S4°E true [176°] log 3 miles and continued to 8:00 P.M. at which time a/c S5°E [175°] log 62 miles. At about 10:00 P.M. the weather being fine and horizon well defined, took a set of stellar observations which placed the vessel to the west of position or in 26°181/2'N, 82°581/2'W. Being confidant of this position and knowing that the current on leaving was setting to the westward and also from experience in going up to Tampa, having there a strong set to the westward, a/c S 10°E true [170°] log then being 92. About 5:30 A.M. Chief Officer took stellar observations and placed position on chart 25° 7'N, 82°45'W. On my going into the chart room and comparing this position with the course steered from the position obtained at 10:00 P.M. in presence of Chief Officer, I found the ship had just made the course set. I also took observation of the sun at 7.15 A.M. which placed the vessel in 82°39'W. At about 7.48 A.M. Chief Officer sighted an object just on the horizon bearing S48°W compass, error 5°E [228° compass=232° true].

8:00 A.M. Chief Officer reported to me that the object seen was a lighthouse, black top, white under [this would fit for the Dry Tortugas light on the Loggerhead reef, on the south east corner of the Dry Tortugas]. I went on the bridge and could just make out that it was a Light House there being a glare on the horizon. I went down to the chart and put the bearing down, before leaving the bridge I told the 3rd Officer to watch for other objects, he replied he saw then another lighthouse. A few minutes after the Chief Officer reported the lighthouse appeared on piles. I went on the bridge and we immediately put the helm to port [that is, turned the vessel to starboard] and hauled the vessel round to N45°W compass error 5°E [315° compass=320° true]. We then picked up a buoy almost abeam bearing S55°E compass [235°compass=240° true] dist. about 1–11/2 miles. I went to put bearing of buoy on chart, but had only been from the bridge a minute or two, when the vessel took the ground.

50'
40'
82°35'W
30'
25'
20'
40'
DRY TORTUGAS
REBECCA SHOAL CHANNEL
NEW GROUND SHOAL
35'
REBECCA LIGHT
THE QUICKSANDS
Tampa
80°
27°
FLORIDA
30'
Variation 5° E
24° 25'N
DRY TORTUGAS
6 FATHOMS
3 FATHOMS

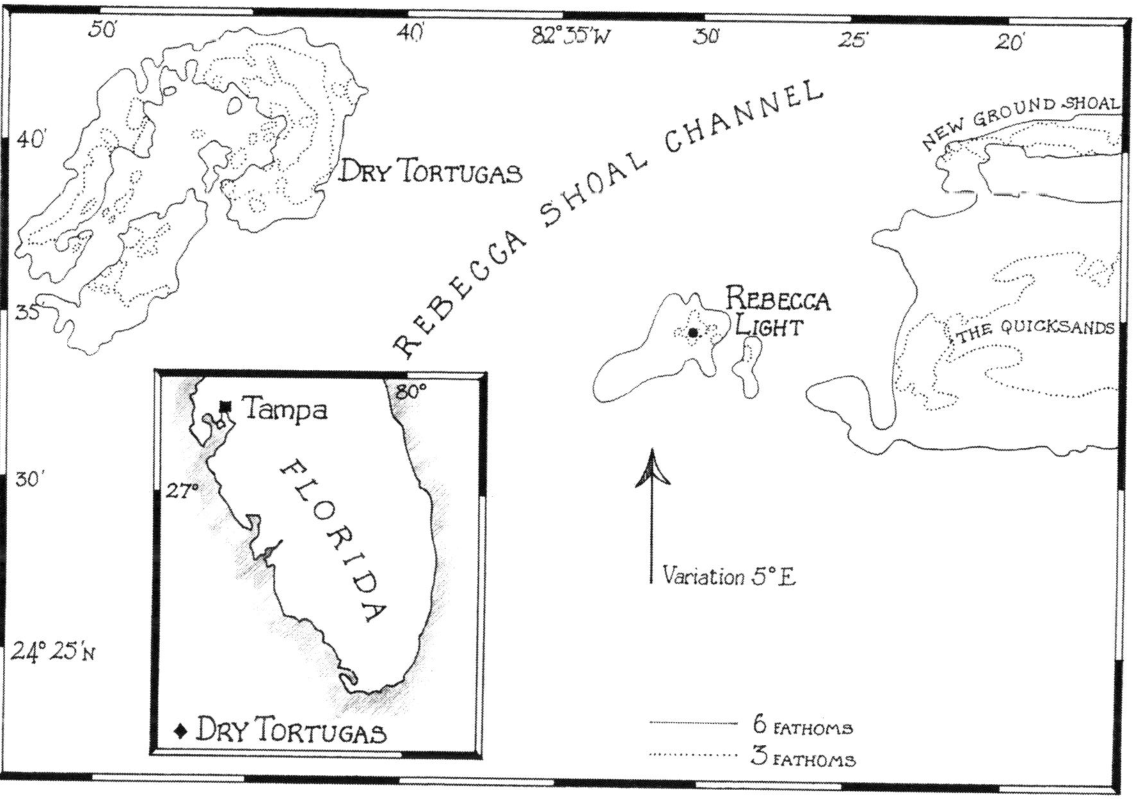

Map 4.

I rushed on the bridge and rang engines full astern, but the vessel would not come off. I kept on working the engines. On taking soundings we found about 61/2 [fathoms] aft shoaling to 3 fathoms forward. Ran[?] up no. 6 tank and after peak, but vessel still refused to move. Called all hands, and commenced to throw coal overboard, and got starboard bower hove aft. Got latter as far as fore rigging, when the winch carried away. Hove away on anchor, and moved engines full astern, but without result. We again hove anchor aft and tried again, but all to no purpose. After getting clear of the coal on deck, about 110 tons, we got derricks up ready to jettison cargo, but about 5:30P.M. the wind commenced to freshen considerably on the vessel's beam. After consulting with Officers, we did not think it prudent to lighten the steamer for fear of her driving further, rocks visible on lee bow. The vessel up to this time making no water.

I cannot account for the difference between the vessel's actual position, and that found by repeated observations, the latter possibly giving us too much confidence.

This account was signed by all the officers. Subsequent entries in the logbook were signed by Colin Hannah and Frederick Ingram, the first mate. When the latter took a boat to the Rebecca Light to seek help, the second mate, R.H. Stuart, signed in his stead.

On 9 October, a tropical storm had formed 800 miles south of the Rebecca Light. On the 10th it was in much the same position, but on the 11th, it had started moving north and developed into a stage 1 hurricane with wind speeds of 70 knots.

13 October. New Ground Shoal.

This is to certify we swung out lifeboats at daybreak and got stream anchor over to try and carry out same on starboard quarter, but owing to strong wind with increasing sea, were unable to do anything. Distress rockets sent up in the night, and signals kept flying during the day. Owing to falling barometer and threatening appearance of the weather, we deemed it imprudent to send a boat away to seek assistance.

Vessel still making no water, but bumping and straining heavily. Used engines at intervals but to no purpose. [The hurricane was 420 miles to the south. It had become stage 2 with wind speeds of up to 95 knots.]

14 October. New Ground Shoal.

This is to certify that during the night the wind kept increasing, and is now blowing a fresh gale, with hard squalls and heavy sea. Weather thick with rain. Vessel bumping, and straining heavily, still making no water, although being driven more upon the reef. Starboard anchor down and vessel's head falling off to northward. About 8:00 P.M. the wind blowing a strong gale, terrific squalls, high sea. Barometer 29.48 inches [999mb], thermometer 82°. Still no water in the vessel, bumping heavily, and apparently driving ahead, heavy strain upon starboard cable, which is now leading aft upon the port side. Ship's head N 1/2 E. [000 1/2=virtually due north.]

[The hurricane was 240 miles to the south. It was now stage 3 with wind speeds of up to 105 knots.]

15 October. New Ground Shoal.

This is to certify that the wind has slightly decreased and barometer risen to 29.56 [1002mb], still blowing hard, with squalls of wind and rain, and heavy sea. Ship has been driven ahead carrying away starboard cable. The vessel is now making water in no. 1, 3 and 4 bilges. Pumps kept going.

10:00 A.M. bent on spare bower [anchor] and in the evening let go both anchors. Very threatening appearance of the weather. [The hurricane was 150 miles to the south, in the region of Cuba. It had become, temporarily, stage 2 again.]

16 October. New Ground Shoal.

Distress signals night and day but no assistance. Strong winds, heavy seas, position of vessel about the same. Barometer 29.47 [999mb], thermometer 82°. Water in all holds and engine room. Pumps still kept going. [The hurricane had moved north west from Cuba, and was 60 miles west of the Rebecca Light. It had become stage 3 once more.]

17 October. New Ground Shoal.

Strong gale, heavy sea, threatening weather. Bar. falling rapidly. Noon bar. 28.2. [956mb], lowest reading 27.95 [947mb]. Thermometer 81°. Terrific weather, and tremendous high breaking sea. Everything being smashed about the decks, unable to do anything. Crew in shelter in cabin.

3:00 P.M. Hurricane center passed over vessel. Holds full of water, tanks full, boats and every movable thing about the vessel smashed or washed away. [As Colin Hannah correctly observed, the hurricane had passed directly over the ship, with winds of up to 105 knots.]

18 October. New Ground Shoal.

Weather moderating slowly. Distress signals night and day. Vessel much damaged by hurricane.

[No sooner had the hurricane passed over *Sierra Morena*, and was 60 miles to the north, the wind speed dropped to 60 knots and the hurricane was then downgraded to a tropical storm.]

19 October. New Ground Shoal.

All hands employed patching up the remains of out only boat to try and get communication. Lt. house apparently taking no notice of our signals. [The tropical storm was now 300 miles to the north. As it proceeded across Florida, and out into the Atlantic, the wind gradually dropped, so that by 23 October the storm had lost its identity.]

20 October. New Ground Shoal.

This is to certify that the Chief Officer and four Able seamen left at 6:00 A.M. for Rebecca Shoal lighthouse in patched boat to try and communicate. Vessel laying in 3 fathoms of water.

4 P.M. steamer *Hero*, Norwegian, bore down and asked if we required assistance. Asked of her to report *Sierra Morena* aground and badly damaged, at first signal station on his route.

21 October. New Ground Shoal.

This is to certify that Chief Officer returned to the ship from Rebecca Lt. House having sent telegrams by *Mangrove* USRC.

Lloyd's List reported:

Liverpool, 21 October, 4:43 P.M. telegram received by Owner from New York states: *Sierra Morena* reported in trouble off Florida.

Key West (by cable). *Sierra Morena*, British Steamer ashore at Rebecca Light; Ran ashore 12 October; she is full of water, bottom badly damaged, lost rudder, lost boats, crew discontented, anxious, wish to abandon ship.

Liverpool, 22 October.

Telegram received by owners from Captain, *Sierra Morena*, Rebecca Shoal. Aground off Rebecca Shoal, New ground 8:00 A.M. 12 October. Bottom seriously injured, holds full of water, tanks are full, engine room flooded, rudder gone, boats washed away, deck fittings damaged. Crew wish to abandon. Weather very bad. Have been unable to communicate. Await instructions.

Official log continues:

23 October. New Ground Shoal.

This is to certify that 16 members of crew left the ship for Key West.

[Signed Colin Hannah and F. Ingram.]

Lloyd's List reports:

Key West, 24 October. *Sierra Morena* is 13 miles from Rebecca Light in 3 fathoms. U.S.S. *Astral* proceeded to *Sierra Morena*, and gave every assistance. Part of crew landed here. Salvage Association.

Official log continues:

26 October. New Ground Shoal.

10 crewmembers left for Key West this day, vessel being full of water, and nothing for the crew to do. Seven members of the crew were left on board to watch vessel at the request of underwriter's surveyor.

26 October. Key West.

This is to certify that the above members of the crew were paid off and returned by Consul to Home Port.

24 November. Key West [written on 27 November].

This is to certify that the remaining members of the crew left the ship on 24 inst. and were paid off yesterday. They left for Home Port this morning, 27 inst.

Lloyd's List reports:

22 December. British steamer, *Sierra Morena* was towed to Key West today.

The Tropical Revolving Storms of 1910

The hurricane that struck the *Sierra Morena* was the last of the season. The season lasts from June to the end of October, the period when the sea is at its warmest. This heat provides the energy to drive the storm as the air, which constitutes it, moves from east to west across the Atlantic, and is set revolving by the earth's rotation.

Table 25. The Saffir–Simpson Scale of Tropical Revolving Storms

Type	Category	Pressure (Millibars)	Wind (Knots)	Winds (m.p.h.)	Surge (Feet)
Depression	T.D.	—	< 34	< 39	—
Tropical Storm	T.S.	—	34–63	39–73	—
Hurricane	1	> 980	64–82	74–95	4–5
Hurricane	2	965–980	83–95	96–110	6–8
Hurricane	3	945–965	96–112	111–130	9–12
Hurricane	4	920–945	113–134	131–155	13–18
Hurricane	5	< 920	> 134	> 155	> 18

There were four tropical revolving storms in 1910:

(1) 20–31 August.

Tropical Storm with maximum wind speeds of 50 knots.
Track: Commencing at the Windward Islands, and moving northwest between Cuba and the Yucatan peninsula, coming ashore at the border between Mexico and the United States.

(2) 5–15 September.

Category 3 hurricane with maximum wind speeds of 105 knots.
Track: Similar to (1)

(3)   23–28 September.

Category 3 hurricane with maximum wind speeds of 105 knots.
Track: Off the eastern seaboard of the United States.

(4)   9–23 October.

Category 3 hurricane with maximum wind speeds of 105 knots.
Track: as described above.

Sierra Morena *Resurgent*

On 18 August 1911, the Sierra shipping company, the original owners, sold the *Sierra Morena* to H. & C. Grayson of the Royal Liver Building, Liverpool, and 11 months after the disaster on the New Ground Shoal, *Sierra Morena* was once more in service. She left Newport News (Virginia) on 12 September 1911. Colin Hannah, David Morrison (the Chief engineer), and the steward remained of the crew who had been aboard during the grounding. *Sierra Morena* called at Norfolk, which is close to Newport News, on the James River, to take on more firemen. On 14 September she sailed for Liverpool, arriving on 4 October, 20 days, 3,235 miles, 162 miles per day at 6.7 knots. On 3 November, she left for Barry, a voyage that took two days.

On 27 November, H. & C. Grayson sold her to Furness, Withy & Co. of Baltic Chambers, West Hartlepool, where she was reregistered, and her name changed to *Graciana*.

S.S. *Graciana*

Colin Hannah made a total of five voyages in *Graciana* between 14 December 1911 and 30 June 1913. None of the agreements were signed by Catherine Hannah, which may indicate that the owners had no objection to masters being accompanied by their wives, as would have seemed to be the case with *Sierra Morena*. However, there is no definite evidence to suggest that Catherine did or did not accompany her husband.

The Chief engineer earned £17:00s per month so Colin Hannah would have earned more than this. £17:00s in 1911 = £46.89 = £562.68 a year, as at March 1999.

Summary of Voyages

Number 1

Departed Barry   14 December 1911
Arrived Buenos Aires   26 January 1912
6,103 miles, 43 days, 142 miles per day at 5.9 knots.

Departed Buenos Aires	17 February
Arrived Bahia Blanca	21 February
540 miles.	

Whilst in Bahia Blanca the British Vice Consul recorded in the agreement:

I hereby certify that the seaman entered on line number 19 [John Robson, 45, born in Aberdeen, living at 49 Maughan Street, Penarth] has been found drowned in this Port of Bahia Blanca, near the Great Southern Railway mole, on this day, 13 April 1912. Proper enquiry and entries made in Logbook and forms duly filled up and forwarded to the Board of Trade.

[Signed] Chas. C. Cumming.

Departed Bahia Blanca	3 April
Arrived Brake	24 May

Brake is on the river Weser, 20 miles below Bremen. 6,850 miles, 51 days, 134 miles per day at 5.6 knots. Departed Brake on 24 May and arrived at Bremen the same day.

Number 2

Departed Bremen	2 June
Arrived Antwerp	4 June
333 miles.	

Departed Antwerp	8 June
Arrived Gothenburg	12 June
616 miles via the Kiel Canal.	

Departed Gothenburg	18 June
Arrived Port Said	?4 July
3,710 miles, 14 days, 265 miles per day at 11 knots.	

Departed Port Said	?4 July
Arrived Muscat	16 July
2,593 miles, 12 days, 216 miles per day at 9.0 knots.	

Departed Muscat	17 July
Arrived Arabistan (?Khuzistan)	23 July
(Arabistan not found in the atlas).	

Departed Arabistan	24 July
Arrived Basra	26 July
(Muscat–Basra: 764 miles).	

Departed Basra	3 August
Arrived Mormugao (Goa)	12 August

Departed Mormugao	21 August
Arrived Port Said	9 September

Departed Port Said	9 September
Arrived Leith (Scotland)	?2 October

3,525 miles, 24 days, 147 miles per day at 6.1 knots.

Departed Leith
Arrived Barrow in Furness (England)   10 October
730 miles.
Voyage terminated in Newport (Wales) on 12 October 1912.
290 miles.

Number 3

The Official Log Book survives for this voyage. It provides an interesting insight into what is now called human resource management in a tramp ship. Each entry is prefaced with "This is to certify that," but it will be omitted following the first extract. The log commences with an entry concerning an event that occurred at 9:30 A.M. on 17 October 1912, the day that *Graciana* left Newport for Swansea, arriving the same day.

> This is to certify that Alfred Lairman [34, born in London, living at 8 Chapel Crescent, Newport] who was shipped as Bosun was found laying on deck helplessly drunk, and frothing at the mouth. Marine Superintendent of Royal Mail found him, and informed me of the fact. We examined the man, and both concluded that it was best to send for an ambulance, as he appeared to be dying. He was taken on shore by police officer. The man has, since our arrival here [at Swansea] written me informing me, that drink was the cause of his illness, and that he got the drink from Stevedores' men. Have signed another Bosun as substitute, the other man's effects and Book [that is his *Continuous certificate of discharge*] will be handed over. [*Graciana* left Swansea for Las Palmas, Grand Canaria, on 22 October 1912, arriving at 5:00 P.M. on 29 October. 1,477 miles, 7 days, 211 miles per day at 8.8 knots. They left for Victoria or Vitoria, Argentina, after twelve hours, at 5:00 A.M. on 30 October.]

> Noon, 4 November, 9°N, 26°W. Limejuice has been served out to the crew.

> 9 November, 8°N, 37°W., W. Thierne, Fireman [aged 20, from Port Elizabeth] is off duty suffering from slight fever. Temp. 101. He is getting every attention and medicine as per Medical Guide. [*Graciana* arrived in Victoria on 13 November, 3,256 miles, 14 days, 233 miles per day at 9.7 knots.]

> 16 November 1912. W. Thierne is still off duty but improving gradually. Temp. 991/2. Giving him medicine for simple fever and nourishing light food. [*Graciana* departed Victoria, part loaded, on 17 November for Rio de Janeiro where she arrived the following day, 280 miles.]

18 November. W. Thierne has resumed duty. [Two months later W. Thierne would be dead, but not because of his illness.]

21 November. Sidney Bradford, Apprentice, is suffering from some skin disease of scalp. Had him attended by Doctor. [*Graciana* was still in Rio de Janeiro.]

26 November. Sidney Bradford is still under the Doctor with his head. It appears to be improving.

[*Graciana* departed Rio de Janeiro for Santos on 3 December where she arrived the following day, 210 miles.]

6 December. Sidney Bradford, Apprentice, who was suffering with eruptions on scalp, is now better.

Noon, 11 December. Samuel Mulley [aged 33, born and living in Ipswich. His wages were £5:00s per month] able seaman, came and requested to be paid off. On my refusing to comply with his request, he has refused duty, for which I fine him as per agreement.

6:00 A.M. 12 December. Samuel Mulley still refused duty, had him before HBM Consul today but he would not consent to go to work, obtaining order for arrest from Consul, and had him [Mulley] put in prison.

12 December. H. Morris [aged 47, born in London, living in Newport, Wales] and Thomas Fee [aged 49, born and living in County Down, both were earning £5:00s per month] Firemen, have been absent without leave since the night of 11 inst.

D Buckley [aged 42, born and living in Cork, £5:00s per month] has been coming and going all day yesterday and today, being under the influence of drink. At noon today, H. Morris returned to the ship. He refused to go to work. Was most insolent and told me to put him in jail if I liked. I accordingly obtained order for his arrest from the Consul, and had him put in prison.

14 December. D. Buckley, fireman, is unable for his work. He goes on shore, gets under the influence of drink, comes on board and demands to see a doctor, claiming that he is sick. Took him before the Consul. Buckley there stated he had a bad tooth. This has been removed and the Consul ordered him to go to work. I may state this man has given me much trouble, both before leaving Swansea, and at this Port [Santos]. I therefore wish to fine him for each day he has been unable to work. [This decision was endorsed when the voyage concluded at London. Buckley also had to pay £0:06s:8d, the fee for having his tooth removed.]

16 December. Thomas Fee, fireman, returned to the ship and resumed duty. He had been locked up since 11 inst. [A fine was levied but the amount is illegible. Again this was endorsed in London.]

17 December. H. Morris, Fireman, and Samuel Mulley AB, being anxious to return to the ship and resume duty, obtained order for their release from Consul today. Mulley has returned on board but Morris has not yet returned.

19 December. D. Buckley, being still under the influence of drink, and refusing to work, coming and going to the ship as he pleases, applied to Consul for order for his arrest, and had him put in jail. H. Morris returned to ship and resumed duty.

24 December. D. Buckley, having promised to go to work, was released from jail and returned on board.

30 December. S. Mulley and H. Morris, have been absent from the ship since 20th and have taken their effects with them. On the advice of HBM Consul, I have taken out orders for arrest of S. Mulley and H. Morris.

3 January 1913. S. Mulley and H. Morris not turning up, signed on Thomas Jones [aged 29 born and living in Woolwich] Sailor, and H. McGarry [aged 39, from Cork] Fireman in their places. Morris's book [*Continuous certificate of discharge*] has been handed to Consul, and return form sent back. [Presumably to the Registrar of Shipping and Seamen. There is no mention of Mulley's papers. On 3 January 1913 at 6.30 P.M. *Graciana* left Santos for Havre.]

4 January 9:00 A.M. The Chief Officer reported to me that he had found a man stowed away. Had the man brought before me. He stated his name was James Ryan, [aged 28, from Liverpool] that he was a fireman, and had come on board the worse for drink, and had woke up and found himself at sea. [He signed the agreement and was paid the going rate for a fireman, £5:00s per month.]

5 January 1913. 22°58' S, 40°17' W. At about 7:15 P.M. 5 inst. A heavy run of coal occurred in port bunker, after which I heard one of the firemen [P. Cunningham aged 35 of Glasgow] who was on watch call out to the trimmer to ascertain if he was all right. On there being no reply, the Chief engineer, who was speaking to me on the bridge at the time, ran down to [the] bunker and called out for William Thierne, the trimmer whose watch it was at the time. On getting no reply he went forward to see if the man had gone there. Finding this was not the case, it became evident the man had got buried in the coal. All hands were instantly at work, both below and on deck, piling coal in stokehold, and getting some on deck. Work was continued incessantly, but owing to the bunker being nearly full of coal at the time, we had to shift about 45 tons.

At about 12.30 A.M. 6 inst. We recovered the body of William Thierne. The body was quite stiff, apparently death had taken place almost immediately after the collapse of the coal. It appeared the coal had got jammed and, notwithstanding the fact the man had been warned by the Chief engineer, and also his own mates, not to venture on top of the coal, must have done so, with the result that when the coal collapsed he, Thierne, went with it. From the appearance of the body, it would seem that death was principally due to suffocation. The lips and face much swollen, and the eyes bulging. After the body was washed, we found several ribs had been broken and the neck apparently so, also other contusions about the body. These may have been done after death, owing to the large pieces of coal rolling down with the body. [This entry in the log was signed by Colin Hannah, the first mate, the first and second engineers, and two firemen.]

6 January, 1913, Noon. 20°47' S, 39°27' W. After proper preparation, the Body of William Thierne was committed to the deep. The Funeral Service, Church of England, being read over.

7 January. The following is a list of the effects of the late William Thierne, fireman. 2 blankets, 1 straw hat, 1 belt, 1 muffler, 3 prs. trousers, 3 vests, 2 jackets, 1 pillow, 1 singlet, 1 shirt, 2 prs. socks, 1 collar, 1 tie, 1 tobacco pouch, 1 handkerchief, 1 tobacco box, 1 Hymn book, 1 Prayer Book, 1 armlet, 1 rug, 1 bag, 1 valise. [There then follows an account of the wages due to the dead man.]

Wages from 17.10.12–6.1.13

2 months @ £5	£10:00s:00d
20 days @ 3s:4p	£3:06s:08d
Total earnings	£13:06s:08d
Less	
To Advance	£2:10s:00d
Cash	£1:00s:00d
Supplies	£0:12s:03d
	£4:02s:03d
Total earnings	£13:06s:08d
Less	£4:02s:03d
	£9:04s:05d
Allotments for 3 months	£7:10s:00d
Balance due	£1:14s:05d

— Assuming his Wife has Received 3 Allotments.

[This means that Mrs. Thierne was living on 50 shillings per month—12 shillings and 5 pence per week. An agricultural laborer earned 18 shillings per week, although Mr. Thierne received his keep aboard ship. Colin Hannah also made a note of the deserters' wages]:

This is to certify the following is the account of wages of S. Mulley, deserted 20.12.12.

2 months @ £5	£10:00s:00d
Wages from 19.10.12 viz. 2 months @ £5 =	£10:00s:00d
2 days @ 3s:4d =	06s:08d
Total earnings	£10:06s:08d
Less	
To advance on joining	£2:10s:00d
Cash	£1:06s:08d
Consul's fees ordering arrest	

Consul's fees ordering release total	10s
Jail fees	13s:04d
7 days off duty @ 3s:4d	£1:03s:04d
Fine for refusing duty	10s
Supplies during voyage	15s:08d
Insurance, 10 weeks @ 4d	3s:04d
Total deductions	£7:12s:04d
Total earnings	£10:06s:08d
Less	£7:12s:04d
Balance in favor of seaman	£2:14s:04d

[The other deserter H. Morris ended up with £3:15s:10d. It is not clear how, or when, the deserters would obtain the money owed to them. *Graciana* arrived at Havre on 30 January 1913, 27 days out, 5,255 miles, 195 miles per day at 8.1 knots.]

1 February, 7:00 A.M. James McGarry, fireman [who had replaced one of the deserters in Santos] is absent from the ship without leave, for which I wish to fine him as per agreement. [This fine was endorsed in London.]

4 February, Noon. Thomas Fee, fireman, reported to me that James McGarry, who has been absent since the 1 inst. was in hospital, having fallen in dock. Reported the matter to the Consul who made enquiries and found McGarry had left the hospital this morning. He is not yet returned on board. [*Graciana* left Havre for London on 5 February, part loaded.]

6 February. 8:00 A.M. Off Dover. James McGarry refuses to work on the plea of pains in his side. He states he twisted himself while on watch. I enquired of him if he did not get hurt when he fell in the dock. He replied he did get his ribs hurt.

Graciana arrived in London on 6 February 1913, 205 miles. The Superintendent of the Mercantile Marine Office, Dock Street, London entered the following in the Log:

> I hereby certify that I have enquired into the circumstances attending the death of William Thiene, and am satisfied that the entries on p.p. 10, 11, and 21 of the official log are correct and true, and that further enquiry is unnecessary.

When Colin Hannah came to fill in the "List of Crew and Report of Character" most of the men who had given him so much trouble were given "V.G. for Ability and General conduct." Although deserters were not rated, Samuel Mulley was: "V.G." Daniel Buckley was given "V.G for Ability and Dec. [whatever that means] for General Conduct." Possibly the whole exercise was a waste of time, and Colin Hannah did not give it his full attention.

Number 4

Graciana left London on 11 February 1913, but her subsequent movements are not clear from the agreement. The first endorsement, on 22 February, is in the china clay port of Fowey, on the south coast of Cornwall, which is only 340 miles from London. The third mate joined here, together with a fireman. *Graciana* also appears to have put into Cardiff on 24 February, because although this is not mentioned by the Mercantile Marine office, the second engineer joined the ship here (he had sailed in *Graciana* on the previous voyage).

Graciana's next port of call was Philadelphia, which she reached on 18 March (3,232 miles), leaving for Baltimore on 25 March, where she arrived on 28 March (376 miles). Five days later, on 2 April, she sailed for Leith, making that port on 19 April, 17 days out, 3,470 miles, 204 miles per day at 8.5 knots. *Graciana* had deck cargo, and this was checked by Customs on 23 April, to ensure that it was within the prescribed limits laid down by the Shipping Acts. This was important, as deck cargo raises the center of gravity of a ship, and affects stability.

Number 5

Graciana left Leith for Middlesbrough (England) on 28 April 1913. Once again her destination was Philadelphia, for where she set off on 7 May, arriving on 28 May, 21 days, 3,550 miles, 169 miles per day at 7.0 knots.

Philadelphia–Baltimore, departed 4 June, arrived 6 June, 376 miles.

Baltimore–Leith, once more with deck cargo, departed 14 June, arrived 30 June, 16 days, 3,470 miles, 217 miles per day at 9.0 knots. This was Colin Hannah's last voyage in *Graciana*.

S.S. *Ascania*

The *Ascania* was a Cunard passenger liner (plate 14) that, at the beginning of 1915, was being used as a prisoner of war ship. She had been built in 1911, and was registered in Liverpool, G.R.T. 9,120, N.R.T. 5,702, nominal horsepower of engines 978. Thus, as is usual with steamships, 62 percent of her volume was available for carrying passengers. The N.R.T. to horsepower ratio was 5.8. She was the largest ship that Colin Hannah had served in.

The master was S. Gronow, 42, whose address was 14 Malpas Road, Wallasey (near Birkenhead). This street runs parallel to Queensway where Colin Hannah lived at number 28, and so the two would have presumably known each other.

The official log survives and in January and the first part of February the entries record that the *Ascania* was in Portsmouth. On 21 February, the log states that she was at Ryde, Isle of Wight, and that the first officer had transferred to the *Andania*. The following day he was replaced by Colin Hannah who recorded that his last

Plate 14. The S.S. *Ascania.*

ship had been the *Andania,* so the two men may have swapped. The crew agreements of the *Andania* for 1914 and the beginning of 1915, however, have no record of Colin Hannah. The log continues:

> Ryde, 20 February 1915. Government tender *Elbe* in coming alongside broke gangway ladder and platform through getting foul of tender rope, and injuring W.A. Lewis [second officer].

> 27 February, W.A. Lewis is off duty, suffering from severe contusions. Surgeon in attendance.

> 1 March, William Worthman, German interned alien, by trade a ships carpenter, died of heart failure following acute malaria. Age unknown.

> 7 March, Herman Crossen, 34, German prisoner of war, died of malaria and hyperpyrexia. Occupation unknown.

> 13 March W.A. Lewis, second officer, discharged by mutual consent.

The log finishes now as a new crew agreement was drawn up.

Crew Agreement

16 March 1915–24 June 1915, Southampton–Portsmouth–Plymouth– Lemnos (Greece)–Alexandria–Gibraltar–London

The crew consisted of 162 men. Of this number, 32 were involved with sailing the ship. Although S. Gronov had been the master of the *Ascania* during the previous agreement, this position was taken initially, by the former master of the *Saxonia* (name illegible), but S. Gronov replaced him on 30 March 1915.

Colin Hannah was first officer with pay of £16:00s per month. There were also second and third officers, a carpenter, a bosun, and his mate. Other crew were:

Able seamen	11
Seamen	8
Quartermasters	4
Deck boys	2

In the engineering department there were 43 in all. In charge was the chief engineer (£22:00s per month) with his five assistants. Other crew were:

Donkeyman	
Firemen	14
Trimmers	9
Greasers	10
Boilerman	1
Electrical attendant	1
Refrigerator greaser	1

The refrigerator greaser was A.E. Bridger who had been an apprentice on the *Ladakh*. Obviously his career had not prospered.

The largest department was that concerned with the domestic offices of the ship.

Chefs	2
Cooks	7
Bakers	6
Butchers	4
Pantrymen	4
Scullery man	1
Storekeepers	2
Scullions	6
Stewards	10
Stewards' boys	5
Waiters	30
(one of whom was a hospital attendant)	
Linen keeper	1
Library steward	1
Watchman	1
Waterman	1

Also in the crew were:

Surgeon
Purser. He was paid £16:00s per month, the same as Colin Hannah.
Purser's assistant.
Marconi operator and assistant.
The majority of the crew earned £7:00s–£8:00s per month.

The destinations of the *Ascania*, as described in the agreement, are nonspecific: "From Ryde to a port or place of destination within the limits of 30° and 70° North latitude."

The following dates and ports are recorded in the agreement:

16 March	Southampton
30 March	Portsmouth
31 March	Ryde (Isle of Wight)
7 April	Portsmouth
14 April	Southampton
10 May	Plymouth
7 June	Lemnos (A Greek island being used as a forward base for the Gallipoli campaign)
9 June	Alexandria

The shipping officer at the British consulate, Paul Cassar, recorded in the agreement the diagnosis of those left behind due to sickness, thus he noted: "R.B. Reed, AB has been left in hospital at Lemnos, suffering from fever."

| 9 June | Gibraltar |
| 24 June | Voyage terminated at London. |

Crew Agreement

30 September 1915–29 April 1916

The agreement stated that the *Ascania* was to be employed

> On Admiralty service on a voyage or voyages in the Coasting, Home or Foreign trades within the limits of 75 degrees latitude to and fro as required for a period not exceeding 24 months, the master having the option of discharging without notice any member of the crew at a port in the U.K. at any time before the termination of the period of the agreement. Agreement to end in the United Kingdom.

Colin Hannah's wages were increased to £18:00s per month. Three people earned more than he: the master, the chief engineer (£23:00s), and the second engineer (£19:00s). The third officer, aged 63, was the oldest member of the crew, but he left the ship on 13 October 1915 at Gravesend, due to sickness. Thirty-seven of the seamen were from the United Kingdom (including Southern Ireland). Other nationalities were:

Dutch	3
Japanese	3
Russian	2
Australian	1
Gibraltarian	1

The engineering department was more racially disparate due to the stokers and trimmers.

United Kingdom (including all the officers)	9
Dutch	9
Belgian	4
Barbados	2
Berbera	2

And one each from: Australia, Canada, France, Greece, Jamaica, Russia, Saint Vincent, and Somaliland.

The majority of those who were responsible for the passengers were from the United Kingdom, mainly London, except for two Swiss, a Dutchman, and a Canadian.

The *Ascania* left London on 4 October 1915, and arrived at Alexandria on 23 December, having called at Gravesend on 13 October. The shipping officer at Alexandria, Paul Cassar, noted that a Dutch fireman, G. Christians, aged 30, was discharged, as he was suffering from venereal disease.

Ascania was back in Tilbury on 13 January 1916. One week later she was at London docks, and on 31 January at Devonport (Plymouth). On 1 March she was at Port Said, and on 16 March at Alexandria where Paul Cassar discharged two men with venereal disease, one of whom was H. Butler, 24, the captain's steward. Another man was diagnosed as suffering from erysipelas, and was also discharged.

Ascania then left for Marseilles, arriving on 25 April, where a new agreement was drawn up.

Crew Agreement

28 April 1916–5 June 1916, Marseilles–Montreal–London

Although the preamble was again nonspecific, and there was no mention of *Ascania* being engaged on Admiralty business, two naval signalmen were on the crew list.

On 20 May 1916, *Ascania* arrived at Montreal. A total of eight men from the Chief steward's department are recorded as being discharged to "Join HM Forces." Despite there being a war, the number of deserters, and men failing to join, are noted in the *Ascania* agreements in the same numbers as occurred in peace time. Thus, in Montreal six men deserted: one Danish seaman and five firemen and trimmers, of whom two were Irish, two Egyptian, and one an Englishman.

Ascania now returned to London, on what was to be Colin Hannah's last voyage, arriving on 5 June 1916, just after his fiftieth birthday, 33 years since he joined the *Penthesilea* with the rank of boy, and just over 18 years since the photograph was taken of the crew of *Ladakh* in Brooklyn (see plate 4, p. 23).

Summary of Voyages

Penthesilea

Rank: boy. Age: 17 years, 6 months. Wages: £0:15s per month.

Table 26. First Voyage in Square Rig

From	To	Departed	Arrived	Days	Miles	Miles per day	Speed
Liverpool	Bombay	8.ix.83	28.xii.83	111	10750	96.8	4.0
Bombay	Rangoon	16.i.84	6.iii.84	49	2117	43.2	1.8
Rangoon	Liverpool	3.iv.84	13.viii.84	132	11660	88.3	3.7

Rank: ordinary seaman. Age: 19 years, 7 months. Wages: £1:15s–£2:00s per month.

Table 27. Second Voyage in Square Rig

From	To	Departed	Arrived	Days	Miles	Miles per day	Speed
Liverpool	Rangoon	20.ix.84	22.i.85	124	11660	94.0	3.9
Rangoon	Liverpool	23.iii.85	6.ix.85	167	11660	69.8	2.9

Table 28. Third Voyage in Square Rig

From	To	Departed	Arrived	Days	Miles	Miles per day	Speed
Liverpool	Bombay	9.x.85	11.ii.85	125	10750	86.0	3.6
Bombay	Liverpool	8.v.86	9.ix.86	124	10750	86.7	3.6
Liverpool	Penarth	1.x.86	3.x.86		250		

Table 29. Fourth Voyage in Square Rig

From	To	Departed	Arrived	Days	Miles	Miles per day	Speed
Penarth	Bombay	21.x.86	19.ii.87	121	10563	87.3	3.6
Bombay	Rangoon	1.iv.87	6.v.87	36	2117	58.8	2.5
Rangoon	Liverpool	28.v.87	26.x.87	151	10750	71.2	3.0

Rank: third mate. Age: 21 years, 8 months. Wages: £3:05s per month.

Table 30. Fifth Voyage in Square Rig

From	To	Departed	Arrived	Days	Miles	Miles per day	Speed
Liverpool	Penarth	9.xi.87	11.xi.87		250		
Penarth	Bombay	18.xi.87	15.iii.88	117	10563	90.3	3.8
Bombay	Rangoon	10.iv.88	10.v.88	30	2117	70.6	2.9
Rangoon	Liverpool	1.vi.88	31.x.88	153	10750	70.3	2.9

Rank: second mate. Age: 22 years, 8 months. Wages: £5:00s per month.

Table 31. Sixth Voyage in Square Rig

From	To	Departed	Arrived	Days	Miles	Miles per day	Speed
Penarth	Rangoon	21.xi.88	1.iv.89	130	11660	89.7	3.7
Rangoon	Amsterdam	27.iv.89	1.xi.89	156	11795	75.6	

Table 32.

From	To	Departed	Arrived	Days	Miles	Miles per day	Speed
Liverpool	Newport	12.xii.89	14.xii.89				

Table 33. Seventh Voyage in Square Rig

From	To	Departed	Arrived	Days	Miles	Miles per day	Speed
Newport	Mauritius	9.i.90	Went ashore, Bideford Bay, 20.i.90				

Caroline Morris

Rank: first mate. Age: 23 years, 11 months. Wages £6:15s per month.

Table 34. Eighth Voyage in Square Rig

From	To	Departed	Arrived	Days	Miles	Miles per day	Speed
Newport	Valparaiso	1.iii.90	12.vi.90	101	8787	87.0	3.6
Valparaiso	Pisagua	18.vi.90	4.viii.90	47	800	17.0	0.7
Pisagua	London	13.ix.90	22.xii.90	100	9890	98.9	4.1

Table 35. Ninth Voyage in Square Rig

From	To	Departed	Arrived	Days	Miles	Miles per day	Speed
London	Valparaiso	2.ii.91	18.v.91	105	9090	86.6	3.6
Valparaiso	South Shields	28.vii.91	21.xii.91	116	9215	79.4	3.3

Passed the examination for master on 12 December 1891. Age: 25 years, 9 months.

Sierra Parima

Rank: first mate. Age: 25 years, 11 months. Wages: £8:00s per month.

Table 36. Tenth Voyage in Square Rig

From	To	Departed	Arrived	Days	Miles	Miles per day	Speed
Penarth	Mauritius	9.ii.92	27.iv.92	77	8228	106.9	4.5
Mauritius	Rangoon	21.vi.92	11.vii.92	20	3215	160.8	6.7
Rangoon	Liverpool	17.vii.92	23.xi.92	119	11660	97.9	4.1

Catherine McDowall and Colin Hannah were married on 28 November 1892.

Table 37. Eleventh Voyage in Square Rig

From	To	Departed	Arrived	Days	Miles	Miles per day	Speed
Liverpool	San Francisco	7.i.93	22.ix.93	105	13667	130.2	5.4
San Francisco	Queenstown	15.vi.93	28.ix.93	105	13412	127.7	5.3
Queenstown	South Shields	4.x.93	9.x.93	5	720	144.0	6.0
South Shields	Swansea	21.xi.93					

Table 38. Twelfth Voyage in Square Rig

From	To	Departed	Arrived	Days	Miles	Miles per day	Speed
Swansea	San Francisco	29.xii.93	24.iv.94	116	13540	116.7	4.9
San Francisco	Liverpool	6.viii.94	8.xii.94	124	13667	110.2	4.6

Table 39. Thirteenth Voyage in Square Rig

From	To	Departed	Arrived	Days	Miles	Miles per day	Speed
Liverpool	Milford Haven.	14.ii.95	16.ii.95	Put in due to stress of weather.			
Milford Haven.	Astoria	18.ii.95	23.vi.95	125	14237	113.8	4.7
Astoria	Portland	25.vi.95	26.vi.95				
Portland	Astoria	29.vii.95	30.vii.95				
Astoria	Liverpool	17.viii.95	23.xii.95	128	14237	111.2	4.6

Cabul

Rank: captain. Age: 29 years, 11 months.

Table 40. Fourteenth Voyage in Square Rig

From	To	Departed	Arrived	Days	Miles	Miles per day	Speed
Antwerp	Cardiff	14.2.96	20.ii.96.	6	500	83.3	3.5
Cardiff	Mauritius	27.2.96	27.v.96	89	8228	92.4	3.9
Mauritius	Astoria	30.6.96	4.xi.96	127	12763	100.5	4.2
Astoria	Hull	5.12.96	3.v.97	149	14480	97.2	4.1

Ladakh

Rank: captain. Age: 30 years, 5 months.

Table 41. Fifteenth Voyage in Square Rig

From	To	Departed	Arrived	Days	Miles	Miles per day	Speed
Liverpool	Calcutta	17.viii.97	15.xii.97	120	11655	97	4.0
Calcutta	New York	23.ii.98	13.vi.98	111	12335	111	4.6
New York	Bombay	29.vii.98	28.xii.98	122	11430	94	3.9
Bombay	Rangoon	31.xii.98	14.ii.99	45	2117	47	2.0
Rangoon	Falmouth	16.iii.99	11.vii.99	117	11340	97	4.0
Falmouth	Bremerhaven	12.vii.99	18.vii.99	6	630	105	4.4

Table 42. Sixteenth Voyage in Square Rig

From	To	Departed	Arrived	Days	Miles	Miles per day	Speed
Bremerhaven	New York	2.ix.99	11.x.99	26	3520	135	5.6
New York	Bombay	16.xi.99	19.iii.00	124	114300	92	3.8
Bombay	Bassein	10.iv.00	10.v.00	29	2059	71	3.0
Bassein	Falmouth	22.v.00	26.ix.00	127	11223	88	3.7
Falmouth	Rotterdam	29.ix.00	1.x.00	2	400	Under tow	8.0

Table 43. Seventeenth Voyage in Square Rig

From	To	Departed	Arrived	Days	Miles	Miles per day	Speed
Rotterdam	Antwerp	31.x.00	1.xi.00	1	121	Under tow	
Antwerp	San Francisco	28.xi.00	23.iv.01	147	13779	94	3.9
San Francisco	Falmouth	18.vi.01	5.x.01	109	13440	123	5.1
Falmouth	Dublin	14.x.01	16.x.01	2	363	Under tow	7.6

Table 44. Eighteenth Voyage in Square Rig

From	To	Departed	Arrived	Days	Miles	Miles per day	Speed
Dublin	Cardiff	23.xi.01	25.xi.01	2	215	108	4.8
Cardiff	Esquimault	17.xii.01	22.iv.02	127	14337	113	4.7
Esquimault	Tacoma	?	17.v.02		90		
Tacoma	Queenstown	10.vi.02	26.x.02	138	15143	110	4.6
Queenstown	London	3.xi.02	7.x.02	4	560	Under tow	5.8

Imaum

Rank: second mate. Age: 36 years, 9 months. Wages: £8:00s per month.

Table 45. First Voyage in Steam

From	To	Departed	Arrived	Days	Miles	Miles per day	Speed
Avonmouth	Galveston	5.xii.02	23.xii.01	18	4820	268	11.0
Galveston	Havre	1.i.03	20.i.03	19	4880	256	10.7
Havre	Newport	27.i.03			450		

Rank: second mate, then first mate. Wages: £8:00s–£11:00s per month.

Table 46. Second Voyage in Steam

From	To	Departed	Arrived	Days	Miles	Miles per day	Speed
Newport	Bombay	4.ii.03	1.iii.03	24	6110	255	10.6
Bombay	Antwerp	18.iii.03	13.iv.03	26	6360	245	10.2
Antwerp	Cardiff	19.iv.03	21.iv.03		570		

Sierra Morena

Rank: captain. Age: 37 years, 7 months. Wages: more than £16:00s per month.

Table 47. Third Voyage in Steam

From	To	Departed	Arrived	Days	Miles	Miles per day	Speed
Glasgow	Galveston	13.x.03	7.xi.03	25	5045	202	8.4
Galveston	Havre	25.xi.03	Dec.				

Table 48. Fourth Voyage in Steam

From	To	Departed	Arrived	Days	Miles	Miles per day	Speed
Hull	Savannah	4.i.04	27.i.04	23	3975	172	7.2
Savannah	Liverpool	13.ii.04	29.ii.04	16	3715	232	9.8

Table 49. Fifth Voyage in Steam

From	To	Departed	Arrived	Days	Miles	Miles per day	Speed
Liverpool	Cardiff	7.iii.04					
Cardiff	Colombo	21.iii.04	18.iv.04	28	6538	234	9.7
Colombo	Negapatam	26.iv.04	29.iv.04		240		
Negapatam	Cuddalore	8.v.04	9.v.04		60		
Cuddalore	Marseilles	12.v.04	10.vi.04	29	6105	211	8.8
Marseilles	Barry	16.vi.04	25.vi.04		472		

Table 50. Sixth Voyage in Steam

From	To	Departed	Arrived	Days	Miles	Miles per day	Speed
S. Shields	Mobile	22.i.05	15.ii.05	24	4970	207	8.6
Mobile	Havre	18.iii.05	6.iv.05	19	4640	244	10.2
Havre	Dunkirk		13.iv.05		143		
Dunkirk	Cardiff	15.iv.05			538		

Table 51. Seventh Voyage in Steam

From	To	Departed	Arrived	Days	Miles	Miles per day	Speed
Cardiff	Sourabaya	3.v.05	1.vii.05	58	8748s	151	6.3
Via the Cape					11493	198	8.3
Sourabaya	New York	1.viii.05	11.x.05	72	10809	150	6.3
Via the Cape					12360	172	7.2
New York	Fernandina	25.x.05	30.x.05	5	790	158	6.6
Fernandina	Savannah	3.xi.05	4.xi.05		148		
Savannah	Norfolk	11.xi.05	18.xi.05		450		
Norfolk	Bremerhaven	18.xi.05	6.xii.05	18	3680	204	8.5
Bremerhaven	London	11.xii.05			409		
London	Barry		25.xii.05		590		

Table 52. Eighth Voyage in Steam

From	To	Departed	Arrived	Days	Miles	Miles per day	Speed
Barry	Mobile	28.xii.05	20.i.06	23	4480	195	8.1
Mobile	Havre	7.ii.06	28.ii.06	21	4640	221	9.2
Havre	Bremerhaven	3.iii.06	7.iii.06		540		

Table 53. Ninth Voyage in Steam

From	To	Departed	Arrived	Days	Miles	Miles per day	Speed
Cardiff	Batavia	31.iii.06	25.v.06	55	8350	152	6.3
Via the Cape					11123	202	8.4
Batavia	Sourabaya	5.vi.06	7.vi.06		386		
Sourabaya	Hong Kong	15.vi.06	2.vii.06	13	1939	149	6.2
Hong Kong	Sourabaya	9.vii.06	25.vii.06	16	1939	121	5.0
Sourabaya	Hong Kong	30.vii.06	11.viii.06	19	1939	102	4.3
Hong Kong	Sourabaya	15.viii.06	27.viii.06	12	1939	162	6.7
Sourabaya	Samarang	1.ix.06	7.ix.06		360		
Samarang	Hong Kong	8.ix.06	17.ix.06	9	2300	256	10.6
Hong Kong	Samarang	26.ix.06	15.x.06	11	2300	209	8.7
Samarang	Hong Kong	18.x.06	31.x.06	13	2300	177	7.4
Hong Kong	Sourabaya	8.xi.06	19.xi.06	11	1939	176	7.3
Sourabaya	Hong Kong	24.xi.06	10.xii.06	14	1939	139	5.8
Hong Kong	Batavia	15.xii.06	27.xii.06	12	1789	149	6.2

Table 54. Tenth Voyage in Steam

From	To	Departed	Arrived	Days	Miles	Miles per day	Speed
Batavia	Philadelphia	4.i.07	15.iii.07	60	10599	176	7.3
Via the Cape					12065	201	8.3
Philadelphia	Savannah	28.iii.07	2.iv.07	5	676	135	5.6
Savannah	Havre	29.iv.07	19.v.07	20	3530	177	7.4
Havre	Hamburg	21.v.07	27.v.07	6	560	93	3.9

Table 55. Eleventh Voyage in Steam

From	To	Departed	Arrived	Days	Miles	Miles per day	Speed
Barry	Punta Arenas	29.vi 07	1.viii.07	32	7163	224	9.3
Punta Arenas	Pisagua	9.viii.07	19.viii.07	10	2240	224	9.3
Pisagua	Sydney	21.ix.07	24.x.07	33	6820	207	8.6
Sidney	Antofagasta	14.xi.07	18.xii.07	34	6717	198	8.2
Antofagasta	Antofagasta	23.xii.07	28.i.08				
Antofagasta	Caldera	6.ii.08	8.ii.08		200		
Caldera	Punta Arenas	6.iii.08	16.iii.08	10	1780	178	7.4
Punta Arenas	Tilbury	31.iii.08					
Tilbury	Antwerp	14.v.08	16.v.08		193		
Antwerp	Swansea		23.v.08		525		
Swansea	Liverpool	29.v.08	31.v.08		236		
Liverpool	Newport	13.viii.08					

Table 56. Twelfth Voyage in Steam

From	To	Departed	Arrived	Days	Miles	Miles per day	Speed
Newport	La Plata	26.viii.08	25.ix.08	30	6100	203	8.5
La Plata	Buenos Aires	6.x.08	8.x.08		25		
Buenos Aires	Bahia Blanca	22.x.08	1.xi.08		540		
Bahia Blanca	Liverpool	3.xi.08	27.xi.08	6520	272	11.3	
Liverpool	South Shields	11.xii.08			882		

Table 57. Thirteenth Voyage in Steam

From	To	Departed	Arrived	Days	Miles	Miles per day	Speed
South Shields	Valparaiso	22.xii.08	4.ii.09	44	7450	169	7.1
Valparaiso	Iquique	4.ii.09	9.iii.09		783		
Iquique	Pisagua	15.iii.09	16.iii.09		40		
Pisagua	Hamburg	20.iii.09	13.v.09	54	10030	186	7.7
Hamburg	Barry	11.vi.09			900		

Table 58. Fourteenth Voyage in Steam

From	To	Departed	Arrived	Days	Miles	Miles per day	Speed
Barry	Santos	24.vi.09	19.vii.09	25	5180	207	8.6
Santos	Iquique	30.vii.09	22.viii.09	23	4262	185	7.7
Iquique	Fiume	6.ix.09	1.xi.09	55	8050	146	6.1
Fiume	South Shields	15.xi.09	2.xii.09	17	3200		7.8

Table 59. Fifteenth Voyage in Steam

From	To	Departed	Arrived	Days	Miles	Miles per day	Speed
North Shields	Iquique	10.xii.09	27.i.10	48	9930	207	8.6
Iquique	Tocopilla	19.ii.10	20.ii.10		130		
Tocopilla	Hamburg	1.iii.10	20.iv.10	51	7123	140	5.8
Hamburg	Barry	29.iv.10	3.v.10	4	900	225	9.4

Table 60. Sixteenth Voyage in Steam

From	To	Departed	Arrived	Days	Miles	Miles per day	Speed
Barry	Saint Vincent	13.v.10	24.v.10	11	2330	212	8.8
Saint Vincent	Bahia Blanca	24.v.10	9.vi.10	16	4065	254	10.6
Bahia Blanca	Valparaiso	29.vi.10	13.vii.10	14	2433	174	7.2
Valparaiso	Caleta Buena	13.vii.10	16.vii.10	3	800		
Caleta Buena	Mejillones	31.vii.10	1.viii.10		140		
Mejillones	Montevideo	3.viii.10	19.viii.10	16	3350	209	8.7
Montevideo	Saint Lucia	20.viii.10	7.ix.10	18	4224	235	9.8
Saint Lucia	Philadelphia	8.ix.10	16.ix.10	8	1500	188	7.8
Philadelphia	Tampa	1.x.10	7.x.10	7	1347	192	8.0
Tampa	Savannah	11.x.10					

On 12 October 1910, *Sierra Morena* went ashore on New Ground Shoal. She was refloated and salvaged.

Table 61. Seventeenth Voyage in Steam

From	To	Departed	Arrived	Days	Miles	Miles per day	Speed
Newport News	Norfolk	12.ix.11					
Norfolk	Liverpool	14.ix.11	4.x.11	20	3235	162	6.7

Graciana

Table 62. Eighteenth Voyage in Steam

From	To	Departed	Arrived	Days	Miles	Miles per day	Speed
Barry	Buenos Aires	14.xii.11	26.xii.12	43	6103	142	5.9
Buenos Aires	Bahia Blanca	17.ii.12	21.ii.12		540		
Bahia Blanca	Brake	3.iv.12.	24.v.12	51	6850	134	5.6
Brake	Bremen	24.v.12					

Table 63. Nineteenth Voyage in Steam

From	To	Departed	Arrived	Days	Miles	Miles per day	Speed
Bremen	Antwerp	2.vi.12	4.vi.12		333		
Antwerp	Gothenburg	8.vi.12.	12.vi.12.		616		
Gothenburg	Port Said	18.vi.12	?4.vii.12	14	3710	265	11
Port Said	Muscat	?4.vii.12	16.vii.12	12	2593	216	9.0
Muscat	Arabistan	17.vii.12	23.vii.12				
Arabistan	Basra	24.vii.12	26.xii.12				
Basra	Marmugao	3.viii.12	12.viii.12				
Marmugao	Port Said	21.viii.12	9.ix.12				
Port Said	Leith	9.ix.12	?2.x.12	24	3525	147	6.1
Leith	Barrow		10.x.12		730		
Barrow	Newport				290		

Table 64. Twentieth Voyage in Steam

From	To	Departed	Arrived	Days	Miles	Miles per day	Speed
Newport	Swansea	17.x.12	17.x.12				
Swansea	Las Palmas	22.x.12.	29.x.12	7	1477	211	8.8
Las Palmas	Victoria	30.x.12	13.xi.12	14	3256	233	9.7
Victoria	Rio	17.xi.12	18.xi.12		280		
Rio de Janeiro	Santos	3.xii.12	4.xii.12		210		
Santos	Havre	3.i.13	30.i.13	27	5255	195	8.1
Havre	London	5.ii.13	6.ii.13		205		

Table 65. Twenty-First Voyage in Steam

From	To	Departed	Arrived	Days	Miles	Miles per day	Speed
London	Fowey	11.ii.13					
Fowey	Cardiff						
Cardiff	Philadelphia		18.iii.13		3232		
Philadelphia	Baltimore	25.iii.13	28.iii.13		376		
Baltimore	Leith	2.iv.13	19.iv.13	17	3470	204	8.5

Table 66. Twenty-Second Voyage in Steam

From	To	Departed	Arrived	Days	Miles	Miles per day	Speed
Leith	Middlesbro'	28.iv.13			140		
Middlesbro'	Philadelphia	7.v.13	28.v.13	21	3550	169	7.0
Philadelphia	Baltimore	4.vi.13	6.vi.13		376		
Baltimore	Leith	14.vi.13	30.vi.13	16	3470	217	9.0

Ascania

Dates are problematic.

Table 67. Twenty-Third Voyage in Steam

From	To	Departed	Arrived	Days	Miles	Miles per day	Speed
Southampton	Plymouth	16.iii.15	10.v.15		118		
Plymouth	Lemnos		7.vi.15		2784		
Lemnos	Alexandria		9.vi.15		520		
Alexandria	Gibralter				1800		
Gibralter	London		24.vi.15		1301		

Table 68. Twenty-Fourth Voyage in Steam

From	To	Departed	Arrived	Days	Miles	Miles per day	Speed
London	Gravesend	4.x.15			23		
Gravesend	Alexandria		23.xii.15		3107		
Alexandria	Tilbury		13.i.16		3085		
Tilbury	London				22		
London	Devonport		31.i.16		329		
Devonport	Port Said		1.iii.16		3027		
Port Said	Alexandria		16.iii.16		140		
Alexandria	Marseilles		25.iv.16		1405		

Table 69. Twenty-Fifth Voyage in Steam

From	To	Departed	Arrived	Days	Miles	Miles per day	Speed
Marseilles	Montreal		20.v.16		3840		
Montreal	London		5.vi.16		3135		

Colin Hannah's Retirement and Death

The *Ascania* was the last ship that Colin Hannah served in. It has not been possible to discover what he did with the remainder of his life: just over thirty years. What is known, however, is that for at least 20 years before his death in 1948, he lived at Summerhill (plate 15) Hardgate, Haugh of Urr, Dumfries and Galloway, with Catherine and his older brother, William.

Plate 15.

The river Urr rises at lake Urr, in the hills above Castle Douglas, and flows into the Solway Firth, sixty miles east of where Colin Hannah was born in Mochrum. "Haugh" means a low-lying meadow by the side of a river, and just above the village is the smaller settlement of Hardgate.

Summerhill was built in 1813, by the Reverend James Biggars, the minister of the Hardgate United Free Church (plate 16). High on the valley side, it commands magnificent views over the surrounding countryside. Since Colin Hannah owned it, an extension has been built at the rear, and bay windows added at the front. The present owner is Roy Paton, who moved to Summerhill in June 1982. Although it is over fifty years since Colin Hannah died, Mr. Paton has been able to speak with people who still remember him. The two aspects of his character that struck them most were his staunch liberalism and his involvement with the church. The latter is born out by the photograph of the 1937 Urr Kirk Session (plate 17, p. 139). Colin Hannah is in the back row, second from the left (looking at the photograph.)

W. Callender, in the front row, first left (again looking at the photograph), and his wife, were probably particular friends of Colin Hannah for he wrote this poem for their daughter:

Mr. and Mrs. William Callender, Crofthead.

I herewith send—but not of brass,
A present for your dear Wee Lass,
And trust the Lord may always bless
Protect and guide Her, from all shoals, so she may pass,
Free on life's tide.

And may she with good health be blest
With trial, grief, nor care, e'er pressed,
And may she aye stand with the best,
Her head erect
But always lean to those oppress't
In any sect.

And now a friend's most earnest prayer,
Is that she may always have a share,
Of her dear Father's sense, thrift and care
Her Mother's pride
And aye that Friend—without compare
With her abide.

Summerhill   Colin Hannah

His constant companion, a Jack Russell terrier, called "Jack" is buried in the garden at Summerhill. When Mr. and Mrs. Paton first moved to the house, they thought they could hear Jack scratching at the door to come in, but they did not worry, as

Plate 16. Hardgate United Free Church.

they felt he was a benign spirit. Two other vignettes: Colin Hannah was the proud owner of an Austin Seven motorcar, and a lady in Hardgate remembers him invigilating at examinations when she was at school.

Catherine died at Summerhill on 12 May 1943 at 7:00 P.M. The cause of death was: pernicious anemia, myocardial degeneration, and heart failure.

The following day, Captain Colin Hannah, Shipmaster (retired) purchased from the Stewartry of Kirkudbright County Council in the Urr burial ground, two lairs for twelve shillings, and Catherine's funeral was held on 15 May. A granite tombstone was erected on which her age was recorded as 70 when it was in fact 75.

Catherine's estate consisted of "Household furniture and other effects" valued at £10:00s, and the balance of an account with Martin's Bank, 4 Water Street, Liverpool, of £109:12s:4d. The total value of the estate in today's terms was about £2,500. Four months after Catherine's death, Colin Hannah revised his will. After the appointment of trustees, namely his bank manager and solicitor in Castle Douglas, he directed that his estate be distributed as follows:

> First. For payment of my debts and funeral expenses, Government duties and expenses of executing the trust hereby created.

> Second. I direct my Trustees to hand over to my nephew, William Bryce, my clothing and personal effects free of Government duty.

> Third. I direct my trustees as soon as possible after my death to pay the following legacies free of Government duty and expenses, but without interest, to Colin Hendrie Howie, Galloway House, Crosby Road, Waterloo, Liverpool, One hundred pounds.

> To my nephew, Colin Critchely, 7 Willis Square, Nothumberland Terrace, Liverpool [Willis Square is not on the current street map of Liverpool], One hundred pounds.

> To my old friend Edward C. Atkinson, [see page 78] 21 Lullymore Terrace, S.E. Road, Dublin, Fifty pounds.

> To my sister-in-law Mrs. Alice McDowall or Hughan [born 1880] 325–327 Crimmies Avenue, Bronx, New York, Two hundred pounds.

> Fourth. I direct my Trustees in the event of my brother, William Hannah, surviving me to give him the option of living in the dwelling house Summerhill, Hardgate, free of rent, with the use of the furniture therein so long as he may wish to do so; declaring however, that in the event of my brother exercising this option he shall be responsible for the maintenance and repair of the said dwelling house, garden and pertinents (*etc.etc.*)

> Fifth. On the death of the survivor of me and the said William Hannah or on my death and the said William Hannah not exercising the option hereinbefore referred to, I direct my trustees to hand over my whole household furniture, plenishing and personal effects to my sister-in-law Mrs. Sarah McDowall or Doyle [born 1878], Phoenixfield, Ballyardle, Newry, Northern Ireland, to be divided as she may see fit between herself and her daughters.

Plate 17.

The Elders of Haugh of Urr Church   C.H. second from left, back row.

Lastly. I direct my Trustees to divide the residue of my estate, including the proceedings of my said property of Summerhill into five equal shares and to pay and make over:

One share to my brother, William Hannah,

One share to my brother, John Hannah [born 1873]

One share to my sister, Janet Hannah or Campbell [born 1876], 30 Raglan Street Renfrew, Ontario, Canada.

One share to the said Sarah McDowall or Doyle,

Three quarters of one share to my nephew, William Bryce, 121 Bonnyton Road, Kilmarnock.

One quarter of one share to my niece Mrs. Mary Bryce or Maclean, residing in Skye.

When Colin Hannah died his estate was valued as follows:

Total of Moveable Estate and Effects:	£5,603
Value of Heritage (i.e., property)	£ 650
Less debts/funeral expenses	£ 78
Total	£6,174

£1 in 1948 = £20.77 as at March 1999. Therefore Colin Hannah's estate was worth £128,234.

Colin Hannah died at Summerhill at on 18 January 1948 at 1:20 P.M. The cause of death was: myocardial failure, arteriosclerosis. Informant: William Hannah.

Captain Hannah was interred in the Urr burial ground with Catherine on 21 January 1948 at 2:00 P.M. The inscription on the granite tombstone (plate 18) reads as follows:

Sacred to the memory of Catherine McDowall, beloved wife of Colin Hannah, master mariner, who died at Summerhill, Hardgate 12 March 1943 aged 70 years. Also the above Colin Hannah, who died at Summerhill 18 January 1948, aged 81 years.

Plate 18. Tombstone of Colin Hannah (*center, foreground*).

Chapter 4

The Voyages of *Ladakh,* 1883–1902

The thirteen crew agreements that were drawn up while *Ladakh* was owned by Edward Bates & Sons provide an insight into the management of a sailing tramp ship. They also reveal something of the lives of the men who crewed her. They were of diverse race and were very badly paid, which probably accounts for the fact that they appear to be entirely rootless, and regard crewing as a means of traveling the world possibly in the hope of finding a better life.

Ladakh Before Colin Hannah

Ladakh was launched by Oswald, Mordaunt & Co., Southampton in February 1883 and passed into the ownership of Edward Bates & Sons on 12 April. She then sailed to her homeport, Liverpool, (460 miles) being reported off Holyhead on 16 April. There was some confusion both about her name: "Ladkh" and that of her master: "Delairig" which should have been Delargy. Having loaded at Liverpool she left for Bombay on 9 May 1883.

Crew Agreement—First Voyage

9 May 1883–24 March 1884, Liverpool–Bombay–Calcutta–London

Total number signing:	47
Failed to join:	4
Sick:	1
Deserted:	0

£1 in 1883 = £45.58 as at March 1999.

Archibald Delargy 35 Cushendall Master

This is a village almost at the northeast tip of Northern Ireland in County Antrim.

J. Dodd	45	Plymouth	First mate	£8:00s
A. Jennings	22	Manchester	Second mate	£5:10s
John Hughes	22	Dundalk	Carpenter	£6:10s
John Farron	33	Sunderland	Sailmaker	£5:00s
George Lamlish	31	Southampton	Steward	£5:00s
W.A. Notley	27	Bristol	Cook	£4:00s

All remained in the ship until the termination of the agreement.

Two apprentices were on board, Frances Joseph Lewis and Frederick Phillip Lander. Both were born in 1867, and their indentures were registered in Liverpool—Lewis on 7 May 1883, and Lander two days later.

Twenty-three able seamen and four ordinary seamen signed the agreement in Liverpool.

Their nationalities were:

English	17
Welsh	1
Scottish	1
Southern Irish	3
Channel Islands (Jersey)	1
American	1
Finnish	1
German	1
Saint Helena	1

The average age of the able seamen was 33, the oldest being 52, the youngest 21. Their wages were £2:15s per month. The average age of the ordinary seamen was 19½, the youngest was 16. Their wages were £1:10s, although the 16 year old was paid £1:00s.

Having left Liverpool on 9 May 1883, *Ladakh* was sighted off the Tusker light (at the most south easterly point of Ireland) the following day, arriving in Bombay on 11 August 1883, 94 days out, 10,750 miles, 114 miles per day at 4.8 knots. She remained here for 30 days, sailing for Calcutta on 10 September, arriving on 28 September, 18 days out, 2,112 miles, 117 miles per day at 4.9 knots.

While in Calcutta for 45 days, eight crew members were discharged by mutual consent, and the German, who was 45 years old, was left behind sick. These men were replaced by 10 others with wages increased to £3:00s per month. Their nationalities were:

English	2
Scottish	2
German	2
American	1

Dutch	1
Swedish	1
Illegible	1

Ladakh sailed for London on 12 November 1883. She was spoken to in 23°S, 4°E (approximately 500 miles south east of Saint Helena) on 19 January 1884, passing the island on the 26th, so she was making slow progress.

Ladakh was off the Lizard on 18 March and entered Falmouth the same day, 126 days out, 11,335 miles, 90 miles per day at 3.7 knots. She was now taken in tow by the tug *Robert Bruce* and was off Deal and Gravesend on 20 March (360 miles). The crew was discharged in London on 22 March 1884.

Crew Agreement—Second Voyage

10 May 1884–17 June 1885, London–Sidney (Australia)–Wilmington–San Francisco–Liverpool

Total number signing:	57
Failed to join:	1
Total number sailing:	56
Deserted:	21

£1 in 1884 = £46.89 as at March 1999.

Thirty-five signed the agreement in London.

Archibald Delargy	36	Master		
J.L. Dodd	26	Plymouth	First mate	£8:10s

He had served in *Ladakh* on the previous voyage.

J. Purkis	28	Portsmouth	Second mate	£6:10s
Thomas Jennings	22	Dundalk	Third mate	£3:10s
John Hughes	23	Dundalk	Carpenter	£6:10s

He had served in *Ladakh* on the previous voyage.

Charles Green	54	Liverpool	Sailmaker	£5:00s
J.M. Fraser	35	Suffolk	Bosun	£4:00s
H. French	33	Hampshire	Steward	£4:10s

Ladakh was his first ship.

Joseph Zima	36	Malta	Cook	£4:10s

Twenty able seamen, four ordinary seamen, and two boys signed the agreement in London.

Their nationalities were:

English	10
Scottish	1
Jerseyman	1
Southern Irish	1
American	1
Swedish	5
Norwegian	2
Danish	1
Dutch	1
French	1
German	1
Jamaican	1

The average age of the able seamen was 32, their wages were £3:00s. The average for the ordinary seamen was 19, their wages were between £2:00s and £1:10s. The average age of the boys was 14½, and they were paid £0:15s.

On 10 May 1884, *Ladakh* cleared London Customs outward bound for Sidney and was towed down channel to be off the Lizard on 13 May. On 7 June, 28 days out, she was in 8°N, 24°W, and by 10 June she had crossed the equator and was in 2°S, 26°W, a distance of approximately 600 miles. She was not spoken to again until she arrived in Sidney on 17 August 1884, a voyage of 99 days, 12,620 miles, 140 miles per day at 5.8 knots.

The "Maritime Intelligence" section of *Lloyd's List* noted:

> The *Ladakh*, August 26 at Sidney reports heavy weather in long, 5°W, shortly after rounding the Cape; several stanchions were carried away, and the spare spars washed overboard; further damage of the same nature was done a few days later.

Ladakh remained in Sidney for 29 days during which time 15 men deserted: 13 able seamen, one ordinary seaman, and the cook. Their nationalities were:

English	5
Scottish	1
Southern Irish	1
Swedish	4
Danish	1
French	1
Maltese (cook)	1
Norwegian	1

They were replaced by 15 others:

English	5
Scottish	4
American	1
Norwegian	3
Jamaican	1
Russian (cook)	1

Ladakh sailed for Wilmington (the harbor for Los Angeles) in California on 16 September 1884. She arrived on 28 November, 73 days out, 6,511 miles, 89.2 miles per day at 3.7 knots. She left for San Francisco on 16 December, arriving on Christmas Eve, eight days out, 369 miles, 46 miles per day at 1.9 knots. Another six men deserted:

Dutch	1
English	1
American	1
Norwegians	3
Russian (cook)	1

They, in turn, were replaced by six others:

American	1
Canadian	1
Swedish	2
German	1
Latvian	1

Ladakh, loaded with wheat, sailed for Queenstown for orders on 29 January 1885 having been in port for 36 days. On 19 March 1885, 46 days out, she was in 47°S, 110°W, this is west of the southern tip of South America, and *Ladakh* was being positioned to sail round Cape Horn.

On 11 May, she was well into the North Atlantic in 21°N, 36°W, and on 6 June was steering east in 48°N, 27°W. (Queenstown is in 51°5'N, 8°3'W.) *Ladakh* arrived off Queenstown on 14 June where, without stopping, she received orders to proceed to Liverpool. After passing Holyhead at 7:40 P.M. on 16 June 1885, she was reported in Liverpool the following day after a voyage of 138 days, 13,667 miles, 99 miles per day at 4 knots.

On 14 July, *Ladakh* sailed for Newport (South Wales), arriving on 16 July, after a voyage of 292 miles. Captain Delargy together with the first mate, carpenter, sailmaker, and steward remained with the ship. Ten able seamen (one of whom had just served in the Bates' ship *Manydown*) were engaged for the run. They were paid £2:10s.

Crew Agreement—Third Voyage

23 July 1885–23 June 1886, Newport (South Wales)– San Francisco–Liverpool

Total number signing:	53
Failed to join:	1
Deserted:	18
Deaths:	2
Stowaway	1

£1 in 1885 was equivalent to £49:73 as at March 1999.

Archibald Delargy	37	Cushendall	Master	
Herbert Tattersall	26	Oxton	First mate	£8:00s
Gustave Wigdahl	21	Illegible	Second mate	£5:00s
A.D. French	35	Longstock	Steward	£5:00s
William Drew	37	Portsmouth	Cook	£5:00s
John Hughes	24	Dundalk	Carpenter	£6:10s
Charles Green	63	Illegible	Sailmaker	£5:10s
T. Colbert	40	Warfield	Bosun	£4:00s

All remained with the ship for the duration of the agreement except the steward and the bosun, who deserted in San Francisco.

Two apprentices were on board: James Taylor, 16; his indentures had commenced on 23 July 1869 at Newport. The other apprentice's name is illegible, but he was 19, and his indentures were signed in Liverpool on 20 September 1882.

Twenty-three able and one ordinary seaman signed the agreement at Newport. Their nationalities were as follows:

English	7
Scottish	2
Southern Irish	2
Ulster	2
Channel Islands	1
Isle of Man	1
American	2
Norwegian	2
Italian	1
Illegible	4

A stowaway, aged 28, from Cork appeared soon after sailing and signed the agreement on 25 July. His wages were 1 shilling per month, presumably a token payment that rendered him subject to the conditions of the agreement.

The average age of the able seamen was 30, the oldest being the Jerseyman who was 49. They were paid £3:00s per month. The ordinary seaman was 18 and his wages were £1:10s per month.

Ladakh sailed for San Francisco, probably loaded with coal, at 1:00 A.M. on 25 July 1885 and was observed passing Lundy. *Lloyd's List* records her as being spoken to in the following positions:

August 1	40°N, 11°W (off the coast of Portugal)
August 13	14°N, 25°W (off the Cape Verde islands)
August 29	6°S, 28°W
September 27	Off Cape Horn in 65 °W

The issue of *Lloyd's List,* 9 September 1885, which notes the position of 13 August, records under the heading "Missing vessels" the following entry:

> The *Yarra Yarra* of Liverpool, O.N. 76,473, sailed from Portland [Oregon] for Queenstown, with wheat, on the 2 February last and from Astoria [at the mouth of the Columbia River on which Portland lies] on the 13 February, and has not since been heard of.

This may well have been a similar ship to *Ladakh,* engaged in a similar trade.

Ladakh arrived in San Francisco on 7 December 1885 after a voyage of 135 days, 13,530 miles, 100 miles per day at 4 knots. The British consul noted that there had been two deaths:

- Donald Ramsey aged 40, from the Isle of Bute had died on 2 November 1885 in 0°10'S, 112°43'W. The cause of death was "consumption," which was the common name for tuberculosis. Robert Koch (1843–1910) had discovered the tubercle bacillus in 1882, so that it was possible in 1885 to make a definitive diagnosis of the disease but not on board a ship. Nevertheless, it was likely that a patient with a wasting disease, who was coughing up blood, may well have had tuberculosis. One wonders how the rest of the crew fared having lived in close proximity with a patient who would have been producing large numbers of tubercle bacilli every time he coughed.
- The other man who died was Hugh McDonald, aged 45, from Dundee. He had died on 23 August 1885 in 2°N, 13°W. The cause of death was given as "general decay," a vivid description of the wretched man's condition no doubt, but meaningless in pathological terms.

While in San Francisco there was the usual mass desertion with 18 of the crew leaving the ship. The majority disappeared in December, but some did not go until January. The stowaway, who presumably had joined the crew officially by this stage, deserted "on the point of sailing." The nationalities of the deserters were as follows:

English	6
Welsh	1
Ulster	2
Southern Irish	2
American	2
German	2
Norwegian	2
Italian	1

Nineteen new crewmembers joined the ship in San Francisco. This number included the cook, 16 able seamen, and 2 ordinary seamen. The average age of the seamen was 32. Their nationalities were:

English	3
Irish	3
Scottish	1
American	1
Bermudan	1
German	1
Gibraltarian	1
Italian	1
Mauritian	1
Norwegian	1
Saint Lucian	1
Swedish	2
Illegible	2

Ladakh sailed for Liverpool on 19 February 1886 having been in San Francisco for 74 days. On 7 June, 108 days out she was in 39°N, 40°W arriving in Liverpool on 23 June 1886, a voyage of 124 days, 13,667 miles, 110 miles per day at 4.6 knots.

The following day there was an inquiry into the deaths that had occurred on the outward voyage by the Superintendent of the Mercantile Marine Office, who wrote in the agreement:

> I certify that I have made inquiry respecting the deaths of the within named
> H. McDonald and D. Ramsey and find the evidence of the Crew satisfactory
> confirming the entries in the Official Log Book.

Crew Agreement—Fourth Voyage

15 July 1886–16 August 1887, Liverpool–Calcutta–London

Total number signing:	51
Deserted:	0
Sick:	1

£1 in 1886 was equivalent to £51.28 as at March 1999.

| John Thomas | 48 | Bristol | Master | |

He had previously been master of the Bates ship *Manydown*.

| Herbert Tattersall | 27 | Oxton | First mate | £8:00s |

He had been first mate on the previous voyage.

Charles Pryce Jones	23	Tranmere	Second mate	£5:00s
Thomas Kelly	42	Liverpool	Carpenter	£5:00s
Charles Taylor	32	Liverpool	Bosun	£4:00.
George Taylor	52	North Shields	Sailmaker	£5:00s

His last ship was also the *Manydown*.

| Joseph Dilworth | 40 | Liverpool | Steward | £4:10s |
| M.J. Watkins | 25 | Swansea | Cook | £4:00s |

Joined *Ladakh* on previous voyage at San Francisco on 16 February 1886.

The third mate and the bosun left the ship at Calcutta by mutual consent. Two apprentices were on board—Edwin Ford and James Taylor. Both were 16. Their indentures were registered in Newport (South Wales)—Ford's on 22 April 1886, and Taylor's on 23 July 1885.

Twenty-one able seamen signed the agreement in Liverpool. They were paid £2:10s per month and their nationalities were as follows:

English	9
Jerseyman	1
Southern Irish	2
Canadian	1
Bermudan	1
Greek	1
Italian	1
Norwegian	1
German (Prussian)	1
Swedish	3

The age of the Norwegian is problematical. His year of birth appears to be 1819, which would make him 67 years old. If he is excluded from the figures, the average age of the crew was 36. The Italian, who was 56 and from Trieste, had served in *Ladakh* for the whole of the previous voyage but would leave when she reached Calcutta. An ordinary seaman was also on board. He was 19 and came from Birkenhead. He too would leave at Calcutta.

Ladakh sailed on 15 July 1886 for Calcutta. On 14 September, she was in 37°S, 6°W, which is in the southern Atlantic, arriving in Calcutta on 9 November, 117 days out, 11,655 miles, 100 miles per day at 4 knots.

Twenty-one of the crew left the ship by mutual consent, and a 40 year old was left behind sick. They were replaced by 21 others, including a new second mate—22 year old Joseph Midgley—who haled from Yorkshire, and a boy—A.J. Reaks aged 16—who had never been to sea gave as his place of birth Calcutta. His pay was 10 shillings per month. The pay of the able seamen was increased to £3:00s per month. Their nationalities were:

English	10
Northern Irish	1
Southern Irish	2
Australian	1
Calcutta	1
German	1
Norwegian	2
Swedish	3

Ladakh remained in Calcutta for 133 days and did not sail for London until 22 March 1887. On 30 July, she was in 43°N, 31°W, this latitude is virtually the same as Cape Finnisterre on the northeast corner of Spain.

By 13 August, *Ladakh* was passing Southend under tow bound for the Victoria Dock in London. Her exact date of arrival is not recorded in the agreement or in *Lloyd's List*, but it must have been either on 13 or 14 August 1887, a voyage of 145 days, 11,685 miles, 81 miles per day at 3.4 knots.

Crew Agreement—Fifth Voyage

28 September 1887–17 June 1889, London–Sidney (Australia)– San Francisco–Manila–San Francisco–Queenstown–Hull (England)

Total number signing:	68
Deserted:	22
Left behind in prison:	2

£1 in 1888 was equivalent to £52.94 as at March 1999.

John Thomas	48	Bristol	Master	
Herbert Tattersall	28	Oxton	First mate	£8:00s

He had served in *Ladakh* since 23 July 1885.

Joseph W. Barry	24	Winsford	Second mate	£5:00s
Thomas Kelly	42	Liverpool	Carpenter	£5:00s

He had signed the previous agreement in Liverpool on 15 July 1886.

| Illegible | 45 | London | Steward | £4:00s |
| M.J. Watkins | 26 | Swansea | Cook | £4:00s |

He had joined *Ladakh* in San Francisco on 16 February 1886.

| Thomas Brown | 49 | Edinburgh | Bosun | £4:00s |
| George Taylor | 58 | North Shields | Sailmaker | £5:00s |

He had signed the previous agreement in Liverpool on 15 July 1886.

All would remain with the ship until the agreement expired in Hull on 17 June 1889 except for the second mate, who would leave in San Francisco by mutual consent on 5 February 1889.

Seventeen able seamen signed the agreement in London on 28 September 1887. Their wages were £2:10s per month. Six had signed the previous agreement: two in Liverpool on 13 July 1886, and four in Calcutta on 18 March 1887. Of these six, four would desert, and one would be left behind in prison. Their nationalities were:

English	8
Northern Irish	1
Channel Islands	1
Canadian	1
New Zealand	1
Swedish	3
Indian (English name)	1
Illegible	1

Three ordinary seamen were aboard, aged 16, 17, and 19. The 16 year old, A.J. Reaks, was a first time voyager when he joined *Ladakh* in Calcutta on 18 March 1887 (giving his nationality as Calcutta). He would desert in Sidney. The ordinary seaman, aged 19, was later promoted to able seaman, but he would desert in San Francisco. A boy, at 14 the youngest to sail in *Ladakh* (and she was not his first ship), would stay with her until the agreement terminated.

Ladakh cleared London Customs on 29 September 1887 and left Gravesend under tow for Sidney the following day. She arrived at Sidney on 18 January 1888, 110 days out, 12,620 miles, 115 miles per day at 4.8 knots.

In *Lloyd's List,* it was reported for *Ladakh* that

> All sails set were blown away in a hurricane shortly after losing the SE trades. The truss bolt of the foreyard was broken, and the port sidelight was washed away.

Ladakh remained in Sidney for 54 days, during which time eight men deserted and two were left behind in prison. Their average age was 22. The nationalities of the deserters were:

English	4
New Zealand	1
Swedish	1

The 16 year old mentioned above, A.J. Reaks, also deserted, as did Michael Ryan, 25, who gave his nationality as Bombay.

The men left in prison were: Thomas Biggs, 26, London, and John Rooney, 44, from Antrim in Northern Ireland. The latter was illiterate. Their wages and effects were left with the shipping master. Nine able seamen joined the ship; every one of whom would desert in San Francisco. *Ladakh* sailed for San Francisco on 13 March, arriving on 7 June, 86 days out, 6,450 miles, 75 miles per day at 3 knots. Twelve men deserted, their nationalities were:

English	3
Guernsey	1
Canadian	1
Swedish	3
Norwegian	2
Russian	1
Illegible	1

Average age 27.

A new agreement was now drawn up and added to the original as a continuation. Twelve able seamen signed it, their nationalities were:

Scottish	2
Welsh	1
Jerseyman	1
American	3
Swedish	3
German	2

Average age 31.

Ladakh's next port was Manila for which she sailed on 12 July after spending 35 days in San Francisco. She arrived on 18 September, 68 days out, 6,230 miles, 92 miles per day at 3.8 knots.

No one deserted here, but the Scotsman and an American, who had joined in San Francisco, left by mutual consent. Two Spaniards also joined the crew. Although they were aged 29 and 33, *Ladakh* was their first ship. They were paid £3:00s, only £1:00s less than the able seamen.

Ladakh returned to San Francisco on 20 October after 32 days in port. She arrived on 6 January 1889, 78 days out, 6,230 miles, 80 miles per day at 3.3 knots.

All those who had originally joined the ship in San Francisco and who had not left in Manila, were discharged by mutual consent, as was the second mate,

Joseph Barry. He was replaced by P. Robinson, 45, from Liverpool. The two Spaniards deserted. Fourteen able seamen were engaged, and their nationalities were:

English	3
Scottish	3
Welsh	1
Swedish	2
Austrian	1
Finnish	1
French	1
German	1
Norwegian	1

Average age 31 years.

After 33 days in San Francisco loading wheat, *Ladakh* sailed for Queenstown for orders on 8 February 1889, arriving on 2 June, 114 days out, 13,580 miles, 119 miles per day at 5.0 knots.

On 8 June, she left for Hull and arrived 17 June, 9 days out, 680 miles, 76 miles per day at 3.0 knots. All except the master, John Thomas, were discharged on the day of arrival, as the agreement had terminated.

Thirteen crew, all English except for one Scotsman, were recruited to move the ship to London 239 miles away. The Scotsman was designated "leading hand" and paid £2:7s:6d for the trip, the others, £1:17s:6d. They were ordered to be on board on 10 July, "Three hours before high water." *Ladakh* arrived at Gravesend on 13 July 1889 and proceeded to the South-West India dock.

Crew Agreement—Sixth Voyage

18 September 1889–27 March 1893, London–Sidney (Australia)–Newcastle (New south Wales)–Bombay–Calcutta–New York–Calcutta–New York

Total number signing:	81 (but ultimately 109)
Failed to join:	4
Deserted:	4
Sick:	5
Left behind in prison:	1

£1 in 1889 was equivalent to £51.28 as at March 1999.

John Thomas	50	Bristol	Master	
P. Robinson	45	Liverpool	First mate	£7:10s
Herbert William Laws	24	Horsey	Second mate	£5:00s
Thomas Kelley	47	Liverpool	Carpenter	£5:10s

He had signed the previous agreement on 15 July 1886.

Illegible	30	Copenhagen	Steward	£4:10s
Illegible	34	Born at sea	Cook	£4:00s
Frank Black	24	London	Bosun	£4:00s
Edward (illegible)	49	Russia	Sailmaker	£5:00s

The first mate left the ship in New York, and the second mate was promoted. The sailmaker and carpenter were also discharged at New York. The cook deserted at Sidney, the steward and bosun were discharged at Calcutta.

Two apprentices were on board, both 16, and their indentures had been registered in London: William Douglas on 18 May 1888, and James Kilner on 15 June 1888.

Seventeen able seamen signed the agreement in London (including one in Gravesend). They were paid £3:05s per month. Their nationalities were:

Swedish	8
English	3
German	3
Norwegian	2
Scottish	1

Average age 22 years.

One of the Swedes had served in *Ladakh* on the previous voyage. Three ordinary seamen signed the agreement: a 19 year old Scotsman, who was paid £2:00s per month, was promoted to able seaman during the voyage, when his wages were increased to £2:05s; an Englishman, who was 20 and paid £2:00s; and Michael Swords from Dublin, who had served in *Ladakh* on her previous voyage and was paid £1:10s. This was raised to £2:00s during the voyage.

Ladakh left London for Sidney on 21 September 1889. On 20 October she was spoken to in 3°N, 23°W, and arrived in Sidney on 31 December, 118 days out, 12,620 miles, 107 miles per day at 4.5 knots. Three able seamen and the cook deserted. The cook was replaced by a Scotsman, Hugh M. Sutherland, from Edinburgh who was 36. After 25 days in Sidney, on 24 January 1890, *Ladakh* moved 70 miles north to the port of Newcastle, which is at the mouth of the Hunter River and was the major coal exporting port of Australia. Six able seamen were engaged here; their wages were £4:00s per month, except for a 19 year old from Falmouth, who was paid £3:05s. A new cook was also appointed, as Hugh Sutherland had been imprisoned. His crime was not recorded in the agreement. The nationalities of these new crewmembers were:

English	4
Scottish	1
French	1
German	1

A 19 year old German, who had signed on at Gravesend, was left behind sick, and an Englishman, aged 37, deserted. After 17 days in Newcastle, *Ladakh* sailed for Bombay on 12 February 1890, arriving on 7 May, 84 days out, 6,095 miles, 73 miles per day at 3.0 knots. *Ladakh* remained in Bombay for 56 days, until 2 July, when she sailed for Calcutta, arriving on 21 July 1890, 19 days out, 2,112 miles, 111 miles per day at 4.6 knots. A Scotsman, aged 19 who had joined at London, was discharged sick, as were two more Scotsmen (one aged 34, the other aged 25), both of whom had joined at Newcastle. The bosun was discharged at Calcutta (by mutual consent) and was replaced by a 31 year old from Antigua. The steward was also discharged, but there is no record of anyone replacing him. Four able seamen were engaged, two Englishmen, aged 46 and 35, a Frenchman, aged 32, and a 38 year old American from New Bedford.

After 81 days in Calcutta, *Ladakh* sailed for New York on 10 October 1890. The "Maritime Intelligence" section of the 12 November issue of *Lloyd's List* reported:

> The ship *Ladakh* while proceeding down the river from Calcutta on October 10 grounded at Rainmaker's Reach, but floated in a quarter of an hour and proceeded; no damage reported.

On 23 December 1890, *Ladakh* passed Saint Helena and arrived in New York on 3 February 1891, 116 days out, 6,800 miles, 59 miles per day at 2.4 knots. *Ladakh* remained in New York for 50 days, during which time 19 crew were discharged by mutual agreement. The first mate left, and Herbert William Laws, the second mate, was promoted with wages of £7:10s per month. The other changes were:

W. Andrews	40	Plymouth	Cook	£5:00s
C. Curwen	21	Harrington	Second mate	£5:00s
M. Torrance	36	Glasgow	Sailmaker	£5:00s
James W. Young	31	Halifax	Bosun	£5:00s

A bosun, appointed a few days earlier, had failed to join, and James Young joined the ship on the day of sailing. Fourteen able seamen also joined, their nationalities were as follows:

English	5
Ulsterman	1
American	1
Austrian	1
Dutch	1
German	2
Guernsey	1
Norwegian	2

Their average age was 29. All were paid £3:14s.

On 25 March 1891, *Ladakh* left New York bound for Calcutta. On 21 April, she was spoken to in 5°N, 27°E (entering the South Atlantic). She arrived at Calcutta on 15 July, 112 days out, 12,335 miles, 110 miles per day at 4.6 knots. *Ladakh* remained here for 85 days, during which time 19 men left by mutual consent, and one due to sickness. The latter was the 19 year old ordinary seaman, who had been promoted to able seaman. He had signed the agreement in London on 19 September 1889 and was discharged on 5 October 1891, three days before sailing. Other replacements were:

C.G. Seacrona	52	Sweden	Sailmaker	£5:00s
William Charley	43	Singapore	Steward	£5:00s
Walter Atkinson	28	Saint Johns	Bosun	£4:10s

A new cook failed to join, and there is no record in the agreement of anyone being appointed to replace him. Seventeen able seamen, and one ordinary seaman also signed the agreement. Three failed to join, and one, who signed on 23 September, was discharged due to sickness on 7 October. The nationalities of those who remained were as follows:

English	6
Scottish	1
Canadian	3
Dutch	1
Finnish	1
Indian	1
Russian	1
Illegible	1

On 18 October 1891, *Ladakh* sailed for New York, and on 21 December, passed Saint Helena. She arrived in New York on 11 March 1892, 144 days out, 6,800 miles, 47 miles per day at 2.0 knots. The "Maritime Intelligence" section of *Lloyd's List* noted:

> Ship *Ladakh* arrived from Calcutta 153 [*sic*] days out, reports was driven off shore three times, with decks constantly flooded, had boats stove in, lost and split sails, and received other damage.

The original agreement had now been signed by 80 crewmembers and was becoming unwieldy, so a supplementary one was drawn up in New York on 18 April 1892. Only Captain Johnson, and the first mate, Herbert Laws, remained from the original agreement. The Swedish sailmaker, who had signed it in Calcutta on 10 September 1891, also remained. The latter two did not sign the new agreement, although Captain Johnson did.

Total number signing (excluding the master):   28
Failed to join: 3
Left behind in prison: 1

Charles Wennnerblom		Age and nationality illegible	Carpenter	£6:00s
Charles Skellon	26	Yorkshire	Steward	£5:00s
Charles Akhurst	20	London	Bosun	£4:10s

Seventeen able seamen, and one ordinary seaman sighed the agreement, their nationalities were as follows:

English	7
Scottish	3
Welsh	1
Australian	1
German	1
Russian	1
Swedish	3
West Indian	1

Their average age was 31. Able seamen were paid £3:14s, and the ordinary seaman was paid £1:10s.

On 23 April 1892, *Ladakh* left New York for Rangoon, arriving on 2 August, 101 days out, 12,340 miles, 122 miles per day at 5.1 knots. She remained here for 29 days. Two able seamen, an Englishman and a Swede, were discharged by mutual consent, and were replaced by two Englishmen, aged 22 and 23.

On 1 September, *Ladakh* sailed for Chittagong arriving on 19 September. This was a voyage of 600 miles, so the distance made good per day was only 31.6 miles at a speed of 1.3 knots. At this time of year the northeast monsoon would have been blowing, which should have made the trip a beam reach. The slow speed, however, suggests there may have been more north than east in the wind, so that *Ladakh* would have had to tack.

On 25 September, a 24 year old, whose name and nationality are illegible, joined the crew as an able seaman. Unfortunately he had to be discharged on 2 November, as he was in Chittagong jail. He was replaced by a Barbadian, who was 26.

Ladakh left Chittagong on 14 November 1892 bound for Dundee. Her positions were recorded in *Lloyd's List* as follows:

24 January 1893 passed Saint Helena.
17 March, off Portland Bill.
18 March at 10:11A.M. off North Foreland.
20th March, off Deal.

The weather was reported as fine, the winds light and variable, and the sea smooth. This suggests that a spring anticyclone had built, and *Ladakh* did not arrive in Dundee until 26 March 1893. Deal to Dundee is approximately 390 miles, so distance run per day was 65 miles, which gives a speed of 2.7 knots. The complete voyage was one of 132 days, 12,021 miles, 91 miles per day at 3.8 knots.

Crew Agreement—Seventh Voyage

21 April 1893–11 October 1894, Dundee (Scotland)–New York–Bombay–Rangoon–Saint Helena–Bremerhaven

Total number signing	49
Failed to join	3
Sick	7
Deserted	11

£1 in 1893 was equivalent to £52.94 as at March 1999.

John Thomas	54	Bristol	Master	
W. Bond	29	Liverpool	First mate	£8:08s
Richard Michael	22	Holyhead	Second mate	£5:00s
William Tullis	49	Dundee	Carpenter	£6:00s
C.G. Seacrona	52	Sweden	Sailmaker	£5:00s
Charles Skellon	27	Yorkshire	Steward	£5:00s
Charles Fairweather	42	Saint Andrews	Bosun	£4:10s

Both the sailmaker and the steward had signed the previous agreement. The former at Calcutta on 11 September 1891, the latter at New York on 18 April 1892. All remained with the ship until the termination of the agreement at Bremerhaven. Under the heading, "Cook," is written, "On Lascar Agreement." This is the only time that this appears in any of the *Ladakh* crew agreements. A Lascar was a sailor from the East Indies, and would have been paid less. (The 1931 *Perseus* agreement (see p. 41) had a separate contract for the Chinese seamen, presumably for the same reason.)

Two apprentices were recorded: Clement William Hepworth, aged 16, his indentures had been registered in Hull on 13 October 1890; and Frederick Lewis Deansfield, aged 19, indentures registered in Swansea on 24 January 1890. He was "Time expired" at the end of this voyage on 13 October 1894.

Twenty able seamen, one of whom failed to join, signed the agreement in Dundee. The oldest was 50, the youngest 19. Their average age was 28, and they were paid £3:00s per month. Two ordinary seamen signed. Their ages were 19 and 21, and their wages were £2:10s. The nationalities of the crew were:

Scottish	12
English	1
Dutch	1
French	1
Finnish	1
German	1
Norwegian	1
Swedish	2
Illegible	1

In the agreement there is a heading, "If in the Reserve, number of commission or RV2." A 42 year old able seaman, Alec Spencer from Aberdeen, had a number in this column: 85,945. The elder of the apprentices had "RVM 457" above his name.

On 24 April 1893, *Ladakh* left Dundee for New York where she arrived on 7 June, 44 days out, 3,085 miles, 70 miles per day at 2.9 knots. Eleven of the crew now deserted:

Scottish	4
Dutch	1
Finnish	1
French	1
German	1
Norwegian	1
Swedish	2

Their average age was 27.

Thirteen men replaced them, but two failed to join. Their nationalities were:

English	1
Southern Irish	2
American	1
Danish	2
Finnish	1
Norwegian	4

Their average age was 24.

After 36 days in New York, *Ladakh* sailed for Bombay on 13 July, arriving on 17 November 1893, 127 days out, 11,510 miles, 90.6 miles per day at 3.8 knots. A 30 year old Irishman was left behind in hospital, and two Norwegians, aged 24 and 25, joined the ship, which sailed for Rangoon on 30 December, where she arrived on 17 February 1894, 49 days out, 2,117 miles, 43.2 miles per day at 1.8 knots. Two Scotsmen, aged 21 and 34, and an American, aged 35, were left behind sick. Another Scotsman, aged 25, and a Dane, 24, were discharged by mutual agreement. They were replaced by three Scotsmen aged 18, 24, and 41, a 45 year old Englishman, and a Dutchman whose age is not recorded.

Ladakh left Rangoon for Queenstown on 16 March 1894 after 27 days in port loading rice.

She had to put into Saint Helena on 14 June to land James Walls, from Paisley, one of the Scotsmen who had joined at Rangoon. The British Consul recorded that he was suffering from "Rheumatism." A possible diagnosis would be acute rheumatic fever with involvement of the heart, which would explain the need to get the patient ashore urgently. A 19 year old American, Oliver Binder, joined the crew, and *Ladakh* sailed for Queenstown on 16 June. She arrived off the port on 26 September, 192 days out from Rangoon, 11,480 miles, 60 miles per day at 2.5 knots. She received orders to sail for Bremerhaven, and was taken in tow off Portland by the tug *Knight of the Cross,* arriving in Bremerhaven on 11 October 1894, 15 days from Queenstown, 846 miles, 56 miles per day at 2.35 knots.

Crew Agreement—Eighth Voyage

7 November 1894–21 April 1896, Bremerhaven–New York–Saint Vincent (Cape Verde Islands)–Hong Kong–Manila–Boston–New York

Total number signing:	70
Failed to Join:	1
Deserted:	15
Left in Prison:	1
Sick:	3
Died:	1

£1 in 1894 was equivalent to £54.70 as at March 1999.

John Doyle	36	Skerries	Master (1)	

Doyle's home is one of Ireland's premier fishing ports, north of Dublin. His previous command had been the Bates ship *Cabul.*

John Johnson	60	Lerwick	Master (2)	

John Johnson's previous command had been the Bates ship *Yarkand.*

W. Bond	34	Liverpool	First mate (1)	£8:00s

He had served in *Cabul* with Captain Doyle.

John Follett	48	Dartmouth	First mate (2)	£8:00s
William Lewis	20	Clapton	Second mate	£5:00s
Thomas Clay	59	Liverpool	Carpenter	£6:00s
C.G. Seacrow	54	Sweden	Sailmaker	£4:00s

| John Oram | 28 | Liverpool | Steward | £5:00s |
| B. Götgen | 56 | Germany | Cook | £4:05s |

Captain Doyle and W. Bond left the ship due to injury. Everyone else remained until the agreement terminated in New York.

Two apprentices were aboard. The first was Thomas Dobson, 20, indentures registered in Swansea, 24 January 1890. His apprenticeship expired on 25 November 1895, at sea, and he was appointed third mate with wages of £2:15s per month. He would serve in *Ladakh* for almost six years. The other apprentice, Clement William Hepworth, was 16. He had served in *Ladakh* on the previous voyage. His year of birth was 1877, and his apprenticeship had commenced in 1890 when he was 14. He completed his articles on 2 April 1896 when *Ladakh* arrived in Boston.

Eighteen able seamen signed the agreement in Bremerhaven. They were paid £2:15s per month. Their average age was 24. The oldest was 39, the youngest 17. Their nationalities were:

English	3
Scottish	1
Dutch	2
Finnish	1
German	6
Russian	2
Spanish	1
Swedish	2

There were also two English ordinary seamen. The elder, R. Harvey, was 22, and although it was his first ship, he was paid £2:00s. He would be lost overboard on the voyage between New York and Hong Kong. The younger, who was 18, and had been to sea before, was paid £1:15s.

Ladakh sailed from Bremerhaven on 16 November 1894 arriving at New York on Christmas Eve, 38 days out, 3,520 miles, 92.6 miles per day at 3.9 knots. *Lloyd's List* reported as follows:

> New York, 28 December. British ship *Ladakh* which was docked in the Erie Basin at the Anglo–American stores, broke from her moorings and drifted into the basin on 26 December. Both anchors were let go which held the vessel until morning, when tugs replaced her in the dock.

She was loading petroleum, which was carried in cases.

While in New York, 13 of the crew deserted. Their nationalities were as follows:

Dutch	2
English	1
Finnish	1

German	5
Spanish	1
Russian	1
Swedish	2

Both the oldest and youngest were among their number. They were replaced by 13 able seamen, one of whom failed to join. They were paid £3:05s, their average age was again 24. Their nationalities were:

English	4
American	2
Austrian	1
Danish	1
Italian	2
Norwegian	2

There was also an ordinary seaman aged 18, John Jay Allan Jr., from Bristol, Rhode Island. *Ladakh* was his first ship, and he was paid only 10 shillings per month. As we shall learn later, he was left behind in prison in Hong Kong. *Ladakh* sailed from New York for Hong Kong on 5 February 1895. *Lloyd's List* reported as follows on 25 February:

> "Saint Vincent, Cape Verde Islands. British ship *Ladakh*, New York for Hong Kong (petroleum) put in here with boats damaged, deck movables washed overboard, and hatches stove in; made jettison of 600 cases. Harvey, one of the crew, drowned. Captain and First Officer have their legs broken. Captain will await instructions from his owners.

Ladakh was 20 days out, 2,800 miles, 140 miles per day at 5.8 knots. She must have met with an unusually deep, and vigorous depression. It cannot have been a hurricane, as the season for these storms is June to October. Nevertheless, on 6 March *Lloyd's List* reported:

> The Captain, Mate and Crew of the *Ladakh* are all doing well, but it is understood that the vessel will have to wait here for another Captain and Mate who are being sent out here.

John Doyle had been born in Skerries in 1855, and obtained his master's ticket in Dublin in 1881. According to *Lloyd's Captains Register,* his first command, in 1889, was the Edward Bates & Sons' ship *Cabul,* and he remained with her until he joined *Ladakh* in 1894. Following his accident, he disappears from the register.

The British Consul in Saint Vincent noted the discharge of W. Bond, the first mate, and also a 22 year old Norwegian able seaman, E. Forsen, who had joined the ship in New York. Both were stated to have been "Injured in service of the ship."

The consul continues: "The master has reported to me the death by drowning during the voyage from New York of R.W. Harvey—his effects have been delivered to me, also his balance of wages amounting to £4:05:05d."

The new captain, John Johnson, arrived, and took command on 2 April 1895. As mentioned above, he had lately been captain of the *Yarkand*, the smallest of Edward Bates & Sons' sailing ships. The new first mate was 48 year old John Follett from Dartmouth. Two able seamen, aged 26 and 23, plus an ordinary seaman, aged 20, all natives of the Cape Verde Islands, also joined the ship.

Ladakh finally left Saint Vincent on 4 April after a stay of 38 days. She arrived in Hong Kong on 15 August, 133 days out, 11,720 miles, 88 miles per day at 3.7 knots. Five able seamen, and one ordinary seaman who had joined in New York, were discharged by mutual agreement. The deputy superintendent of the mercantile marine office also noted in the Agreement:

> I also certify that J.J. Allan has been discharged and left behind at Victoria Gaol [Jail] and the accounts as rendered by the master show that he is in debt to the ship. I further certify that J.J. Allan declines to sign the release on the ground that he has some effects on board. This has been proved to be false by an entry in the Official Log Book duly attested by nine members of the Crew.

Six able seamen joined the crew. Three were English, one was from the Isle of Man, and two were French. Their average age was 27. On 27 September 1895, after 42 days in port, *Ladakh* left Hong Kong for Manila, where she arrived on 3 October, 6 days out, 632 miles, 105 miles per day at 4.4 Knots.

On 25 October, the two able seamen from the Cape Verde Islands deserted. They were replaced by two men whose country of origin has not been identified. They were 24 and 19. *Ladakh* left Manila for Boston on 19 November 1895, after spending 47 days in port. Thomas Dobson completed his apprenticeship on 25 November and was appointed third mate. As mentioned earlier, he would remain in *Ladakh* until 2 November 1900. On 14 December, she was reported off Anger (Strait of Sumatra) arriving in Boston on 1 April 1896, 132 days out, 13,632 miles, 103 miles per day at 4.3 knots. Captain Johnson, together with the two able seamen who had joined at Manila, and Thomas Dobson, remained with the ship. Everyone else, including the second mate, the petty officers, 17 able, and one ordinary seaman were discharged by mutual consent on 2 April 1896.

On 14 April 1896, 15 Bostonians, whose average age was 44, were engaged to take *Ladakh* to New York to load, a distance of 380 miles. Their wages are recorded as $14.00, "By the run to New York." They left on 17 April and arrived on 19 April. The Bostonians were recorded as deserters on 22 May. This is difficult to understand, as they had been engaged as a scratch crew to move *Ladakh* to New York.

Crew Agreement—Ninth Voyage

1 May 1896–15 July 1897, New York–Hong Kong–Iloilo (Philippines)–Queenstown–Liverpool

Total number signing: 44
Failed to join: 6
Sick: 2

£1 in 1896 was equivalent to £56.59 as at March 1999.

John Johnson	62	Dartmouth	Master	
John Lucas Follett	48	Dartmouth	First mate	£8:00s
Thomas Dobson	21	Liverpool	Second mate	£5:00s
J.E. Hermanson	24	Liverpool	Bosun	£4:00s
Charles Nelson	25	Sweden	Carpenter	£5:10s
J. Adrian Anderson	29	Sweden	Sailmaker	£4:15s
John Logan	30	Liverpool	Steward	£5:00s
Thomas Johnson	28	Sunderland	Cook	£4:00s

All remained with the ship until the agreement expired at Liverpool in July 1897. Seventeen able seamen, two ordinary seamen, and two boys signed the agreement in New York. Their nationalities were:

Danish	4
German	4
Finnish	2
Norwegian	2
Swedish	2
American	1
Canadian	1
English	1
Scottish	1
Welsh	1
Illegible	2

The average age of the able seamen was 30. The youngest was 22, the oldest 45. Their wages were £3:10s per month. The average age of the ordinary seamen and boys was 22. The ordinary seamen were paid £2:15s, and the boys £2:05s and £2:00s.

Ladakh sailed from New York bound for Hong Kong on 23 May 1896. She arrived on 20 November, a passage of 181 days, 13,709 miles, 76 miles per day at 3.2 knots. While in Hong Kong, eight crew were discharged by mutual consent, and two were left behind sick. They were replaced by 11 others, two of whom failed to join. The wages of the able seamen were increased to £3:00s per month. Their average age was 34. The oldest was 45, the youngest 25. Their nationalities were:

English	2
Norwegian	2
Swedish	2
Canadian	1
French	1
Illegible	1

Ladakh left Hong Kong for Iloilo in the Philippines, to load sugar, on 2 January 1897, having spent 42 days in port. She arrived on 12 January, 894 miles, 89.4 miles per day at 3.7 knots. She sailed for Queenstown, for orders, on 3 February, after 22 days in port. She passed Anjer on 2 March, and arrived at Queenstown on 6 July 1897, 154 days out, 12,673 miles, 82 miles per day at 3.4 knots. *Ladakh* sailed for Liverpool on 12 July, arriving on 14 July, 255 miles.

Herbert Holdsworth would join her in a month's time.

Colin Hannah Joins *Ladakh*

Crew Agreement—Tenth Voyage

14 August 1897–18 July 1899

See Chapter 1.

Crew Agreement—Eleventh Voyage

9 September 1899–1 October 1900, Bremerhaven–New York–Bombay–Bassein (Burma)–Rotterdam

Total number signing	55
Failed to join	2
Deserted	26
Sick	3

£1 in 1899 was equivalent to £54.70 as at March 1999.

Colin Hannah			Master	
Thomas Dobson	25	Liverpool	First mate	£7:10s
Fred Midgley	24	Yorkshire	Second mate	£5:10s
R. Blair	49	Liverpool	Sailmaker	£5:05s
T. Girtz	38	Germany	Carpenter	£5:10s
James Anderson	49	Liverpool	Steward	£5:00s
John Gillitzer	33	Germany	Cook	£4:10s

All remained with the ship until the termination of the agreement in Bremerhaven. Twenty-two able seamen, one ordinary seaman, and a bosun signed the agreement for the voyage to New York. The bosun's wages were £4:00s, the able seamens' £3:05s, and the ordinary seamens' £2:00s. Their nationalities were as follows:

German	7
Swedish	5
Danish	3
Italian	2
Russian	2
Chilean	1
Dutch	1

Ladakh sailed for New York on 2 September 1899. On 15 September, she was spoken to when in 51°N, 21°W. It is possible she took this northerly route to lessen the chance of meeting the hurricanes that blow at this time of year, predominantly between the Atlantic islands and the Caribbean, although the eastern seaboard of America may also be a danger area. She arrived in New York on 11 October, a voyage of 26 days. While in New York the crew deserted en masse. They were replaced by 24 men, two of whom failed to join. The able seamen were paid "One shilling per day for 85 days and £3:14s [per month] thereafter." Their nationalities were as follows:

American	4
English	4
Norwegian	4
Canadian	2
Danish	2
Swedish	2
Northern Irish	1
Scottish	1
Illegible	2

Ladakh sailed from New York on 16 November 1899, having spent 36 days in port. She was spoken to on 14 December, steering south, in 2°S, 30°W (off Brazil) and reported "All well." On Christmas Day, she was in 24°S, 27°W (just south of the latitude of Rio de Janeiro). At the turn of the century, she would have been approximately 600 miles off the east coast of Brazil. She arrived in Bombay on 19 March 1900, after a passage of 124 days, 11,430 miles, 92 miles per day at 3.8 knots. Three men deserted, an Englishman, a Canadian, and one whose nationality is illegible. Also, two were left behind sick. They were replaced by two men, one from Mauritius, and the other an Englishman.

Three weeks later, on 10 April, *Ladakh* sailed for Bassein in Burma, to load rice, arriving on 10 May 1900. Bassein is situated approximately 60 miles from the mouth of the most easterly of the five rivers that constitute the delta of the Irrawaddy. Three more crew now joined the ship, a Dane, a Norwegian, and a Swede. They had to be brought from Rangoon, where they had signed a supplement to the main agreement. On 22 May 1900, *Ladakh* sailed for Falmouth for orders, having spent only 12 days loading. This would suggest the rice was loaded loose, rather than in bags. This latter task could take weeks, as it had to be done by hand, and entailed carefully stowing thousands of bags in such a way that they would not shift in bad weather. This is not to say that loose cargoes did not also have to be carefully stowed, but the problem was obviously much more straightforward.

On 7 August *Ladakh* passed Saint Helena, steering northwest, and reached Falmouth on 26 September 1900, 127 days out, 11,223 miles, 88 miles per day at 3.7 knots. She left on 29 September for Rotterdam, and must have had a fair wind, as she arrived on 1 October 1900.

The current agreement terminated, and all members of the crew, except Colin Hannah, were discharged, including Thomas Dobson who had served in *Ladakh* for almost six years. It was not quite his last engagement in the ship, however, as he would help to move her from Rotterdam to Antwerp the same day.

Usually, when an agreement terminated, the crew found places in other ships, but if they could not, or did not wish to, the owner of the ship, in which they had just served, had to defray the cost of their passage to a United Kingdom port. He also had to arrange for the payment of their wages there. The British Vice Consul recorded in the agreement:

> I further certify, that the within named [there then follows the names of nine men] have been transmitted from this Port to London. The UK master to comply with the requirements of section 186, subsection 201 of the Merchant Shipping act, 1894.

All nine men collected their wages from the mercantile marine office, Dock Street, London East between 5 and 8 October 1900. There was a deduduction, for what was described as "Cartage Fare" of 1/8d (one shilling and eight pence). It is not known why this charge was made when the owner was supposed to pay the cost of the crews' passage home.

Ladakh now proceeded to Antwerp, under tow, to discharge her cargo of rice. Although this voyage would only last one day, a new agreement was drawn up in the format of a *Half Yearly Agreement and Account of Voyages and Crew of a ship engaged in the Home Trade Only*. The crew consisted of Colin Hannah and Thomas Dobson, plus 13 Dutchmen whose average age was 43. One of them was bosun, with wages of £1:10s for the trip, the cook and the able seamen were paid £1:05s. On 1 October 1900 the crew were discharged, including Thomas Dobson.

Crew Agreement—Twelfth Voyage

20 November 1900–10 October 1901, Antwerp–San Francisco–Dublin

Total number signing	49
Failed to join	3
Deserted	18
Sick	0

£1 in 1900 was equivalent to £52.94 as at March 1999.

Colin Hannah			Master	
W.W. Bailey	44	Dublin	First mate	£8:00s
E.B. Curphy	24	Liverpool	Second mate	£5:10s
C. Crossly	23	Bury	Third mate	£4:00s
C.L. Nilsen	27	Danish	Carpenter	£5:05s
R. Blair	50	Liverpool	Sailmaker	£5:05s
H.C. Smith	29	London	Steward	£5:00s
P. Dupont	40	Belgian	Cook	£4:00s

The cook was disrated to ordinary seaman on 14 August 1901, two months before he left the ship. He was replaced by T. Pritchard, 23, of Carnarvon. All stayed with the ship until the termination of the agreement on 17 October 1901. The sailmaker had signed the previous agreement, and thus spent just over two years in *Ladakh*. Twenty-one able and ordinary seamen, including a 16 year old deck boy from Antwerp, who was promoted to ordinary seaman, signed the agreement for the voyage to San Francisco. The able seamen were paid £3:00s per month, while the ordinary seamen and deck boys were paid £1:10s. No bosun was appointed. Their nationalities were as follows:

Norwegian	4
Canadian	3

All from the Maritime Provinces

Belgian	2
London	2
Swedish	2

Naturalized Americans

of German origin	2
American	1
Chilean	1
Finnish	1
Danish	1
Dutch	1
Welsh	1

On 28 November 1900, *Ladakh* sailed for San Francisco. The following day, she was off Saint Catherine's Point, Isle of Wight, and was not sighted again until 10 January 1901, when she was spoken to in 3°S, 27°W (off the coast of Brazil) steering south southwest. She arrived at San Francisco on April 23, 147 days out, 13,779 miles, 94 miles per day at 3.9 knots. Eighteen of the crew deserted. The three who remained with the ship included the two Belgians, the 16 year old (who had been promoted to ordinary seaman), and the 15 year old ordinary seaman, who had been disrated to boy on 30 November 1900. The Welshman also remained in *Ladakh* and was subsequently promoted to cook.

Twenty new crew were engaged, but three failed to join. Their wages were increased to £5:00s per month for able seamen and £3:10s for ordinary seamen, the boy earning the same amount. No bosun was appointed. Their nationalities were:

American	7
English	3
Southern Irish	2
Belgian	1
Canadian (Nova Scotia)	1
Northern Irish	1
Swedish	1
Illegible	1

Ladakh sailed for Falmouth for orders on 18 June 1901, loaded with wheat. She had spent 56 days in San Francisco. Two of the Americans, who had been engaged as able seamen, were disrated to ordinary seamen before the ship sailed. An 18 year old American, who had started the voyage as an ordinary seaman, was disrated to boy on 26 June, and another able seaman (nationality illegible) was disrated to ordinary seaman on 13 July 1901. *Ladakh* arrived in Falmouth on 5 October, 109 days, 13,440 miles, 123 miles per day at 5.1 knots. She remained there until 14 October, when she left, in tow of the tug *Stormcock*, for Dublin to unload the grain. When she arrived, on 16 October 1901, all of the crew, except the first mate, were discharged.

Ladakh was now to be moved from Dublin to Cardiff in ballast, and an agreement was drawn up for *A Ship engaged in the Home Trade only*. The preamble to this stated that the voyage was to be:

> From Dublin to Cardiff or any loading port in the Bristol Channel and there until the vessel be safely moored in floating dock or shored in graving dock, as ordered by the master on arrival, sails furled, anchors batten [*sic*] on board, ropes coiled up, decks and bulwarks washed down, and all left snug to the master's satisfaction.

Also mentioned in the agreement is the fact that, "The runners signing this agreement to pay their own expenses back to Dublin." As well as Colin Hannah and the first mate, William Price, a cook, steward, bosun, and eleven able seamen were engaged, six of whom were illiterate. The majority were from Dublin, and all were paid £2:05s "Per run." The average age of the able seamen was 49. *Ladakh* left Dublin on 23 November and arrived at Cardiff two days later.

Crew Agreement—Thirteenth Voyage

16 December 1901–7 November 1902, Cardiff–Esquimault–London

Total number signing: 43
Failed to join: 1
Deserted: 12
Sick: 1

£1 in 1901 was equivalent to £52.94 as at March 1999.

Colin Hannah			Master	
John Hines	36	Bude	First Mate	£8:00s
George Black	26	Kircudbright	Second mate	£5:00s
Jahn Adalfston	23	Finland	Carpenter	£4:15s
H.G. Smith	30	London	Steward	£5:00s
A. McLean	52	Aberdeen	Cook	£4:00s
Alexander Smith	35	Liverpool	Sailmaker	£5:00s

All remained with the ship until the agreement terminated in London on 8 November 1902.

H.G. Smith had signed the previous agreement on 20 November 1900, and thus served in *Ladakh* for almost two years. Alexander Smith, in the column in the agreement headed "Ship in which he last served, and year of discharge therefrom" has entered "Same, 1899." This implies that he had not been to sea since he was discharged from *Ladakh* on 18 July 1899 at Bremerhaven, at the conclusion of the agreement signed initially on 17 August 1897. He had also been with Colin Hannah in *Cabul* in 1896. A 45 year old American from Maine was appointed bosun with wages of £3:15s per month. Nineteen able seamen, one of whom failed to join, and three ordinary seamen, signed the agreement. The nationalities of the able and ordinary seamen were as follows:

Danish	6
Finnish	3
Norwegian	4
English	2
Southern Irish	2
Welsh (Anglesey)	1
Canadian (Winnipeg)	1
German	1
Northern Ireland	1

One of the Danes is of interest, as he was the oldest crewmember, at 65 years, to have sailed under Colin Hannah. His name was Thomas Swan, and his birthplace was given as "Hallanbar" or "Kallanbar" (neither has been found in the atlas). He stayed with the ship until the agreement terminated in 1902, at which time he could have been 66. The able seamen were paid £3:00s per month, and the ordinary seamen £2:00s. One, whose rank is illegible, presumably boy, was paid £1:00s

On 17 December 1901, *Ladakh* left Cardiff for Esquimault, arriving on 22 April 1902, 127 days out, 14,337 miles, 113 miles per day at 4.7 knots. Esquimault is a harbor adjacent to Victoria, the capital of Vancouver Island. It is on the northern shore of the Strait of Juan de Fuca, which separates Canada from the northwestern American state of Washington. It also leads into Puget Sound, on the eastern side of which is Seattle and, further down, the port of Tacoma, which is where *Ladakh* was ultimately bound. After Esquimault she called at Port Townsend, on the American side of the Strait, and which serves as a port of entry for Tacoma (and Seattle). *Ladakh* arrived at Tacoma to load wheat on 17 May 1902.

Twelve crew deserted, 11 in Esquimault and one in Tacoma. Also, the Northern Irishman was left behind sick. These crewmembers were replaced with 13 others, whose nationalities were:

English	4
American	3
French	2
German	1
Italian	1
Swedish	1
Welsh	1

One of the Englishmen was appointed bosun's mate with wages of £5:00s. The able seamen were paid £4:00s, and the ordinary seamen £3:00s. One of the Americans, who was 18 and on his first voyage, was initially paid as an ordinary seaman, but his wages were subsequently reduced to £2:10s.

Ladakh left Tacoma for Queenstown for orders on 10 June 1902 having been in the port for 24 days, 49 days since she had arrived in Esquimault. On 18 September, she was spoken to in 1°S, 20°W, midway between Brazil and Gabon. On 26 October she arrived at Queenstown, 138 days out, 15,143 miles, 110 miles per day at 4.6 knots. *Ladakh* left for London, under tow, on 3 November. The following day she was reported passing the Lizard in tow by "One of Jolliffe's tugs" and on the 5th she was off Prawle Point in South Devon. She arrived at the Victoria Dock, London, on 7 November 1902, 560 miles, 140 miles per day at 5.8 knots. As this was *Ladakh*'s last voyage in Edward Bates & Sons' ownership, all the crew were discharged, including Colin Hannah.

Subsequent Fate of *Ladakh*

After 19 years in the ownership of Edward Bates & Sons, *Ladakh* was sold to Italian owners on 17 December 1902. The certificate of registry records that, on this date, only two of the original shareholders still had an interest in the ship. Edward Percy Bates had died on 31 December 1899, and his 20 shares had been left to Gilbert Thompson Bates. The latter must also have acquired the 12 shares of Wilfred Imrie Bates, as he then held 50 shares, and Sydney Eggers Bates was still recorded as owning 14 shares.

The new owner was G. Maresca of Castelammare, which is at the southern end of the Bay of Naples. He renamed *Ladakh, Ninfa.* Until 1913, L. Lauro was master in which year G. Maresca replaced him. The last year in which *Ninfa* appears in *Lloyd's Register of Shipping* is 1917, when she is reported as being "In port, damaged." In 1920, she was sold to Cuban owners, converted to steam, and used to carry molasses in bulk, probably to be used in the manufacture of industrial alcohol. Her name was changed to *Mambi.*

On 23 May 1943, *Mambi* was a part of convoy NC 18, off Cuba, when she was torpedoed by U-176 with the loss of 23 men. U-176 was commanded by Korvetten Kapitän Reiner Dierkson, who was born on 24 March 1908, at Esenhausen, Baden Württenberg. Between 4 August 1942 and 13 May 1943, he sank 11 ships with a total tonnage of 53,307. On 13 May 1943, after sinking *Mambi,* he also sank the American ship *Nikeliner.* Only two days later, U-176 met her end, when she was sunk, on 15 May, north east of Havana, in position 23°21'N, 80°18'W, by depth charges from an American Kingfisher aircraft (VS-62/1), and the Cuban patrol boat SC 13. All hands, 53 men in total, were lost.

Summary of Crew Agreements

During the time *Ladakh* was in Edward Bates & Sons' ownership, 13 crew agreements were drawn up. All have been examined. The short term agreements, for crews moving *Ladakh* between nearby ports for loading or unloading, are not included, nor are the 15 Bostonians who were engaged to move her from Boston to New York on 24 April 1896, although they were included in the main agreement.

Total number signing: 765 (excluding 12 apprentices)
Failed to join: 34

If the deck officers, captains and mates, and the petty officers, sailmakers, and carpenters are excluded from the total number signing, and if the one carpenter who did fail to join is taken into account, this figure is 4.9 percent of the total.

Total number sailing: 731

Their nationalities were as follows:

English	228
Scottish	58
Welsh	12
Isle of Man	2
Channel Islands	8
Northern Irish	17
Southern Irish	28

Total from the British Isles: 353 (48.3 percent)

American	52
Canadian	16
Australian	2
New Zealand	1

Total English speakers: 424 (58.0 percent)

Swedish	69 (9.4 percent)
German	51
Norwegian	46
Danish	21
Finnish	16
Dutch	11
French	11
Italian	8
Russian	9
West Indian	8
Belgian	5
Indian (with English names)	4
Austrian	3
Cape Verde Islands	3
Mauritius	3
Spain	3
Chilean	2
Gibraltarian	1
Greek	1
Latvian	1
Saint Helena	1
Singapore	1
Illegible	26
Not identified	2

Average age of all crewmembers: 30.1 years

Sick: 26 (3.6 percent)

This figure includes the two who died on board due to illness.

Lost overboard: 2 (0.27 percent)
Injured "In service of the ship": 3 (0.41 percent)

Number of crew who signed more than one agreement, excluding captains: 34 (4.7 percent)

Of whom: 5 were first mates;
4 were carpenters;
3 were sail makers;
3 were stewards;
1 was a cook;
12 were able seamen, of whom six deserted and one was left behind in prison; and
6 were ordinary seamen, of whom one deserted.

Served in other ships owned by Edward Bates & Sons:

Of the five captains of *Ladakh* only Archibald Delargy did not join from one of Bates's ships.

John Thomas	*Manydown*
John Doyle	*Cabul*
John Johnson	*Yarkand*
Colin Hannah	*Cabul*

Thirteen other crewmembers had served in the following ships:

Cabul	5
Kistna	2
Yarkand	2
Herat	1
Kelat	1

First time voyagers: 10 (1.4 percent)

These may be divided into a younger and an older group. The former is made up of seven crew members with an average age of 17.3 years, the youngest being 14. The older group contains the two Spaniards, aged 29 and 33, who joined in Manila on 16 October 1888, and deserted in San Francisco on 7 January 1889. Also a steward, who joined in Liverpool on 8 May 1884, and stayed for the duration of the agreement.

There was one stowaway, from Cork, aged 28.

Deserted: 146

If masters, mates, carpenters, and sailmakers are excluded, this is 22 percent of the total who sailed in *Ladakh*. San Francisco was the most popular city for deserters, followed by New York:

San Francisco	55 (37.7 percent of deserters)
New York	46 (31.5 percent)
Sidney	27 (18.5 percent)
Esquimault and Tacoma	12 (8.2 percent)
Bombay	4 (2.7 percent)
Manila	2 (1.4 percent)

Average age of deserters:　　28.2 years.

Nationalities of deserters:

English	24 (10.5 percent of the English)
Swedish	20 (29.0 percent of the Swedes)
German	18 (35.3 percent of the Germans)
Norwegian	16 (34.8 percent)
Danish	10 (47.6 percent)
American	6 (11.5 percent)
Canadian	6 (37.5 percent)
Russian	5 (55.5 percent)
Scottish	5 (8.6 percent)
Dutch	4 (36.4 percent)
Finnish	4 (25.0 percent)
Southern Irish	4 (23.5 percent)
Italian	3 (37.5 percent)
Spanish	3 (100 percent)
Cape Verde Islands	2 (66.6 percent)
Chilean	2 (100 percent)
Indian (but with English names)	2 (50 percent)
Northern Irish	2 (11.8 percent)
Welsh	2 (16.7 percent)
Belgian	1 (20 percent)
Channel Islander	1 (12.5 percent)
Maltese	1 (100 percent)
Not stated	1
Illegible	1

The number of men signing agreements with a cross was 73. This is 11 percent of crew (excluding officers and petty officers). The figure is probably an underestimate, as many signatures are made with what appears to be an illiterate hand.

Wages

The average value of the £ (compared with 1999 values), between 1883 and 1902, was £52.40. (Equivalent 1999 values are in brackets for comparison.)

First mates:	usually £8:00s per month, but occasionally £7:10s. £96:00s a year (£5,030).
Second mates:	usually £5:00s per month, occasionally £5:10s, and on one occasion, £6:00s. £60:00s a year (£3,144).
Carpenters:	varied between £4:15s and £6:10s. Average was £5:13s. £67:16s a year (£3,553).
Sailmakers:	varied between £4:10s and £5:10s. Average was £5:00s. £60:00s a year (£3,144).
Stewards:	varied between £4:05s and £5:00s. Average was £4:16s. £57:12s a year (£3,018).
Cooks:	varied between £3:10s and £4:10s. Average was £4:00s. £48:00s a year (£2,515).
Bosuns:	varied between £3:15s and £5:00s, but usually £4:00s. £48:00s a year (£2,515).
Able seamen:	varied between £2:10s and £4:00s, but on one occasion £5:00s. Average was £3: 03s. £37:16s a year (£1,981).

In 1886, average wages, in all industries (excluding agriculture), were 21.2 shillings per week, which is £55:00s a year. Thus cooks, bosuns, and able seamen, were paid less than the average, although they were provided with food and accommodation. Any families at home, however, would have had a thin time. The lowest wages on land were those of agricultural laborers who earned £42:00s, which was slightly more than an able seaman.

Summary of Voyages

Archibald Delargy, Master

Table 70.

From	To	Departed	Arrived	Days	Miles	Miles per day	Speed
Southampton	Liverpool	?	?		460		
Liverpool	Bombay	9.v.83	11.viii.83	94	10750	114	4.8
Bombay	Calcutta	10.ix.83	28.ix.83	18	2112	117	4.9
Calcutta	Falmouth	12.xi.83	18.iii.84	126	11335	90	3.7
Falmouth	London	18.iii.84	20.iii.84	2	360	Under tow	

Table 71.

From	To	Departed	Arrived	Days	Miles	Miles per day	Speed
London	Sidney	10.v.84	17.viii.84	99	12620	140	5.8
Sidney	Wilmington	16.ix.84	28.xi.84	73	6511	89.2	3.7
Wilmington	San Francisco	16.xii.84	24.xii.84	8	369	46	1.9
San Francisco	Liverpool	29.i.85	17.vi.85	138	13667	99	4.0
Liverpool	Newport	14.vii.85	16.vii.85	2	292		

Table 72.

From	To	Departed	Arrived	Days	Miles	Miles per day	Speed
Newport	San Francisco	25.vii.85	7.xii.85	135	13530	100	4.0
San Francisco	Liverpool	19.ii.86	23.vi.86	124	13667	110	4.6

Total mileage: 85,673. Days at sea: 817 = 2.24 years. Average miles per day: 100.6.Average speed: 4.2 knots.

John Thomas, Master.

Table 73.

From	To	Departed	Arrived	Days	Miles	Miles per day	Speed
Liverpool	Calcutta	15.vii.86	9.xi.86	117	11655	100	4.0
Calcutta	London	22.iii.87	14.viii.87	145	11685	81	3.4

Table 74.

From	To	Departed	Arrived	Days	Miles	Miles per day	Speed
London	Sidney	30.ix.87	10.i.88	110	12620	115	4.8
Sidney	San Francisco	13.iii.88	7.vi.88	86	6450	75	3.0
San Francisco	Manila	12.vii.88	18.ix.88	68	6230	92	3.8
Manila	San Francisco	20.x.88	16.i.89	78	6230	80	3.3
San Francisco	Queenstown	8.ii.89	2.vi.89	114	13580	119	5.0
Queenstown	Hull	8.vi.89	17.vi.89	9	680	76	3.0
Hull	London	?	13.vii.89		239		

Table 75.

From	To	Departed	Arrived	Days	Miles	Miles per day	Speed
London	Sidney	21.ix.89	31.xii.89	118	12620	107	4.5
Sidney	Newport.	24.i.90			70		
Newport	Bombay	12.ii.90	7.v.90	84	6095	73	3.0
Bombay	Calcutta	2.vii.90	21.vii.90	19	2112	111	4.6
Calcutta	New York	10.x.90	3.ii.91	116	6800	59	2.4
New York	Calcutta	25.iii.91	15.vii.91	112	6800	60	2.5
Calcutta	New York	18.x.91	11.iii.92	144	6800	47	2.0
New York	Rangoon	23.iv.92	2.viii.92	101	12340	122	5.1
Rangoon	Chittagong	1.ix.92	19.ix.92	19	600	31.6	1.3
Chittagong	Dundee	14.xi.92	26.iii.93	132	12021	91	3.8

Table 76.

From	To	Departed	Arrived	Days	Miles	Miles per day	Speed
Dundee	New York	24.iv.93	7.vi.93	44	3085	70	2.9
New York	Bombay	13.vii.93	17.xi.93	127	11510	90.6	3.8
Bombay	Rangoon	30.xii.93	17.ii.94	49	2117	43.2	1.8
Rangoon	Queenstown	16.iii.94	26.ix.94	192	11480	60	2.5
Queenstown	Bremerhaven	26.ix.94	11.ix.94	15	846	56	2.4

Total mileage: 164,665. Days at sea: 1999 = 5.48 years. Average miles per day: 82.4. Average speed: 3.4 knots.

John Doyle, Master.

Table 77.

From	To	Departed	Arrived	Days	Miles	Miles per day	Speed
Bremerhaven	New York	16.xi.94	24.xii.94	38	3520	92.6	3.9
New York	Saint Vincent	5.ii.95	25.ii.95	20	2800	140	5.8

Total mileage: 6,320. Days at sea: 58.

John Johnson, Master.

Table 78.

From	To	Departed	Arrived	Days	Miles	Miles per day	Speed
Saint Vincent	Hong Kong	4.iv.95	15.viii.95	133	11720	88	3.7
Hong Kong	Manila	27.ix.95	3.x.95	6	632	105	4.4
Manila	Boston	19.xi.95	1.iv.96	132	13633	103	4.3
Boston	New York	17.iv.96	19.iv.96	2	380		
New York	Hong Kong	23.iv.96	20.xi.96	181	13709	76	3.2
Hong Kong	Iloilo	2.i.97	12.i.97	89	894	89	3.7
Iloilo	Queenstown	3.ii.97	6.vii.97	154	12673	82	3.4
Queenstown	Liverpool	12.vii.97	14.vii.97	2	255		

Total mileage: 53,896. Days at sea: 699 = 1.92 years. Average miles per day: 90.5. Average speed: 3.77 knots.

Colin Hannah, Master.

Table 79.

From	To	Departed	Arrived	Days	Miles	Miles per day	Speed
Liverpool	Calcutta	17.viii.97	15.xii.97	120	11655	97	4.0
Calcutta	New York	23.ii.98	13.vi.98	111	12335	111	4.6
New York	Bombay	29.vii.98	28.xi.98	122	11430	94	3.9
Bombay	Rangoon	31.xii.98	14.ii.99	45	2117	47	2.0
Rangoon	Falmouth	16.iii.99	11.vi.99	117	11340	97	4.0
Falmouth	Bremerhaven	12.vii.99	18.vii.99	6	630	105	4.4

Table 80.

From	To	Departed	Arrived	Days	Miles	Miles per day	Speed
Bremerhaven	New York	2.ix.99	11.x.99	26	3520	135	5.6
New York	Bombay	16.xi.99	19.iii.00	124	11430	92	3.8
Bombay	Bassein	10.iv.00	10.v.00	29	2059	71	3.0
Bassein	Falmouth	22.v.00	26.ix.00	127	11223	88	3.7
Falmouth	Rotterdam	29.ix.00	1.x.00	2	400	Under tow	8.0

Table 81.

From	To	Departed	Arrived	Days	Miles	Miles per day	Speed
Rotterdam	Antwerp	31.x.00	1.xi.00	1	121	Under tow	
Antwerp	San Francisco	28.xi.00	23.iv.01	147	13779	94	3.9
San Francisco	Falmouth	18.vi.01	5.x.01	109	13440	123	5.1
Falmouth	Dublin	14.x.01	16.x.01	2	363	Under tow	7.6

Table 82.

From	To	Departed	Arrived	Days	Miles	Miles per day	Speed
Dublin	Cardiff	23.xi.01	25.xi.01	2	215	108	4.8
Cardiff	Esquimault	17.xii.01	22.iv.02	127	14337	113	4.7
Esquimault	Tacoma	?	17.v.02		90		
Tacoma	Queenstown	10.vi.02	26.x.02	138	15143	110	4.6
Queenstown	London	3.xi.02	7.xi.02	4	560	Under tow	5.8

Total mileage: 136,187. Days at sea: 1,359 = 3.72 years. Miles per day: 100.2 Average speed: 4.2 knots.

Summary for the Period in Edward Bates & Sons' Ownership

February 1883–7 November 1902 for a total of 19.66 years.

Time spent at sea:	13.28 years (67.5 percent).
Total mileage:	446,311 nautical miles (513,258 statute miles).
Average mileage per day:	92.0 nautical miles (105.8 statute miles).
Average speed:	3.84 knots (4.42 statute miles per hour).

Ports visited:		
	New York	7 times
	Bombay	5
	Calcutta	5
	San Francisco	5
	Falmouth	4 (for orders)
	Liverpool	4
	London	4
	Queenstown	4 (for orders)
	Rangoon	3

Sidney (Australia)	3	
Bremerhaven	2	
Hong Kong	2	
Manila	2	
Antwerp	1	
Bassein	1	
Boston	1	
Cardiff	1	
Chittagong	1	
Dublin	1	
Dundee (Scotland)	1	
Esquimault	1	
Hull (England)	1	
Iloilo	1	
Newport (South Wales)	1	
Newport (Australia)	1	
Rotterdam	1	
Saint Vincent	1	(Stress of weather)
Tacoma	1	
Wilmington	1	
Total: 29		

Cargoes Carried by Ladakh for Which There Is Documentary Evidence

Wheat

San Francisco–Liverpool	29 January 1885
San Francisco–Hull	8 February 1889
San Francisco–Dublin	18 June 1901
Tacoma–London	10 June 1902

Rice

Rangoon–Bremerhaven	16 March 1894
Bassein–Rotterdam	25 May 1900

Petroleum

New York–Hong Kong	5 February 1895

Sugar

Liverpool–Iloilo	3 February 1897

Selected Bibliography

Corlett, Ewan, 1980, *The Iron Ship,* (Bradford on Avon: Moonraker Press).

Derby, W.L.A., 1970, *The Tall Ships Pass* (Newton Abbott: David & Charles Reprints).

Gropallo, Tomaso, 1964, *Il Romanzo della Vella* (Genova: Edizioni Maralunga).

Hyde, Francis E., 1957, *Blue Funnel* (Liverpool: University of Liverpool Press).

Jones, W.H.S., 1956, *The Cape Horne Breed* (London: Jarrolds).

Keay, John, 1977, *When Men and Mountains Meet* (London: John Murray).

Lubbock, Basil, 1921, *The Colonial Clippers* (Glasgow: John Brown & Son).

________, 1929, *The Last of the Windjammers* (Glasgow: John Brown & Son).

Milsom, C.H., 1988, *Blue Funnels in the Mersey* (Isle of Man: Sea Breezes Publications).

Thornton, R.H., 1945, *British Shipping* (Cambridge, England: Cambridge University Press).

Villers, Alan, 1971, *The War with Cape Horn* (London: Hodder and Stoughton).

The Oxford Companion to Ships and the Sea, 1976 (Oxford: Oxford University Press).

Reed's Marine Distance Tables, 1965 (East Molesey: Thomas Reed Publications).

The Times Atlas of the World, 1994 (London: Times Books, Harper Collins).

Index

Able Seaman
    Qualifications, 20
Ascania, xi–xii, 26, 117–19, 135

Baltic Exchange, 9
Barque, 1
Barquentine, 1
Bassein (Burma), 10, 20, 127, 167, 169,
    181, 183
Bernard Hall, 30–33, 35, 41

Cabul, 8, 19, 20, 85–88, 126, 162, 164, 172,
    176
    C.H. master of, 85–88
Callender, William, 137
    Poem (by C.H.) for his daughter, 137
Cargo Liners, 29
Cargoes
    Ladakh, 10–11, 169, 183
    Summary, 10–11
Census, 1881, 66
Coal
    Price of, 77
    Trimmer killed by, 114–15

Death by drowning, 21, 165
Deaths at sea due to disease, 149
Deck cargo, 117
Disciplinary offences defined, 15–16
Discipline
    Regulations for maintaining, 15
Dobson, Thomas, 19, 21, 22, 24, 27, 166,
    167, 169
    Apprenticed on *Ladakh*, 163, 165
Drunkeness, 16, 112

Edward Bates & Sons, 6–9, 20
    Business philosophy, 3
    Sailing ships owned by, 8
    Steam ships owned by, 8–9
Erikson, Captain Gustav, 11

Food
    Scale of provisions, 14

German prisoners of war
    death of, 119
Gray, William
    Photographer, 6
Greyhound Inn, 62–63
Grievance procedure of crew, 13–14
Gross and Net tonnage of steam ships,
    4–5
Gross tonnage
    Defined, 4

Hannah, Catherine
    Death of, 139
    Sails in *Sierra Morena*, 95, 96, 100, 102
Hannah, Colin
    Agricultural laborer, 19, 66
    Brothers and sisters, 66–67
    First mate examination, 74
    First officer in *Ascania*, 119
    Marriage, 81, 125
    Parents, 19, 66
    Place of birth, 19, 66
    Second mate examination, 71
    Signs August 1897 (*Ladakh*)
        agreement, 19
    Will, 139

Hannah, Mary, 19, 66
Hannah, Thomas, 19, 66
Hertzogin Cecilie, 11
Holdsworth, Gladys, 60
    Remembers Herbert and Jane, 61
Holdsworth, Herbert
    Address in 1897, 17
    Analysis of voyages in Alfred Holt Co.,
        45–51
    Average time spent at sea/annum, 51
    Awarded Mercantile Marine Medal, 47
    Becomes purser, 30, 32
    Birthdays and Christmases spent at
        home, 34, 51
    Character, 60, 61
    Days spent at sea, 1897–1905, 34
    Death, 62
    Death certificate, 62, 64
    Edith, 28
    Emma Jane, sister, 61
    Joins Alfred Holt & Co., 39
    Joins *Ladakh*, 17
    Leaves *Ladakh*, 24
    Mathew Clement, brother, 28
    Parents, 28
    Will, 65
Holdsworth, Jane (H.H.'s wife)
    Death, 65
    Sends postcard during long absence, 51
Holdsworth, Jane Holland Wood
    Letter from Emma Jane Holdsworth, 61
    Suffers from bovine tuberculosis, 62
Holdsworth, Jane Pennington, 28, 49
Holdsworth, Mathew (H.H.'s father), 28
    Death, 37
    Marries Jane Pennington, 28
Holt, Alfred, 39–41
    Character, 40–41
    Compound steam engine, 40
    Research and development, 40
Holt, Richard Durning
    Son of Alfred Holt, 41

Iloilo (Philippines), 10, 166, 167, 181, 183
Iron
    As ship building material, 3, 78, 85

Kistna
    Ship owned by E.Bates & Sons, 3, 8,
        176

Ladakh
    Appearance, 6
    Breaks moorings in Erie basin, N.Y.,
        10, 163
    Building of, 1883, 143
    Cargoes, 10–11, 169, 183
    Certificate of Registry, 4
    Dimensions, 5
    Distance and mileage sailed, 9
    Driven offshore trying to enter New
        York, 158
    Grounds while leaving Calcutta, 157
    Load line, 15
    Number of men in a watch, 20
    Official number, 4
    Origin of name, 6
    Owners, 5
    Photograph of, 2
    Storm Damage near Cape Verde
        Islands, 164
    Sold to Italian owners, 174
    Speed made good, 5–6
    Time spent in harbor, 11
Lubbock, Basil
    Author, *The Last of the Windjammers*, 3
Marine steam engine
    Development of, 39–40
Maury, M., American hydrographer, 3
Maydown
    Ship owned by E.Bates & Sons, 3
McKay, Donald
    Sailing ship designer and builder, 39
Mercantile Marine Medal, 47
Meriones, 48, 49, 54

Net tonnage
    Defined, 4

Offences enumerated, 16
    Bernard Hall, 31
Orders, calling at ports for, 10, 13, 26, 72,
        82, 147, 155, 167, 169, 171, 173, 182

Oswald, Mordaunt & Co.
    Builders of *Ladakh*, 3, 143
    Shipbuilders, 85
Overtime
    Payment for, in *Bernard Hall*, 31

Packet ship, 29
Penthesilea, 67–74, 78, 88, 122, 123
    Ashore in Bideford Bay, 73–74
Pernicious anemia, 54, 65, 139
Perseus, H.H.'s last ship
    Crew agreement, 44
Pisagua, 75, 77, 100, 101, 125, 131, 132
Plimsoll, Samuel, 14–15
Purser
    Duties of, 30

R.W. Leyland & Co., 3, 6
Rice, 10, 26, 72, 81, 85, 162, 167, 168, 183

Sails
    Fore and aft, 1
Ship (technical term), 1
Sickness
    Seamen left at St. Helena, 72
Sierra Morena
    Catherine Hannah sails in, 95, 96,
        100, 102
    Name changed to *Graciana*, 92, 110
Sierra Parima
    Hurricane in Mauritius, 80–81
    Puts into Milford Haven due to
        weather, 84

Small Pox
    First mate in *Imaum* suffers from,
        90–92
Square sails, 1
Steam engine, compound, 40
Stowaways, 69, 148, 149, 176
Sugar, 10, 14, 80, 167, 183
Summerhill, 134–136

Talthybius, 47, 54
Tonnage
    Dead weight and displacement, 5
    Defined, 4
Trade winds, 3
Tramping, 1, 8, 9–10, 29, 124, 143
Trimmers, 32
Tropical storms, 106, 107, 109

Value of the British pound, 17

Wage costs
    Bernard Hall, 33
    For *Ladakh*, 20, 178
Wages, 11, 17
    In all industries, 178
    Master's, 19, 93
Wavertree, 6
Wheat, 10, 82, 83, 147, 149, 155, 171, 173,
    183
Wolseley, R.B., 20
Wright, Kenneth
    Performs autopsy on H.H., 62, 64

About the Author

William L.H. Scarratt was born in 1937 and for twenty-three years was a consultant histopathologist in Plymouth, Devon, England. In 1983 he launched a 35-foot sailing sloop that he had built himself and spent his holidays cruising the Channel Islands, Brittany, and Southwest Ireland with his family. On retirement he exchanged this boat for a 16-foot Salcombe yawl and pursues interests in maritime history, geology, botany, bookbinding and building half models of ships and boats. He lives in Devon with his wife, a retired architect.